Writers
on
Writing

VOLUME II

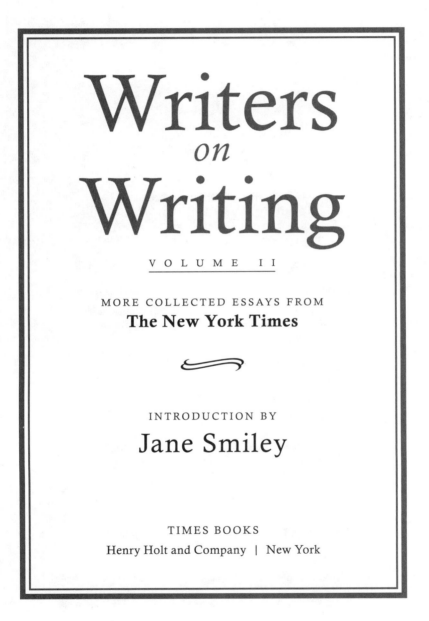

Writers
on
Writing

VOLUME II

MORE COLLECTED ESSAYS FROM
The New York Times

INTRODUCTION BY

Jane Smiley

TIMES BOOKS
Henry Holt and Company | New York

Henry Holt and Company, LLC
Publishers since 1866
115 West 18th Street
New York, New York 10011

Henry Holt® is a registered trademark of
Henry Holt and Company, LLC.
Collection copyright © 2003 by *The New York Times*
Introduction copyright © 2003 by Jane Smiley
All rights reserved.
Distributed in Canada by H. B. Fenn and Company Ltd.

The Library of Congress has cataloged Volume I as follows:

Library of Congress Cataloging-in-Publication Data
Writers on writing : collected essays from the New York times;
introduction by John Darnton.—1st ed.
p.   cm.
ISBN 0-8050-6741-8
1. Authorship.   I. New York times.

PN137 .W734 2001
808'.02—dc21   00-053509
ISBN 0-8050-7361-2

Henry Holt books are available for special
promotions and premiums. For details contact:
Director, Special Markets

First Edition 2003

Designed by Paula Russell Szafranski

Printed in the United States of America

1   3   5   7   9   10   8   6   4   2

An extension of this copyright page can be found on pages 266–67.

Contents

Introduction by *Jane Smiley*   *ix*

Poems Foster Self-Discovery   *1*
   by *Diane Ackerman*

A Path Taken, with All the Certainty of Youth   *9*
   by *Margaret Atwood*

Essentials Get Lost in the Shuffle of Publicity   *13*
   by *Ann Beattie*

Timeless Tact Helps Sustain a Literary Time
   Traveler   *19*
   by *Geraldine Brooks*

Yes, There Are Second Acts (Literary Ones) in
   American Lives   *25*
   by *Alan Cheuse*

Footprints of Greatness on Your Turf   *31*
   by *Frank Conroy*

New Insights into the Novel? Try Reading
   Three Hundred   *37*
   by *Chitra Divakaruni*

Returning to Proust's World Stirs Remembrance   *43*
   by *Leslie Epstein*

Contents

Forget Ideas, Mr. Author. What Kind of Pen Do
   You Use?   49
   by *Stephen Fry*
In Paris and Moscow, a Novelist Finds His
   Time and Place   55
   by *Alan Furst*
Recognizing the Book That Needs to Be Written   61
   by *Dorothy Gallagher*
How to Insult a Writer   67
   by *Herbert Gold*
Calming the Inner Critic and Getting to Work   71
   by *Allegra Goodman*
A Narrator Leaps Past Journalism   77
   by *Vivian Gornick*
They Leap from Your Brain Then Take Over
   Your Heart   83
   by *Andrew Greeley*
When Inspiration Stared Stoically from an Old
   Photograph   89
   by *Kathryn Harrison*
A Career Despite Dad's Advice   93
   by *Michael Holroyd*
Seeing the Unimaginable Freezes the
   Imagination   99
   by *A. M. Homes*
Hemingway's Blessing, Copland's Collaboration
   by *A. E. Hotchner*   105
Returning to the Character Who Started It All
   by *Susan Isaacs*   111
Negotiating the Darkness, Fortified by Poets'
   Strength   117
   by *Mary Karr*

Contents

Hometown Boy Makes Waves   *125*
    by *William Kennedy*

As Her Son Creates His Story, a Mother Waits
    for the Ending   *133*
    by *Beth Kephart*

The Glory of a First Book   *137*
    by *Brad Leithauser*

Easy on the Adverbs, Exclamation Points and
    Especially Hooptedoodle   *143*
    by *Elmore Leonard*

A Famous Author Says: "Swell Book! Loved It!"   *147*
    by *Elinor Lipman*

Hearing the Notes That Aren't Played   *153*
    by *David Mamet*

Heroism in Trying Times   *157*
    by *Patrick McGrath*

Shattering the Silence, Illuminating the Hatred   *163*
    by *Arthur Miller*

Overcome by Intensity, Redeemed by Effort   *169*
    by *Honor Moore*

A Novelist's Life Is Altered by Her Alter Ego   *175*
    by *Marcia Muller*

Computers Invite a Tangled Web of
    Complications   *181*
    by *P. J. O'Rourke*

Saluting All the King's Mentors   *187*
    by *Jay Parini*

Why Not Put Off Till Tomorrow the Novel You
    Could Begin Today?   *191*
    by *Ann Patchett*

Contents

The Eye of the Reporter, the Heart of the
  Novelist   195
  by *Anna Quindlen*
A Retreat from the World Can Be a Perilous
  Journey   201
  by *Jonathan Rosen*
After Six Novels in Twelve Years, a Character
  Just Moves On   207
  by *James Sallis*
Fiction and Fact Collide, with Unexpected
  Consequences   213
  by *John Sedgwick*
Confession Begets Connection   219
  by *David Shields*
A Storyteller Finds Comfort in a Cloak of
  Anonymity   225
  by *Susan Richards Shreve*
Autumnal Accounting Endangers Happiness   231
  by *Richard Stern*
Family Ghosts Hoard Secrets That Bewitch the
  Living   237
  by *Amy Tan*
A Bedeviling Question in the Cadence of English   245
  by *Shashi Tharoor*
Still Replying to Grandma's Persistent "And Then?" 251
  by *Frederic Tuten*
A Pseudonym Returns from an Alter-Ego Trip,
  with New Tales to Tell   257
  by *Donald E. Westlake*
Before a Rendezvous with the Muse, First Select
  the Music   261
  by *Edmund White*

Introduction

Jane Smiley

As tempting as it is for a writer to tell secrets, it is even more tempting to tell them in the *New York Times*. The forms of temptation abound: to join the company of other secret revealers, to get something off your chest, to impart a piece of wisdom that has resisted going into a novel or a poem, to cogently remember a time or an event. For a poet, I imagine there is the temptation to state rather than evoke. For a novelist, there is the temptation to stop dissembling. And so, this collection of *Writers on Writing* pieces is really a collection of temptations yielded to, a collection of secrets divulged in spite of what might happen. Because, as we know, the potential punishments for telling secrets and yielding to temptations, are manifold—the very least of them is the possibility that the man the audience thinks is the Wizard will be exposed as a mere Kansan plying his machine; perhaps the greatest, for a writer, is that investigation of one's mode or method will scatter the Muses and render one speechless (and income-less)—these pieces are also artifacts of dangers passed, penalties evaded.

Am I plying on the hyperbole here? Maybe. But writers of all kinds are superstitious about their gifts and about their relationship to their readers. They know in their hearts that their literary personae are not quite what they themselves are—to pick an extreme example, the narrator of Justine, by the Marquis de Sade, was far more ruthless and imaginative than the Marquis himself. The rest of us writers are not quite so funny nor so compassionate nor so tough nor so enterprising nor so discerning in our lives as we are in our books. If we were, then our friends and family would esteem us as highly as some of our readers do. And so it is an act of some bravery to lay aside the persona at the behest of a newspaper and come forth as oneself, dull, sublunary, just a guy or a gal, with quirks and crochets and odd habits.

As a reader, though, I have only thanks for these writers. I thank Arthur Miller for revisiting the era before "the Good War," when it was not a good war, but just a prospective war, as chaotic and strange and unknown as every war. I thank him for telling the truth after six decades of cultural public relations. I thank Ann Patchet for embracing a laziness many novelists feel and making it so funny that I hope she is blessed by it forever. I thank Mary Karr for her reaction to the turmoil of September 11, 2001—I thank her for keeping her wits about her and knowing that poems would be the perfect thread of order to lead her into the future. I thank David Shields for reading his bad reviews and Elmore Leonard for being practical. Every piece in here contains some helpful nugget, some generous revelation.

Because that's what all these writers were asked to do—they were asked to be generous, to give something away that perhaps they had never given away before, some item of craft or privacy or self-doubt to be read over breakfast and digested along with the bagels and the bad news. They were asked to a make a piece in the newspaper where the weary citizen of interesting times might rest and take a deep breath and contemplate the inner life. Most collections, written over several years and then gathered together, have a disappointing uniformity of tone or method. Not this one. Each writer's choice of what would be divulged is unique. Sashi Tharoor addresses the issue of writing about India in English rather than in another Indian language—an issue of considerable significance in a world where language loss vies with species extinction as a cause for concern. Amy Tan wrestles with the way her mother's life, even after its completion, utterly resists containment in an obituary or in the daughter's mind. Diane Ackerman ponders (I think quite boldly) the two processes of poetry writing and psychotherapy as they coexist in her life. The biographer Michael Holroyd turns his attention to his father and his youthful self with the same precision that he has used to document the lives of his other subjects. Frank Conroy touches on the uncanny coincidences of literary minds thinking alike. Susan Richards Shreve confesses to a deception that will surely inspire a whole generation of young writers.

Nor do we have uniformity of tone here—there is the comic (Donald E. Westlake), the lyrical (David Mamet), the skeptical (Ann Beattie), the affectionate (Beth Kephart), the bemused (James Sallis), the inspired (Leslie Epstein), and a treasury of others. These are examples, not preferences. The pieces in this book are so diverse as to not really be comparable.

How to read this book? At one sitting, as I did, or over a

single weekend, giving oneself over to the friendliness of these authors. Read it like eavesdropping or like twisting the knob on an old radio and tuning in stations from far and wide. Read it like an explorer, then wander among the authors' other works. Most of all, read it in a way that allows the varied voices of the company to come and go, to blend, to harmonize with and to echo one another, because it isn't often that forty-six authors sing in chorus.

Writers
on
Writing
VOLUME II

Poems Foster
Self-Discovery

~

Diane Ackerman

The drawing on the jacket startled me, and I found my
lips pursing in a silent wow. After twenty book covers, I
had a sense of what's fashionable and always enjoyed discovering how a visual artist reimagined my book. A special
favorite was the cover for *A Natural History of the Senses*,
which featured a Waterhouse painting of a woman enrap-
tured by a single rose. Her head was embossed; you could
thumb her hair. But this new cover, for *Origami Bridges:
Poems of Psychoanalysis and Fire*, existed on a higher plane,
as a visual knot for contemplation.

What looked like a simple photograph of an analytical
couch and an analyst's chair on a field of light gray, on second
glance was meticulously folded origami. Then a pattern
emerged: the artist had used manuscript pages of the book. A
small paper bridge, connecting upper and lower parts of the
couch, though flimsy looking, strengthened the whole. The
analyst's chair balanced on tiny points, the way a racehorse

1

balances atop tiny ankles. Couch and chair touched almost imperceptibly at one corner, and their shadows gradually merged.

The closer I looked, the more I saw. The designer had created a Rorschach test. It was a powerfully strange, symbolic cover. But then, creating the poems was the strangest writing experience I'd ever known.

This wasn't a planned book, but one that geysered up naturally over a year and a half, during which I wrote poems daily. I began writing them to corral the unruly emotions that arose during intense psychotherapy, a process I explain a little in this excerpt from "Omens of Winter":

> *Poems arrive as meteorites.*
> *Collecting them, I try my best to impart*
> *impulses, the Morse code of the heart,*
> *but I do not understand the vernacular*
> *of fear that jostles me until art occurs,*
> *or why knowing you from afar*
> *spurs hours of working myself into the stars.*
> *Well, I do know, but I fight its common sense:*
> *I try to stabilize us through eloquence.*
> *It's an old story, better told than I tell,*
> *how artists shape what hurts like hell*
> *(usually love) into separate empires*
> *of lust, tenderness, and lesser desires*

An unusual aspect of my therapy was that my analyst and I lived in different towns. Once a month or so I would visit him in his office. Most weeks we spoke by telephone, however, which in some ways allowed greater intimacy and risk, although it deprived us of the lavish visual cues that can be so telling. The voice is lavish, too. I had been a tele-phone crisis-line counselor for several years, and so I felt comfortable dealing with steep emotions by phone, a drama that has its own fascinating dynamics. Deprived of visual cues, I learned to listen athletically. I describe that kind of detailed listening at length in *A Slender Thread* (a book I wanted to call "Squirrels and the Dark Night of the Soul," but the publisher balked).

Although I don't know my doctor's background, he was a profoundly nuanced listener. Somehow this combination of methods worked remarkably well. A telephone receiver is perforated like a confessional screen, you miss the shame of eye contact, the other's voice seems to originate inside your head; mental portraits of the other form while you're talk-ing, and so on. As in traditional psychoanalysis, you don't see the analyst. But in this case the analyst doesn't see you either.

A therapist usually provides a safe place in which to meet, his space, full of his belongings, with furniture arranged for his physical and aesthetic comfort, where he's in charge of airflow and cushions, and where he's used to the ambient noises: from heating pipes that sound like a giraffe choking on an abacus to a window ledge where doves seem to be warming up for light opera. No, à la telephone, you have to find your own private space, free from interruption, and that's not always easy. For example, in one poem, the roofers begin hammering midsession.

For all of these reasons, our calls sometimes felt dream-like, worldless, timeless, and we often seemed to connect at the level of the unconscious. Then, when we did meet face-to-face, other elements came into play. Among them the chance to refresh my visual memory. On those days, I hungrily studied his features, as if for a boardwalk portrait, noting details that later cropped up in poems.

I sent him all the poems that emerged, hot off the heart, and they became an important part of the therapy, another place where we could meet. There's a tradition of using artworks in this way, children's drawings especially, and it opened up some unexpected avenues. So much of life falls between the seams of the sayable. It's ironic that poets use words to convey what lies beyond words, that poetry becomes most powerful where simple language fails, allowing one to bridge the conscious and unconscious, and even festoon that bridge with sensations and subterranean desires. In a poem by Emily Dickinson, all that may occur in a single word, phrase or even line break. Metaphor thrives in the spaces between words. Of course, psychotherapy and lyrical poetry address many of the same issues, and they both create a space where one can explore one's relationship with oneself and others. Both require rules, tremendous focus, entrancement and exaltation, the tension of spontaneity caged by restraint, the risk of failure and shame, the drumbeat of ritual, the willingness to be shaken to the core. So, though refreshingly different from each other, the two overlap in companionable places.

As I revised each poem, I necessarily restructured some of the feelings the poem captured. That process was also illuminating, as I sense it must have been for Anne Sexton as she drafted poems to her therapist (with whom, as it turned out, she was having an affair). My chief goal with this book, however, was to write the best poetry I could; its usefulness in therapy was felicitous but secondary. That's why I sent out, and subsequently published, the poems in literary journals without telling the editors much about them. They are, after all, simply deeply felt poems about one of the most important relationships in one's life.

I wrote many more than ninety-three poems during that year and a half, and chose to include the ones I thought succeeded best. A poet must select certain of her poems for a reason, overt or hidden, and no doubt the ones I chose form a mosaic of feeling that seems real and continuous to me. No doubt they're prongs that hold a mineral experience in memory. My favorite poems are the ones best able to conjure up the emotions and mood that sponsored them. In that sense, they're bookmarks that allow me to refeel. And reading anyone's poetry, I'm a sucker for phrasemaking, suggestiveness, sleights of mind, rhyme, close description, rigorous pungency. So I also chose poems with stylistic elements that pleased me.

It didn't occur to me at the time, but one association I have with origami comes from a trip to Honduras with the doctors of Interplast. In fascination and awe, I watched dozens of operations on severely afflicted children, mainly with cleft mouth and palate.

Working with a child's unique deformity and available flesh, the surgeons deftly reassembled faces like the folding of origami. Their own faces read: If I fold this piece here, and slide that piece there, and angle this other piece between them, and snip a little behind here, and then fold this other edge down . . . and so on, resolving the geometrical puzzle of a cleft face.

One doctor would start a child on the long road to healing, part of whose ultimate goal was being able to smile—coin of the realm for all children—and another doctor would continue the work when Interplast returned the following year with a new crew of volunteers. On my trip, I helped out as a circulating nurse, someone who bridges the sterile and unsterile fields in the operating room, and I became acutely aware of the surgeons' origami, their creative joining of papery flesh.

Curiously enough, at a certain point, I stopped needing to write analysis poems. No doubt much could be said about their order and evolution, the complex role they played and why at a certain stage I no longer required their intermediacy. There may have been a gradual change in how I processed pain, a psychic change that short-circuited my being inspired to write them. Maybe I wasn't feeling the same miasma I had to name if I hoped to manage and explore it.

Through the poems, little by little, my therapist began to meet and talk with the poet, an essential part of my sensibility that first emerged when I was a small child forging elaborate imaginary worlds and the "Secret Society of Selves" I write about in several poems. Maybe once he knew the poet self, I could return to writing poems about other facets of life, poems I didn't share with my therapist.

When I read the manuscript straight through, I'm surprised by the evolving tones of the relationship, something only visible in hindsight. While writing *Origami Bridges*, I was finishing a prose book, as well, *Cultivating Delight: A Natural History of My Garden*, and some of the poems' moods and themes appear in it. The poems influenced the prose. The reverse was not true, however. The creative flow traveled only in one direction.

I'm currently writing a prose memoir. Will that book enter the charmed circle of psychotherapy and function in a similar way? I don't know. I'm not writing it for that purpose, but being in therapy has made it possible to write. Many important things have happened in analysis since *Origami Bridges* was finished, and as a result I relish it for the time capsule it is: before Exodus, a chapter from the garden.

A Path Taken,
with All the Certainty
of Youth

⌒

Margaret Atwood

How is it that I became a writer? It wasn't a likely thing for me to have done, nor was it something I chose, as you might choose to be a lawyer or a dentist. It simply happened, suddenly, in 1956, while I was crossing the football field on the way home from school. I wrote a poem in my head and then I wrote it down, and after that, writing was the only thing I wanted to do.

I didn't know that this poem of mine wasn't at all good, and if I had known, I probably wouldn't have cared. It wasn't the result but the experience that had hooked me: it was the electricity. My transition from not being a writer to being one was instantaneous, like the change from docile bank clerk to fanged monster in B movies. Anyone looking might have thought I'd been exposed to some chemical or cosmic ray of the kind that causes rats to become gigantic or men to become invisible.

I wasn't old enough to be at all self-conscious about what

had just happened to me. If I'd read more about writers' lives, or indeed anything at all about them, I would have concealed the shameful transformation that had just taken place in me. Instead I announced it, much to the shock of the group of girls with whom I ate my paper-bag lunches in the high school cafeteria. One of them has since told me that she thought I was very brave, to just come out with something like that; she thought I had a lot of nerve. In truth I was simply ignorant.

There was also, as it turned out, the dismay of my parents to be reckoned with: their tolerance about caterpillars and beetles and other nonhuman life forms did not quite extend to artists. As was their habit, they bit their tongues and decided to wait out what they hoped would be a phase, and made oblique suggestions about the necessity of having a paying job.

One of my mother's friends was more cheerful. "That's nice, dear," she said, "because at least you'll be able to do it at home." (She assumed that, like all right-thinking girls, I would eventually have a home. She wasn't up on the current dirt about female writers, and did not know that these stern and dedicated creatures were supposed to forgo all of that, in favor of warped virginity or seedy loose-living, or suicide—suffering of one kind or another.)

If I had suspected anything about the role I would be expected to fulfill, not just as a writer, but as a female writer—how irrevocably doomed!—I would have flung my leaky blue blob-making ballpoint pen across the room, or plastered myself over with an impenetrable nom de plume, like B. Traven, author of *The Treasure of the Sierra Madre*, whose true identity has never been discovered. Or, like Thomas Pynchon, I would never have done any interviews, nor allowed my photo to appear on book jackets; but I was too young then to know about such ruses, and by now it is far too late.

In biographies there is usually some determining moment in early life that predicts the course of the future artist or scientist or politician. The child must be father to the man, and if he isn't, the biographer will do some cut-and-paste and stick on a different head, to make it all come out right. We do so wish to believe in a logical universe. But when I look back over the life I led until I began writing, I can find nothing in it that would account for the bizarre direction I took; or nothing that couldn't be found in the lives of many people who did not become writers.

When I published my first real collection of poetry at the age of twenty-six—"real" as opposed to the small pamphlet I myself had printed up on a flatbed press in a friend's cellar, as was the fashion among poets in those days—my brother wrote to me: "Congratulations on publishing your first book of poetry. I used to do that kind of thing myself when I was younger."

And perhaps that is the clue. We shared many of the same childhood pursuits, but he gave them up and turned to other forms of amusement, and I did not.

There I was, then, in 1956, still at high school, without a soul in sight who shared my view of what I should, could and ought to be doing. I did not know anyone who was a writer, except my aunt, who wrote children's stories for Sunday school magazines, which to my snobbish young mind did not count. None of the novelists whose books I had read—none that wrote for adults, that is, whether trashy books or literary ones—were alive and living in Canada.

I had not yet seriously begun to search for others of my

kind, to ferret them out of their damp caves and secret groves, so my view at the age of sixteen was that of the general citizen: I could see only what was made clearly visible to me. It was as if the public role of the writer—a role taken for granted, it seemed, in other countries and at other times, or so said the potted biographies in the school textbooks—this role had either never become established in Canada, or had existed once but had become extinct.

To quote A. M. Klein's "Portrait of the Poet as Landscape"—a poem I had not yet read, but was to stumble upon shortly and to imprint on, much as a newly hatched duck may imprint on a kangaroo:

> *It is possible that he is dead, and not discovered.*
> *It is possible that he can be found some place*
> *In a narrow closet, like a corpse in a detective story,*
> *Standing, his eyes staring, and ready to fall on his*
>   *face . . .*
> *We are sure only that from our real society*
> *He has disappeared; he simply does not count . . .*
> *. . . is, if he is at all, a number, an x,*
> *a Mr. Smith in a hotel register,—*
> *incognito, lost, lacunal.*

Essentials Get Lost in the Shuffle of Publicity

Ann Beattie

I have come to dread book tours because they so often coincide with world events and with personal events that are sad, preoccupying and bizarre. I was promoting a book when the O. J. Simpson jury suddenly announced that it had reached a verdict. My husband and I were having lunch in the bar of our Seattle hotel. We were of course riveted to the television. Between beverage and entrée came the pronouncement: not guilty. What?

But there was little time for me to question my husband, whom I hold personally responsible for explaining all things inexplicable. I had to race back to the room to be interviewed. This is, for writers, the equivalent of the tiger led from its moated promenade to its zoo cage at night.

The interviewer had heard the news, and it certainly was something. But he had recently interviewed another writer (a friend, as it happens) who had made quite an impression by announcing forcefully that he didn't have to keep doing what he was doing, and if his book didn't find an audience, he could and would quit. What did I think of that?

I thought he was probably burned out from his book tour. But the interviewer hardly listened to me; he still seemed stunned at the vociferousness of the writer who might quit. I said that writing and going on increasingly unproductive book tours took a toll. I suggested that the writer might have been having a bad day. I secretly felt that he was right, that the point comes when you realize it's not worth it anymore. Maybe it's fun for a first-timer. But to a writer who can't be reinvented, who can't be anything but the work she creates, I have serious doubts about the value of a book tour.

Even without it, things are complicated enough: we're our own preliminary editors; we teach; we review; we do committee work; we suffer the slings and arrows of outrageous numbers of blurb requests. I wrap and mail my old running shoes and send them to faraway cities for celebrity auctions benefiting charities that I've never heard of but that are as plentiful as flu.

It's now a familiar feeling that while I'm publicizing a book, I'll be pulled in two directions. I'll force myself to get through an interview when I'm preoccupied with what might be happening nationwide in the wake of the Simpson decision. Years before, I remember arriving for a photo shoot in New York and hearing not the usual make-placid-writers-hyper music but the radio, giving news of a plane burning in the desert: President Jimmy Carter's failed mission to free the captives from Iran. And, a lifetime before that, getting in a cab, as a college-girl-winner of the *Mademoiselle* contest, on her way to some ridiculous, scheduled event, giving the address and hearing the disgusted reply, "Don't you know Robert Kennedy's been shot?"

I was photographed on vacation in Florida before *Picturing Will* came out. The picture of me smiling appeared on page 1 of the *New York Times Book Review*. I was wait-listed for the first flight out the next morning: my father had had a stroke. Too often, things out of my control have called my attention to my book's meager place in the larger scheme. Quite simply, awful things have happened with such regularity that I am now able to skip humility and proceed directly to ludicrousness.

After continued prodding from the Seattle journalist, I said that life on the road could turn into a house of mirrors of a writer's real life. Whereas you might by nature be merely perplexed, you discover, reading your remarks, that you have stated opinions bitterly and emphatically. Though your friends appreciate your humor ("malevolent angels," Harry Mathews once called my husband and me), you sometimes stop yourself in midsentence before an audience, having morphed into Judge Judy.

Though you know you're looking at a distortion—those photographs aren't really you; those questions don't concern anything you've given serious thought to, so it's difficult to judge the veracity of your response—you've nevertheless been made to see yourself as an emphatically dithering person with big ears and a nasty squint. My friend the writer, I thought, must have been having a nasty-squint day.

I knew about those: six books sold the previous night (three to a former student still protesting his grade, one to a skinhead who also collects butterflies, "only the wings," one to someone who says, "Just your name; no inscription," one to a person who likes your work "because it's not too serious"), dead cellphone, missed plane, loved one with a mysterious pain in his chest that is now shooting down his left arm, review faxed from publicity department that criticizes not only your current novel, but your entire presumptuous career, annotated, "Oh well!"

It's easy to make a book tour sound like appalling fun, and of course complaining in this culture is not condoned (search the self-help shelves, and get into the right sort of chat room), but I can, for a moment, ignore the naysayers about my naysaying. I have a question: What did I ever think I was doing out there, and what do I think I'm doing now?

Clinging to youthful assumptions by trying to be the good girl? Formerly, I was young. I approached travel as if it were a school assignment. I accepted the fact that a book tour was part of the process and must also have assumed that it made sense. My first "tour," in 1976, when my first two books were published simultaneously, took me only to New York for a day or two, where I was interviewed by several publications in my hotel room. I didn't read anywhere. I don't recall that there were many readings in those days, except a few at colleges.

By 1980, when my fourth book was published, I was sent to bookstores (ah, for the late, great Books & Company), where amazing crowds showed up. That book's prominent, glowing review didn't hurt. (I still remember asking my editor, Rob Cowley, what "faute de mieux" meant. Poor man, he had to answer me.) Bookstore owners were loyal. They wanted my books before the reps described them; they also wanted a visit. Looking back, it seems we were all having our version of the '80s party, that time when the economy was expanding like bread baked with triple yeast, and we had nice, expensive cheese to spread on it, cholesterol be damned.

Audiences read. They talked to me about Raymond Carver and Joy Williams. They recommended writers I hadn't heard of. They were there to talk about writing, and they offered information instead of asking random questions. Though they didn't write (or were modest), I felt as if we were in this together.

There are still dedicated lovers of literature, but increasingly, when people approach me, they want anecdotes about writers, or they want me to recommend a writers' colony. They ask whether I'll lend my services to a fund-raiser. (Good-bye, shoes.) They have tried to sell me raffle tickets, which is bleakly amusing: a request signifying more than the questioner realizes.

There's an industry out there, sprung up around writers. To many, writing is not so interesting as being a writer, and when writers go on tour, it reinforces people's belief that it's all a package: you create something (details saved for future memoir), you get out there and network and promote it all the way to success, because success is the American Way.

In my opinion, writers have been overexposed, caricatured, asked specious questions to elicit amusing answers, their faces printed on coffee mugs. There are too many of us, and M.F.A. programs graduate more every year, causing publishers to suffer snow-blindness, which has resulted in everyone getting lost. There are those who maintain that bookstore chains have made things more difficult for individual writers. We are all inundated with endless appearances from writers who become Mary Poppins every time they publish again: they drop out of the sky to be booked anywhere and everywhere, say sensible things (the opposite is also nice, and will suffice), then disappear.

Writers are afraid not to be out there, for fear they'll be completely lost in the shuffle, but paradoxically, by getting out there we add to the problem. Nothing is made better by audiences', and the media's, silly attempt to glamorize writers. Any photographer will tell you it's a nightmare assignment to shoot some writer at home (they don't do anything), just as it is the writer's nightmare to realize that her unglamorous life will be symbolized by the ordinariness of her desk. No wonder Annie Leibovitz took me to a Laundromat and photographed me in front of a dryer.

It would be wrong not to be humbled, at times humiliated, by my years on the road. But it would also be wrong to deflect a serious issue with humor. When I started out, I wasn't a so-called literary writer. I was a writer. The more we are separated into smaller categories, the more the audience is condescended to; the more attention is focused on the writer's life, at the expense of considering the work, the more we will continue to perpetuate the delusion that the writer is there—conveniently there, out on the road—to be projected upon. To come to conclusions about the writer is irrelevant to the writer's work. We can only hope that our work transcends us.

⌐

After I published this piece, some people who believed in my work were hurt (one friend said that he was not hurt, but that many people called to ask him how I could do such a thing as omit mention of his loyalty and enthusiasm through the years). I am truly sorry about that. I meant to discuss problems, but if I had it to do over again, I'd certainly say that it means a lot to me that certain people have gone out of their way to support my writing. I stand corrected about this, also: Harry Mathews did not say that my husband and I were malicious angels. He called us mischievous angels.

Timeless Tact
Helps Sustain
a Literary Time Traveler

~~~~~

Geraldine Brooks

My writing desk is a tankard-scoured tavern table that once saw service in an eighteenth-century inn. When I look up, the waved and bubbled window panes of my study offer a view that has changed very little in the two hundred years since the glass was set in place. A small paddock rises gently to an apple orchard, the trees laced with white blossoms. An elderly stallion flicks at flies with a long, supple tail.

At this time of year boughs of unfurling oak leaves hide the black slash of electric wires. And that's helpful; for every morning, after I turn off the urgent chatter of news radio— its breathless headlines and daunting traffic reports—I make my way up to this little room and attempt to leave my own time behind.

For most of 1999 I tried to live in 1666. I wanted to imagine what it was like to be a young woman in a tiny English village of 250 souls in the year bubonic plague struck. The story is based on what took place in a real village named Eyam in the Pennine Mountains.

I stumbled upon Eyam by chance one summer day, hiking with my husband through the picturesque countryside of Derbyshire. Inside the village church a display told of how the villagers had decided to quarantine themselves to arrest the plague's spread. I found the story moving, but I don't think I would have tried to write a novel about it if we hadn't come to live a few years later in a tiny village of 250 souls in the Blue Ridge foothills of Virginia.

You live differently in a small place. I had been a city person all my life: my homes had been in the dense urban tangles of Sydney, New York, Cairo and London. Though each of those cities is very different, I was much the same in all of them. People say cities breed acceptance of diversity, but I didn't learn that lesson there. It took a village to teach me tolerance and a measure of tact.

If you meet a person who lives near you in a big city and you don't like her, that's fine: you can conduct your life so that you never have to speak with that person again. But in a village of 250, you don't have that luxury. You will see each other, day following day. You will sit side by side at town meetings or at other people's dinner tables. You will work together on school committees or at the annual fair. You're stuck with each other.

At first I disliked this. Used to choosing my friends for their like minds and agreeable opinions, I found it hard to be thrust into relationships with supporters of the death penalty or the NRA, of prayer in schools or unbridled property rights. But in time I learned that it wasn't necessary to always speak to someone about the things on which we disagreed. We could find common ground in an interest in heirloom potato varieties or the vicissitudes of puppy training. Within a year or two I was surprised that several of the folk I'd disliked on first meeting had somehow turned into valued friends.

And there were other friends, too: friends I'd never have made in the city. In urban neighborhoods like finds like: the wealthy gather at the leafy end of town, the impoverished struggle on elsewhere, often invisible to the affluent. But all of our village's half-dozen streets are leafy: all share wide, glorious views of pastures and hillsides. Millionaire or minimum-wage worker, we cluster in the enforced coziness of our eighteenth-century townscape.

To be sure, this intimacy isn't always good news. It takes more to sour a friendship here than it would in the city, but when a relationship goes bad, it does so with spectacular consequences. We'd lived here for about a year when one neighbor started having an affair with the husband of another. Since their houses were across the street from each other, discretion was impossible. Everyone knew; everyone had an opinion. Especially the aggrieved wife. She made her feelings plain by carefully whittling a scarlet A and affixing it to her rival's door.

These lessons about rage, passion and tolerance made me think of plague-stricken Eyam: how extraordinary it must have been to bring a community to a decision as dramatic as quarantining itself to keep infection within village bounds. And how horrible to find that as a consequence of your sacrifice two out of three of your neighbors were dead within a year. How would any kind of social order, faith or relationships survive?

I was well into writing about all this when I came across a letter that Henry James had sent to an author of historical fiction. In it he declared that any attempt to write about a time more than fifty years removed from one's own was worthless and should not even be attempted.

"The historical novel is, for me, condemned," he wrote to Sarah Orne Jewett in 1901. "You may multiply the little facts that can be got from pictures and documents, relics and prints, as much as you like—the real thing is almost impossible to do, and in its essence the whole effect is as nought: I mean the invention, the representation of the old consciousness, the soul, the sense, the horizon, the vision of individuals in whose minds half the things that make ours, that make the modern world, were nonexistent."

At first these words rattled me. But then I realized I'd heard very similar opinions many times before, in quite a different context, when I worked as a journalist covering the Middle East and Africa. "They don't think like us," white Africans would say of their black neighbors, or Israelis of Arabs, or upper-class Palestinians about their desperately poor refugee-camp brethren. "They don't have the same material expectations." "They don't value life as we do." "They don't care if their kid gets killed—they have so many of them."

I knew they were wrong. A woman keening for a dead child sounds exactly as raw in an earth-floored hovel as it does in a silk-carpeted drawing room. So what if my 1666 heroine lacked "half the things that make our modern world"? Henry James was wrong to imply that consciousness—the soul—is shaped by things. It is shaped, surely, by emotions and by the way emotions lead one human being to deal with another. And these emotions—fear, depression, love, exhilaration, the desire to live and to see your children live—these I do not think my seventeenth-century woman experienced any differently in her tiny village than I do in mine.

Write what you know. Every guide for the aspiring author advises this. Because I live in a long-settled rural place, I know certain things. I know the feel of a newborn lamb's damp, tight-curled fleece and the sharp sound a well-bucket chain makes as it scrapes on stone. But more than these material things, I know the feelings that flourish in small communities.

And I know other kinds of emotional truths that I believe apply across the centuries. I delivered my son in a modern hospital, but his birth was a bloody, protracted, life-threatening obstetrical emergency. Of what I know from this, which matters more? That the doctor used precision-engineered forceps, or that I was terrified of losing my child?

Five years after that long night, I can't tell you one detail of the things in that delivery room, but I can break into a sweat remembering the consciousness of those hours. So that consciousness is what I used in my fiction. As for the things: I was easily able to refer to a seventeenth-century midwifery textbook to find that in a delivery like mine the midwife might have resorted to a thatcher's hook.

It is impossible to know whether Henry James's harsh words discouraged Sarah Orne Jewett, who had sent him her latest novel for comment. The year after their correspondence she was injured in a carriage accident. The book she had sent to James was the last she ever wrote.

Now the lives of the two writers have themselves passed beyond James's fifty-year mark, and he would not have us presume to speculate. But I can't help imagining Sarah, the carriage, the slide of horses' hooves on the slippery Maine mud, the disarray of long starched skirt as she flew from her seat, the crunch of vertebrae as she landed. . . .

It is human nature to imagine, to put yourself in another's shoes. The past may be another country. But the only passport required is empathy.

Yes, There Are Second Acts (Literary Ones) in American Lives

〜〜〜

Alan Cheuse

In memory of the stupendously best-selling late bloomer James A. Michener, the Center for Writers at the University of Texas gives a ten-thousand-dollar prize, endowed by Random House, to a writer who, like that Pennsylvania-born world-traveling novelist, published his or her first book after age forty. I recently received a letter soliciting a nomination for that award, which got me thinking about the work and lives of some of my own favorite writers who were late starters.

There's Sherwood Anderson, who in his early forties managed a paint factory near Cleveland. One day after work he suffered a nervous breakdown, left home and began walking up the railroad tracks toward the big city, where he would eventually rent a room. There, in a week of furious labor, he wrote the masterly story "Hands," which served as the opening of his great story cycle about small-town midwestern life, *Winesburg, Ohio*.

There's Henry Miller, who in his fourth decade quit Brooklyn for Paris, where he would write his way into literary infamy. And Harriet Doerr, who, in her mid-sixties and recently widowed, applied to the Stanford writing program and eventually wrote the beautiful, prizewinning novel *Stones for Ibarra*. And Michener himself, in his late thirties, ending his career as a military journalist when the war ended, putting together a story collection and moving to New York City, where he served as an editorial assistant by day and a YMCA volleyball spotter by night, until the afternoon he won the Pulitzer Prize for *Tales of the South Pacific*.

That letter about the prize bearing Michener's name set me to meditating on the benefits and liabilities of starting a writing career, as I did myself, relatively late in life.

Like millions of people, I had always thought I wanted to be a fiction writer. But I didn't do much to make that happen. In college I dabbled at stories. Traveling in Europe after graduation, I kept a notebook, I went to bullfights, I drank the same Spanish brandy as Hemingway and gazed on the same Mediterranean waves as Byron. After returning home I spent a couple of years working at various jobs, such as caseworker in a Manhattan social-services unit and assistant fur-page editor at *Women's Wear Daily*. But I produced nothing resembling serious fiction.

"Keats had done his best work and died before he was the age that you are now," my first wife chided me.

She's got a point, I thought. My chance for becoming a prodigy had passed, and I was still doing nothing about what I once thought of as my greatest passion. I was in my late twenties, surely an adult, I thought, and so I ought to find myself an adult profession. Three years of graduate work later, and a Ph.D. in comparative literature nearly in hand, I took a job at Bennington College, the tiny—and then famously expensive—liberal arts institution in southwestern Vermont.

"You'll like teaching there," my graduate literature professor Francis Fergusson told me; he had founded the drama division at Bennington some decades before coming to Rutgers to teach the likes of me. "It's not a real college."

He was right, and mostly in good ways. At Bennington I was free to create my own courses, and after a few years I noticed that I was teaching a cycle of courses in the history of narrative, beginning with the Gilgamesh Epic and continuing on through Homer and Virgil and Chaucer and Dante and Boccaccio and Cervantes and the English novelists and the French and the Russians right on up to the work of the moderns.

My pals were the writers on the faculty—Bernard Malamud, Nicholas Delbanco, John Gardner—rather than the critics. But I wasn't a fiction writer yet, just someone still dreaming about it. So it really stung when one night while at dinner at the Gardner house with a room full of novelists, Joan Gardner went around the table asking about everyone's work in progress and when she got to me said: "That's all right, Alan. Everybody doesn't have to be a writer."

In my eighth year, the college that had nurtured me fired me. But that's another story. The main thing is that after some grieving I found myself elated, prepared to let go of teaching and take a dare I handed myself.

I vowed that I would publish a short story before I turned forty.

I moved to Tennessee, where my second wife took a teaching post at the state university. We made a pact. She would serve as our small family's main breadwinner for five years, and I would have that time to begin writing seriously.

In the half-finished basement room of a starter house on the outskirts of Knoxville, I set my manual Kmart portable typewriter on a Kmart picnic bench and placed that bench under the basement's only window, with a view out under the house's rear deck toward a small ditch and some young redbud trees that marked the rear line of our property. I sat down and found myself ready to begin.

Time alone hadn't made the difference in me. An actor prepares. So does a writer. But in a different way. With hindsight, I could see that living was not enough. The current spate of memoirs about abuse and divorce and other sorts of misery to the contrary, having bad things happen to you doesn't necessarily make you into a writer. Long life, short life, who hasn't lived through enough awful events to make for potential material? So it wasn't misery, though I had suffered my share by then. It was all the reading that I had done that had prepared me.

Which is not to say that all serious readers automatically become writers, or that studying art appreciation can make you a painter, or listening to Beethoven turn you into a composer. But you can't tap your own greatest potential as a composer without knowing Beethoven's music, and you can't write seriously without reading the greats in that peculiar way that writers read, attentive to the particularities of the language, to the technical turns and twists of scene-making and plot, soaking up numerous narrative strategies and studying various approaches to that cave in the deep woods where the human heart hibernates.

This gift and talent for reading like a writer comes early to many people in the field, so early in some that they don't even know they possess this special awareness. Keats had of course done his best work and died at an age far short of mine before I first sat down at that Tennessee picnic table. But then, for whatever reason, some of us are slow learners. Nearly two decades had passed since I had graduated from college, and it had taken me that long to prepare. But apparently now I was ready.

So I started typing. When I looked up from my work, those redbud trees had burst into blossom, and I had written a novella too long to publish in any magazine and a short story that after a couple of revisions I sold to the *New Yorker*, which published it less than a month before my fortieth birthday. In a quick succession of years I produced three novels, a memoir and two story collections, writing without stumbling because, as I thought of myself then, I had done plenty of stumbling before I started writing and perhaps I had gotten all of that out of the way.

Not strictly true, as the next decade would show me. I've made a few false starts since then, and unlike a much younger writer, I know that I had better not make too many more or else I'll find myself in deep trouble. But possessing that kind of insight is one of the advantages of starting late. As is one's understanding of Henry James's remark that it's better to have success as a writer in mid-age rather than in youth because at least then, when you're dropped by a fickle public, you have a life to go back to.

Footprints of Greatness
on Your Turf

Frank Conroy

The house was empty save for myself and the dog. I was in the bedroom reading V. S. Naipaul's recent book *Half a Life* and came to page 114:

> All that he had now was an idea—and it was like a belief in magic—that one day something would happen, an illumination would come to him, and he would be taken by a set of events to the place he should go. What he had to do was to hold himself in readiness, to recognize the moment.

A sense of eeriness came over me, a moment of temporal displacement. I went downstairs and ran my finger along the bookshelf until I found an old paperback of *Stop-Time*, which I had last read perhaps fifteen years before. I opened it and began to scan. It didn't take long. At the bottom of page 23 I found: "I waited, more than anything else, waited for something momentous to happen. Keeping a firm grip on reality was of immense importance. My vision had to be clear so that when 'it' happened I would know. The momentous event would clear away the trivia and throw my life into proper perspective. As soon as it happened I would understand what was going on, and until then it was useless to try."

The same concept, more elegantly and concisely expressed by Naipaul writing in his late sixties than my own first-person effort at about twenty-five, but close for all that. I felt excitement, and pleasure. Naipaul had just won the Nobel Prize, and I allowed myself to believe that since we had come up with roughly the same idea, to depict the inner states of mind of our young, striving characters (mine a good deal younger, but no matter), my own work took on, perforce, an added luster. A kind of accidental authentication forty years after the fact.

The next day I gave my colleague Jim Galvin both excerpts (unattributed) to read, which he did, standing by my desk in my office.

"So?" he asked, handing me back the sheet of paper. "Yeah? What am I supposed to say?"

"Do you think they're related?"

"Sure. I would've said *The Beast in the Jungle*, but the language is too modern."

"It's Naipaul on top. Me on the bottom."

He did not seem surprised, and again mentioned *The Beast in the Jungle*.

I should explain that all my life when a book or a story comes up in conversation, a work I should have read but haven't, I rarely admit my ignorance and do nothing to correct the misapprehension in the other person that I have. (I do not believe I am alone in this vice.) At least I knew the author and quickly obtained a copy of the story. On page 431 of the Penguin Classics edition of Henry James's *Selected Tales* I found the following, written around 1900:

"Of the way you did feel? Well, it was very simple. You said you had had from your earliest time, as the deepest thing within you, the sense of being kept for something rare and strange, possibly prodigious and terrible, that was sooner or later to happen to you."

James's language does indeed seem less modern, but the same idea, device, psychological insight or whatever one wants to call it, is clearly there. James decided to run with it, to take the detail and use it as the basis for a rather long, complicated and very sad story about the relationship between a particular man and a particular woman.

I suspect that many, many writers have found themselves dealing with characters they have created who are waiting for something to happen, something "magic" (Naipaul) or something "momentous" (me) or something "prodigious" (James) that once recognized would change everything.

I don't know enough about computers to do the kind of subtle word-plus-sense search needed to find those authors. Perhaps no search with that tight a focus is even possible, but in the end it would only be a curiosity, because we already know that literature from the beginning has been circling around the human condition, and that writers inevitably notice similar things from slightly different angles. How could it be otherwise?

Most writers are aware, or become aware, that writing is a curious business, involving odd currents running every which way under the surface. It's not an entirely rational process, says E. L. Doctorow, and I agree. It can sometimes seem a bit spooky even.

Many years ago I lost my only copy of chapter 2 of my novel *Body and Soul*. Sometime in the frantic end-of-term business, the packing, the drive across the country, the unpacking, etc., the handwritten pages had disappeared. My wife and I searched for a week, calling all the motels, practically dismantling the interior of the car, running around in circles until we finally gave up.

I called my old friend Robert Stone and told him I was scared to death. I had to write the chapter again, and I didn't know if I could do that. My entire life I had written whatever I was writing with only the foggiest notion of where it would go, and I found it hard to imagine writing any other way. Bob understood instantly and told me I could do it.

"You know that long thing of mine you liked so much?" he asked.

"'Helping?'" I would never forget it. A complex, multi-leveled story of great power.

"I had that old computer then, and I just pushed the wrong button and lost the whole damn thing. Two months' work."

"Yes, but you could type it in again," I said stupidly.

"No, no. I composed it on the computer. It only existed in the machine."

"Holy mackerel."

"You can do it."

So I went back and read chapter 1, which was all I had, and began to write. (It had been a couple of months since I'd worked on chapter 2, and my memories of it were foggy, to say the least.) I completed the new chapter 2, and went on into 3, 4, 5 and so on over the next year without giving the matter much thought.

If it is strange to write something and discover that someone has been there, like Naipaul or James, it is only slightly less strange to write something in which the someone is yourself. The original chapter 2 finally turned up, long after I needed it, when I was halfway through the book. I should say that writing the second chapter 2 took about as long as writing the first one, and felt, subjectively, very close to being new work, rather than a conscious reconstruction.

What an interesting afternoon then, when I put them side by side and read them simultaneously page by page. The major events were pretty much the same, although I hadn't been aware of remembering them so well, the pacing of the events was very close, almost congruent, the relationship of dialogue, exposition and description in terms of space used for each quite close, but the language was different. The words were different.

I was struck by the fact that the two texts could be so similar in many ways and yet dissimilar in language.

I've thought about this rare experience over the years, particularly when one or another case of alleged plagiarism comes up in the news. As Thomas Mallon points out in his book on the subject, *Stolen Words*, it is tricky territory to say the least. A writer like Doris Kearns Goodwin can mix up her handwritten index cards and make other mistakes. Reliance on research assistants is always dangerous, and old-fashioned filing cards constitute an additional danger. Stephen E. Ambrose, doing what might be called book manufacturing, incorporates chunks of people's books and doesn't seem to think he's done anything wrong. Of course historians and biographers must work from past sources, and slips will occur.

The situation in fiction is different, where the assumption is that the author is creating the language, working hard to find the right words to express what he is feeling, thinking and discovering. Borrowing whole phrases, sentences and paragraphs is a deeper sin in fiction, I think. But writers like D. M. Thomas, who acknowledges his debt to a Russian novel about Babi Yar and proceeds to lift whole stretches of prose written by another sensibility—such writers are rare. Out and out liars like my friend Jerzy Kosinski are perhaps even rarer; shamelessness of pathological proportions in his case.

The temptation is simply to assemble language and forgo the hard work of trying to penetrate it. No doubt everything has been brought up before, by someone else, or even by oneself; but if the language is truly worked, freshness is still possible. Worked language is how the writer can "make it new" in the words of Ezra Pound. Every time I pick up a book—even a murder mystery—I assume that's what the writer is trying to do. Otherwise, why bother?

New Insights into the Novel? Try Reading Three Hundred

⟨◦⟩

Chitra Divakaruni

When Neil Baldwin of the National Book Foundation called to inquire if I would agree to be one of the fiction judges for the 2000 National Book Awards, I responded with an immediate and enthusiastic yes. It was a great honor. An opportunity to influence the course of American letters and uphold the standard of art. Under the enthusiasm a certain trepidation gnawed at me: Would I be able to do the job, and do it well? And what about the novel I was halfway through writing? But I blithely shrugged it off.

Until the three hundred-plus volumes we were to judge showed up at my doorstep.

To keep up with the grueling schedule the judges had been set, I read nonstop, pausing only to jot down notes and questions before picking up a new book. I'd immerse myself in the worlds of the novels until words ran together. When I closed a book, sometimes it took me a moment to remember where I was. It was a reading experience unlike any I'd ever undertaken, even during graduate school at Berkeley.

Mingled with the pressure and the seriousness of the endeavor was a sense of illicit pleasure, of holiday. I loved to read, that was one of the reasons why I was a writer. Now I could pursue my passion without guilt while I let the dishes mildew in the sink and fed the children unhealthy micro-wave dinners and did not return phone calls from boring people. I was influencing the course of American letters, after all.

What I didn't realize was that this five-month marathon reading session would change my understanding of the novel form and force me to see my own writing differently.

Perhaps this was because I'd never before read, in such large numbers, books that I didn't actively choose. Many were by writers I hadn't heard of, and while several of them delighted me, a large number did not. Interestingly, though, in each case I began to see distinct patterns being repeated. (This was true, to an extent, of the short stories in the group as well. But it is my sense that the story, perhaps because of its brevity and its closeness to poetry, is a more experimen-tal form, and thus more actively committed to breaking pat-terns.)

First, I noticed how good the beginnings of most of the novels were. Drama, conflict, interesting characters, memo-rable gestures, snappy dialogue, significant themes: they were all there. Reading the initial pages, I would swing between delight and despair. How on earth would I judge among all these great works?

But after the first fifty pages or so, in many novels there was a downhill rush. (Was this because the initial energy was difficult to maintain? Or because—particularly in the case of first-time writers—the beginning had been work-shopped and polished many times, but not the later portions? Or because the novel was sold on the strength of its first few chapters, after which the writer slackened off and the editor didn't care?)

The unsuccessful novel reminds me of a top that has been spinning for a while. One can see the chapters begin to wander in loose, uneven circles. Pacing grows shaky. Events are rushed through, so that they are a mere catalog of plot happenings, or scenes lose momentum as the narration gets snagged on an idea. Characterization becomes wobbly. Motives do not convince. Actions no longer reveal new dimensions of personality. Language falters. And finally the novel topples over into a contrived or commonplace ending and comes to a skittery halt.

The successful novel, on the other hand, has a shape much like a bell. We begin at the top of the bell, its tight curve. Every detail has purpose here: the way a woman tilts her head, the slant of light as one exits the subway, the repetition of a phrase. As soon as we have gained our bearings, we notice things beginning to open up, flaring outward the way a bell does.

John Gardner rightly insisted that a good novel must be a "vivid, continuous dream." To this I would add that there must be in it a sense of expansion. This may be through the development of new and layered narrative voices; it may be through a fuller realization of a stylistic device introduced earlier; through metaphor or symbol or a series of ironic juxtapositions; or through methods as yet unthought of.

The characters are layered, too. At any moment an incident might tug the top layer from person and reveal an astonishment of traits below. Lists, recipes, letters, e-mail, found poetry, excerpts from other writers, real and imaginary: any or all of these begin to add depth and texture, to create a pattern. The pattern may not be obvious or conventionally symmetrical. It may be held in tense balance, aesthetics battling with a desire to push the boundaries of the acceptable. It stirs us, maybe even disturbs us.

Still, we feel confident that the author has an overall design in mind, a large and generous design, the way the first bell maker must have had: a three-dimensional design, with enough space inside it to create resonance and allow its melody (perhaps a cacophonic melody) to echo in the reader the way, it is said, that the tolling of a perfectly made bell creates a corresponding vibration inside the chest of each listener.

It is this resonance, finally, that separates the successful novel from the others. The cast of major characters may be small or large, clowns or kings. The backdrop may be modest (a room) or ambitious (a continent). The vocabulary may be simple or flamboyant, literary or colloquial. The melody may be created by a single flute, or performed by an entire orchestra. But through it all, there's a sense that what we're seeing is not all that this is about.

The novel continuously opens into something larger than the specifics that form the boundaries of the story, though paradoxically these specifics must be concrete and convincing if we are to intimate a larger truth through them. Reading it becomes a three-dimensional experience, beginning in the book and ending in ourselves. Such a novel, while it is a mirror of, and a commentary on, a particular event, people, country or time, is on some level about each one of us, our central truth. Each successful novel gives a special flavor and shape—and tone—to this truth, but does not limit it to these. In this it is similar to the bell, which shapes sound without enclosing it.

The National Book Awards were finally done. Bursting with energy, resolve and newfound wisdom, I returned to my half-written novel the way a mother flies, after an enforced separation, to her darling child. But what was this? In place of the (bell-shaped, I am convinced) work of art I had lovingly constructed was—no, not a spinning top, but a limp, wrinkled balloon out of which air was leaking even as I watched. (Dare I introduce, so late in the essay, a new analogy? I do it to underline the fact that there's always a new way in which one can mess up a novel.)

I've now gone back to the beginning of my novel for an extensive rewrite. I'm not sure how well I'll be able to use the vision I gained in shaping my work. There's a great gap, after all, between understanding and practice. But I'm finding the process—after the initial pain involved in discarding almost two hundred pages—strangely satisfying. Pinned to the wall by my writing desk is a modified quote from Browning:

Ah, but a girl's reach should exceed her grasp,
Or what's a heaven for?

Returning
to Proust's World
Stirs Remembrance

⟿

Leslie Epstein

About a year and a half ago I pulled down the first volume of my Random House Proust and read the familiar words that described how Marcel used to fall asleep. I had no idea why I had done so. After all, I'd read through the unadorned Scott Moncrieff translation forty years earlier, lying in the guest room of my Uncle Julie's house with a thermometer in my mouth for what I suspect was an imaginary fever. I read Kilmartin's touch-up in the early '90s.

Why should Dobbin once more plod these same pages? I think it was Cervantes's translator who said that all men should read the story of the Don three times: in youth, in middle age and toward the end. That's true for any book with the power to change the way we feel about life. But eighteen months ago my foothold was not on the sheer cliff of senectitude but upon that plateau that Proust himself might have called "entre deux âges." Too soon! Yet there I stood, like a sleepwalker, that first volume, all 1,040 pages of it, heavy in my hand.

I compensated for the impulsiveness of my project with the deliberation with which I intended to carry it out. I would read through the three volumes, two pages at a time, not more, not less; and I would do so the last thing each night. The trouble with Proust of course is that you are always losing your way: the parentheses don't close, the verb can't be found, and the key pronoun crouches in the proliferating subordinate clauses.

"The hell with it," you say and push on through the blur, a headache gathering at the corners of your eyes. But reading à la Épsteîn means there is never more than a page to go. Parse Proust's paragraph, untangle the syntax (to discover that the knot was often not in his text but your cortex), and the colored stones in the kaleidoscope have fallen into place. There is no better way to prepare for an adventure with time than to make a simultaneous commitment of five minutes and five years.

And so to bed. Like a box of Godivas on my pillow rests the clothbound book. What bonbons it contains! Here, on the Vivonne, the water lilies ceaselessly drift from bank to bank, like—permit me to paraphrase from memory—the peregrinations of a neurasthenic patient.

Here, too, is Aunt Léonie, who has banished half her friends for belittling her afflictions (Come, Léonie, you should go out for a brisk walk) and the other half for taking them seriously. Look, there is poor Swann, who has taken to buying Odette the most expensive gifts. *Pourquoi?* So that he might love her more. *Comment?* Well, just as a man who is not quite certain he loves the sea soon comes to adore it "after paying triple for an oceanfront room."

Let us go to a party filled with monocled men. A general wears his like a shell splinter; another chap's gaze seems glued to his, like a specimen on a slide; and up swims a third, M. de Palancy, who resembles a carp and so, upon the principle of the part substituting for the whole, carries with him everywhere this fragment of his aquarium. A photograph, Proust tells us, acquires dignity only after its subject no longer exists. How to introduce the Baron de Charlus? Perhaps by describing his fine attire but not failing to notice the nearly imperceptible red spot on his tie, "like a liberty which one dares not take."

I ought, at the first mention of that sinister character, to stop, just as I turn down, at light's out, each second page. It is not a bad idea to keep a nightly appointment with a noble mind; it has the power to purify even the most wasted day.

One morning, about a month after I had started reading *À la recherche du temps perdu,* I sat down at my desk and, after the usual Talmudic fiddling with the sports pages, started to write. What emerged on my legal pad had nothing to do with the novel that was already under way. In that work my narrator had arrived in Rome just in time to witness the triumphal parade of Mussolini's army and the spectacle of the vanquished Ethiopians being led through that same Arch of Titus that had been erected to celebrate the defeat of the Jews.

What I saw before me now was a teenager in a Buick convertible driving along the Pacific Coast Highway with a woman trying to protect her blowing hair and another adolescent who had his arms around the family spaniel to make sure it would not jump from the car. A double take. Why, that fellow at the wheel resembled me. Wasn't that my mother looking into her compact mirror? The curly blond hair, the blue, glittering eyes and, yes, the gap in his teeth when he smiled: that was my brother. We were driving to Malibu to meet the man who wanted to marry my mother.

I put down my Pelikan pen. Where had these people come from? Was I sleepwalking again? I had never, in decades of fiction, written a single word about my own life. My past had taken the form of history, the pain of my childhood preposterously transformed into the suffering of the Jews. Now I understood why I had walked in a trance to the bookshelf and pulled down the volume of Proust. I needed Marcel's courage and Marcel's example. If he could write about how he would wait in literal breathlessness for his mother's good-night kiss, perhaps I could depict my own past with its equivocal caresses.

I finished the first story and then a second and third. I began to see that a novel might be under way. By then I understood that there was another reason I had sought out Proust, one inextricably bound up with the passage of time. When Marcel returns to Parisian society after a hiatus of many years, he encounters his old friends at the Princesse de Guermantes's. He hardly recognizes them. Trembling they are, and pale, the women bent as if their dresses had already become entangled in their tombstones, their heads drooping in trajectories, the momentum of whose parabolas nothing will be able to check. Even the tremor on their lips seems to him a last prayer.

I, too, had recently returned to the neighborhood in which I'd grown up and saw once again the generation of actors and actresses, the writers and agents, who had so dazzled me once with their wit, beauty and bright spirits. Now they were huddled at the edges of the Palisades, as if at the end of a continent, over which a wind was blowing them—like pumice-stone dolls, as Marcel puts it—unrelentingly down.

As Marcel puts it. That is the purpose of literature: to organize our experience, to prefigure it and to provide both the recognition of, and consolation for, the necessity of growing old. I sensed that Proust, or my memory of Proust buried in that final volume, had helped me deal with the shock of what awaited me each time I returned to the West.

But I could not know that a greater shock lay just ahead. Midway through the fourth story, while I was working on a scene in which the boy who resembled me wraps a towel about the woman who resembled my mother after she has emerged shivering from an all too familiar pool, the telephone rang. My mother had had a heart attack, a bad one, out of the blue. I arrived at her bedside the next day. She was up, she was chipper, she wanted her glasses to read the *New Yorker.* But a second attack two days later tore a hole in that already damaged muscle, and the blood swished back and forth for a few hours, until she, I think to her own surprise, slipped away.

Three days later Uncle Julie died, too. We held one funeral. We held the other. Again the survivors appeared before me, though this time I did not give a thought to the glamorous lives they had led: these were just ladies from my mother's bridge group and other ladies and gentlemen from the Plato Society, for which to the end my mother had been writing a paper on the Ottoman Turks.

I returned to my home in the East. Old newspapers, old letters, students and students' stories. Also waiting was the yellow pad, similar to the one I am writing on now, and the abandoned sentence: my mother's double, in her white bathing cap, her bathing costume, blue-lipped from the cold.

My Pelikan was waiting, too. Proust could no longer help me. I was alone in the room. Somewhere Matisse has written that the great thing about art is that no matter what happens to the painter, whatever the interruptions or vicissitudes of his life, the daffodil or the patch of sunlight is still waiting utterly unchanged, so that he can make it complete. I picked up my pen. I finished the scene. I finished the story. I do not believe anyone can find that moment—I cannot find it myself—at which I was forced to suspend the sentence. All is seamless. With those words, and with these, I console myself.

Forget Ideas, Mr. Author. What Kind of Pen Do You Use?

Stephen Fry

Here is a truth to which all writers can attest: Readers are more interested in process than in product.

Authors know this for certain, because authors undergo Trial By Event, "event" being publisher-speak for anything from a chilly book signing in a half-empty general store with one paperback carousel next to the soda cabinet to a grand festival colloquium held before an audience of readers so literary that you just know they have terriers called Scott and Zelda and a parrot called Trilling.

No matter how well-read the audience may be, when it comes to the Q&A, it is always the same. After a few polite interrogatory skirmishes for form's sake come the only questions that matter to the reader.

"Do you write in longhand or on a computer?"

If longhand: "Pencil, ballpoint or old-fashioned ink pen?"

If computer: "PC or Mac? Which font do you prefer?"

No doubt if you were to reveal that you dictated your

work, there would come a fresh slew of questions. "Into a machine or to a secretary?" "Sony or Panasonic?" "Male or female?"

As it happens I have never heard an author say that he did use dictation; this seems to be a method of the Erle Stanley Gardner generation that has fallen into desuetude. Perhaps the rise of computer speech-recognition will change this. But if I did happen to be sharing a festival stage with a literary dictator, I would be fascinated by his answer. You see, writers (perhaps especially writers) want to know how to write, too.

Musicians tend not to face these questions because it is not generally held that everyone has a symphony in him somewhere. Language however belongs to us all. Is there a hint of resentment in readers? "We all speak English. We all write e-mails and letters every day. What's your secret? Just give us enough detail, and we can be inducted into the coterie, too." It is almost as if some people feel that they were off sick or at the dentist's the day the rest of the class was told how to write a book, and that it isn't fair of authors to keep the mystery to themselves.

I exaggerate for effect. Not every reader wants to be a writer, and literary festival audiences are hardly the most reliable sample group from which to extrapolate.

I once shared a stage with Gore Vidal in Manchester, England, which was a very great honor indeed, although he did not appear to appreciate it. No, but, tush. Mr. Vidal was asked if he felt there had ever been an age in recent history that could boast so few good writers as the present. "There are as many good writers as ever there were," he replied, and I wish I could reproduce on the page the trademark patrician Gore-drawl that transforms his lightest remark into a marmoreal epigram. "The problem is that there are so few good readers."

The rise of digital cameras and desktop editing software is starting to create the same effect with filmmaking, by the way. A director is now as likely to be asked by a film fan, "Do you prefer anamorphic or super-35?" or "Do you favor the bleach bypass process?" as once he would be asked, "What's Robert Redford really like?" or "Does Clint do his own stunts?"

A loss of innocence or a thrilling indication that soon we will all be artists? I don't know. I do know that, as I suggested earlier, writers are just as interested as readers in the trivial detail of another writer's day.

For example, I read somewhere that Graham Greene used to leave his last sentence of the writing day unfinished. In this way he always had something straightforward to do the next morning. I have copied this idea and find that something as simple as completing a sentence works very well as a way of priming the pump at the start of the day. Such a technique doesn't transform one into a literary master any more than growling bad-temperedly, beetling your brows and using an ear trumpet will enable you to write great symphonies, but every little bit helps.

My latest novel, *Revenge,* caused me a very specific hair-raising and sleep-depriving problem. I had planned it out in my head, which is about as much planning as I ever do, not being an index-card, scenario or flow-chart sort of a person. It was to be a story of wrongful imprisonment and subsequent vengeance. As I thought the narrative through, a little voice started whispering wicked thoughts into my ear.

"This isn't very original," it would say. "I've heard it before."

At first I didn't pay much attention. When did any of us last read an original story? Original writing is the issue. Treatment is all. But then one night I sat bolt upright in bed and screamed in horror. The truth had suddenly exploded into my consciousness.

The story, the plot I had been working out with such pleasure, was not just unoriginal, it was a straight steal, virtually identical in all but period and style to Alexandre Dumas's *Count of Monte Cristo*.

What does a writer do on such occasions? Abandon his narrative and embark upon another? I was already three chapters in, and those authorial juices that take so long to summon up were flowing nicely. Should I rely on the fact that *The Count of Monte Cristo* is one of those novels that few (myself included at that point) have actually read? I was in one heck of a pickle, let me tell you.

I arose early the next day and drove into the medieval university town of Cambridge, where there are more bookshops than people, and bought every copy of the Dumas original I could find, for now a new, more benign voice was whispering in my ear.

"I bet Dumas pinched the story, too."

And sure enough, in an introduction to one of the editions I found, came the welcome news that the story of a wrongly imprisoned sailor who escapes the Chateau d'If was, in Dumas's day, a kind of urban legend that he had gratefully lifted.

If we're talking process incidentally, Dumas's publishers paid him by the line. Can you imagine anything so foolish? This is why his work is crammed with dialogue.

"Pass the mustard."

"Eh?"

I said, "Pass the mustard."

"You want some custard?"

"No, mustard."

"Oh."

Each carriage return a happy ring on the cash register.

Anyway, once I was assured in my own mind that the out-line of the story was not original to Dumas, I continued with the book, deciding that a "literary reworking" or "homage" was perfectly acceptable, and that I could not in all serious-ness be charged with that most unforgivable of literary crimes, plagiarism.

As a further safeguard I changed the names of my pro-tagonists to anagrams of the originals. Thus Edmond Dan-tès, who reinvents himself as Monte Cristo, becomes in my story Ned Maddstone, who reinvents himself as Simon Cotter. Baron Danglars is turned into Barson-Garland and so on. Edmond's affianced Mercedes transforms herself (in an unforgivable example of automobile paronomasia) into Portia.

Interestingly, and I had not meant in any way to trap or test, my French translators were the only people to pick up on the story's similarity to Monte Cristo. Since then, in new editions, including the current American one, we have proudly announced the book's connection to Dumas. No one, however, has noticed the jeu d'esprit of anagrams and awful puns. All that work for nothing. If you have an hour or so to kill, you might like to pick up a copy (you can read it on a bookshop sofa, far be it for me to vulgarly hawk for business) and see how many you can spot.

Oh, I use a Mac, by the way. Times Roman, 14 point. Very traditional.

In Paris and Moscow, a Novelist Finds His Time and Place

⌒⌐⌐⌐⌐⌐◗

Alan Furst

A few months after I published my fourth book, I decided to become a writer. I would move to Paris and, as it's said, write my novel. "Isn't that," said a friend, "rather, uh, bohemian?" Perfect, I thought, she's not wrong, that's exactly what it is. But why not? I would sit in cafés, smoke Gauloises, look out over a courtyard and write a long, difficult, ambitious book with a doubtful future. My early novels had been acquired by the National Library of Oblivion, they were happy and at peace now, I was free to do whatever I wanted. And what mattered most of all was that I'd found something I wanted to write about.

The idea came, as usual, by accident. I'd gone to the Soviet Union in 1983 to do a travel piece for *Esquire* magazine and discovered that the country was a police state. Yes, I knew that, but I was, in some special American way, emotionally innocent of what it meant. When you handed in your passport at a Moscow hotel, there was a curtain

hanging over the window, so you didn't see the security offi-
cer's face, just the hands. The Soviet authorities weren't subtle about it, they wanted you to be afraid of them, and it
made me mad.

Moscow was a tense, dark city, all shadows and averted
eyes, with intrigue in its very air, a city where writers should
have turned out spy novels by the yard. So then, where was
the Russian le Carré? Dead or in jail, if he or she existed at
all. In fact I believed that Russian writers were not allowed
to write spy novels—or political novels of any sort.

Fine, I thought, I'll write them. And since I felt that
Moscow and its satellite states in Eastern Europe were in
some sense stuck in 1937, I would write about 1937. I had a
recording of the Django Reinhardt–Stephane Grappelli sessions at the Hot Club of France, recorded in 1937. There, I
thought, right there. And what kind of novel would you
write about Russia in 1937? Why, a spy novel, what else? So
I would write historical espionage novels. Was that a genre?
Not that I knew about, but it was now. I could write about
Bulgaria and Romania, Byelorussia and the Ukraine. Even
Bohemia, up on the German border with Czechoslovakia,
important in the autumn of 1938. So, yes, Bohemian at last.

Back in the United States, I went where all historical
novelists must go, to the library. My favorite place. I have a
theory that writers don't actually want to write books, they
want to read them, but, discovering that they are unavail-
able to be read, because they are unwritten, they write
them. Anyhow, I discovered a treasure trove. There were
volumes and volumes on the history of espionage: Russian
espionage; Russian espionage in the 1930s; Russian espionage in the 1930s in France; Russian espionage in the
1930s in France, but the other guy got it wrong.

And that was only part of it. Because I now realized that my favorite writer, Anthony Powell, was a novelist of the midcentury, his late youth and his war spanning the 1933 to 1944 period I'd taken for my own. For me, Anthony Powell is a religion. I read *A Dance to the Music of Time* every few years, as well as others, especially *Venusberg*, a political fantasy of the Baltic.

There was more. Genre novels—by Eric Ambler, six of them prewar, and Graham Greene—and just plain novels, with characters wound up and set moving through the European political realities of that era. Christopher Isherwood's *Prater Violet*, for example, and Arthur Koestler, Josef Roth, Babel, Bulgakov—especially *The White Guard*.

It's funny, the apartment in Paris actually had a garret, a room beneath the roof with a slanted ceiling, and I'd lie up there and read, and sometimes I'd turn on the radio, and there would be, "This is the BBC." News of war (Iraq) faded in and out and crackled with static. Damn.

And then, along with the espionage history and the fiction—used as social and psychological history—there was political history. The ascent of Hitler in 1933. Stalin's first purge, 1934. Spanish Civil War, 1936. Munich and Kristallnacht, 1938. Invasion of Poland, 1939. Fall of France, 1940. Invasion of Russia, 1941. With stories, endless stories. I don't happen to be able to write plots; they come out like plots. So what I do is use the stories that happened, then create the sorts of characters who could have taken part in those stories.

Fact is, during this period in particular, history twisted and turned in more intricate and desperate ways than anything a novelist could think up. In March I finished a new book, called *Blood of Victory*. The title is taken from a speech by a French senator at a conference on petroleum in 1918. He said that oil, "the blood of the earth," had become in time of war "the blood of victory." And the central story of the book follows a real story of the period: the attempts of the British secret services in 1940 to impede the exportation of Romanian oil to Germany. This will be the seventh book in the series, and the number of available stories just grows with research.

Research. Once upon a time I toyed with the idea of a career in academia, as a medievalist. But academia toyed with me, and I gave up on the Middle Ages, because I didn't think of myself as somebody who would spend his life doing research. I leave the moral of the story to you, but eventually I became addicted, and I now see it as a vocational privilege.

Still, there is something to be said for the 300-page interior monologue in italics—at least you won't get letters informing you that the British Beaufighter aircraft was not in service until the end of October. It's hard to avoid that sort of thing in 350 pages of manuscript, even with good editing and copyediting. I think it was Randall Jarrell who once defined the novel as a work in prose of a certain length that has something wrong with it.

The word wrong takes on a particularly spicy flavor when you write for a living. At the beginning of my book *Dark Star,* some of the action is set in Prague, and I wanted the 1937 name of the railroad station there. Given the custom of the time, it would have been either a version of the Parisian Gare du Nord, North Station, no doubt seductively exotic-looking in Czech, or the name of a nineteenth-century hero, just as good.

When I finally found it, however, I discovered that the station had been named for Woodrow Wilson. I knew why, but that didn't help at all. You can't have your hero scuttling through the back alleys of Prague in the rain and show up there. So, eventually, his train "left the central station at 9:30."

And that's the easy part, facts, because the hard part is the words. Basically, if you write novels, you sit alone in a room and fight the language. For example, in one of my books I had what I came to think of as the billowing problem. Everything was billowing—smoke, parachutes, curtains, clouds. And what horrifies you, in retrospect, is that every single time you thought it was just a terrific word. Now, go and try to replace it. I knew enough, at that point, to avoid the malady I call thesaurusitis, the symptoms of which are ghastly: "'Oh, no!' he ejaculated," and like that. So in the final version, the curtains stay where they are, the clouds drift, the parachute billows on page 28, while the smoke billows on page 228, and you hope nobody notices.

No big deal, any of this, just the daily turmoil of a writer's life. A little penury, a little sciatica—still no big deal. It's an honor to be in this profession, fiction-writing. I see now and then that some people are concerned about its future, the novel, but I'm probably one of the worst people in the world to ask about that. I don't even own a computer. I work on a descendant of the magnificent IBM Selectric, using a typeface that has a sort of 1940s look to it, and I write 1940s-style novels about the 1940s.

Curious thing about the IBM Selectric, a writer's machine if ever there was one. I discovered, in Paris, that there's an IBM Selectric underground. Somebody I met at a party told me about it, and I went out the Boulevard Richard Lenoir, off in the commercial part of the 11th arrondissement, where I followed the owner of an office supply store to the first basement, then the second, down a long hallway to a padlocked wooden door, which he opened with a key on a chain attached to his belt. He turned on a light and there, on metal shelves, stood a dozen well-used IBM Selectrics.

"I keep them around," he said. "There's always somebody who wants one."

Recognizing the Book That Needs to Be Written

~~~~~~

Dorothy Gallagher

Years ago, I picked up a copy of Sarah Orne Jewett's collection of stories *The Country of the Pointed Firs*. These are wonderful stories. But what struck me at the time, and what has stayed with me, is a letter from Jewett to Willa Cather that Cather quotes in her preface to the book:

> The thing that teases the mind over and over for years, and at last gets itself put down rightly on paper—whether little or great, it belongs to Literature.

The thing that teases the mind . . . A writer is always preoccupied with identifying the material that is essential to her work, the book that needs to be written. If there is such a core of material, bits and pieces of it will find their way into everything she writes, even into an editor's assignment. And she waits for that moment of synthesis when the subject finds the vehicle for its expression.

For me, that moment first came in the late 1970s. I learned then about an obscure Italian-American anarchist named Carlo Tresca. By that time Tresca had been dead for more than thirty years, murdered in 1943. I had never heard of him, but I recognized him at once. He was the embodiment of my subject. In writing his life, I would at last be dealing with the material that was necessary to me.

And to say what that is, I will turn to another writer, Robert Warshow, who died young, in the 1950s, still in his thirties, but who produced in his short life a number of brilliant essays on American cultural life that are collected as *The Immediate Experience.* In one essay Warshow wrote about the crucial effect of the American Communist movement on the intellectual life of the country in the 1930s.

There was a time, Warshow wrote, when virtually all intellectual vitality was derived in one way or another from the Communist Party. "If you were not somewhere within the party's wide orbit"—and he was referring to the days of the Popular Front, the Spanish Civil War, the rise of Fascism: the time of the party's greatest influence in America and in Europe—"then you were likely to be in the opposition, which meant that much of your thought and energy had to be devoted to maintaining yourself in opposition. In either case, it was the Communist Party that determined what you were to think about and in what terms."

The world has moved on, and very quickly, too. Fanatical ideologies have taken different forms, and even as we watch at this moment, we see the categories of political and social thought that defined the world through the 1980s dissolve and re-form in strange and terrifying ways. But it was the idiom of the Communist Party that I took in with my mother's milk: it was my introduction to intellectual experience and to the dense web of loyalties and enmities that ideology so dangerously generates; and it continues to engage me as nothing else does.

And, really, why wouldn't it? Unquestioning belief in an abstract idea is a peculiar feature of our species that transcends the ages. The historian Martin Malia called Communism "the great political religion of the modern age . . . promising egalitarian redemption at the end of history." Worse, almost, than the horrific acts committed in its name, Communist ideology appropriated the language of the best hopes and ideals of humanity. And every horror was called by the name of its opposite, as George Orwell noticed.

Many immigrant Jews, as my own family did, lived in fairly isolated enclaves, among people who had come from the same part of the world—Eastern Europe, Russia—and who largely shared their views. It was possible for that immigrant generation to live an entire life in America with little connection to the people and country of their emigration.

If my grandfather kept the God of the shtetl, my mother's generation found life's meaning in the Bolshevik revolution. It was left to their children, who were the first generation born in America, to connect with the new world. And for many years that was my business: finding a foothold on this ground. When I felt firmly grounded, the past asserted itself, and I eventually found Carlo Tresca, an anarchist, whose political viewpoint had led him very early to see the dangers of Bolshevism. He became my vehicle and guide to what had always been waiting at the back of my mind.

Writing is problem-solving; whether in fiction, biography or memoir, certain basic questions have to be resolved. In biography, at least, a writer leans heavily on materials gathered in research. Working with a trove of documents is constraining, but also in some ways liberating, as working a puzzle is liberating. The clues are in your files, and if you've done your job as a researcher, you have the tools to solve the puzzle. But when I turned to memoir—the shamelessly naked core of a writer's necessary material—I found myself traveling as light as any writer of fiction.

I have never written fiction, and memoir may be as close as I ever get to it. No more than a biography or a novel is memoir true to life. Because, truly, life is just one damn thing after another. The writer's business is to find the shape in unruly life and to serve her story. Not, you may note, to serve her family, or to serve the truth, but to serve the story. There really is no choice. A reporter of fact is in service to the facts, a eulogist to the family of the dead, but a writer serves the story without apology to competing claims.

This is an attitude that some have characterized as ruthless: that cold detachment, that remove, that allows writers to make a commodity of the lives of others. But a writer who cannot separate herself from her characters and see them within the full spectrum of their human qualities loses everything in a haze of nostalgia and sentimentality. Bathos would do no honor to my subjects nor, most important, bring them to literary life, which is the only way they could live in the world again.

At first I intended to write only one piece, the story of the agonizing last years of my parents' lives, a five-year period during which I had made some notes. The original version of the story I wrote was about 150 pages long. Everything was in it, but it didn't work. I hadn't solved any of the problems that the story demanded. But I was lucky, and eventually a solution came to me.

The right voice in which to tell the story came to me, and when it did, many other things fell into place. And I wound up with a story that is ten or twelve pages long and yet contains everything I wanted to say. After that first piece, I went on to make a book of stories about my family that I called *How I Came into My Inheritance and Other True Stories*, without notes this time, with only treacherous memory and a few letters to guide me.

Now you may ask: Just what is the relation of your memoir to the truth?

It is as close as it can be.

The moment you put pen to paper and begin to shape a story, the essential nature of life—that one damn thing after another—is lost. No matter how ambiguous you try to make a story, no matter how many ends you leave hanging, it's a package made to travel.

Everything that happened is not in my stories; how could it be? Memory is selective, storytelling insists on itself. But there is nothing in my stories that did not happen. In their essence they are true.

Or a shade of true. There is a piece in my memoir that I call "Cousin Meyer's Autobiography." I did not really write this story. My cousin, whose real name was Oscar, left a self-printed memoir of some hundred pages. The first liberty I took with it was to change his name to Meyer in order to avoid confusion with my uncle whose name was Oscar.

Cousin Meyer's memoir was a treasure; it told of some extraordinary events in his life that dovetailed with the central material of my book. I took his hundred pages, reduced them in the way you would reduce a sauce, I turned them a little, say from north to northeast. The result may not be the story he wanted people to read. I took his story over, I insisted on my interpretation, I even added some lines that he did not write.

Did I have a right to do that? Some would say not, and really I would have no defense. Nevertheless, if cousin Meyer, so incensed by my interference, returned from the dead to object, I would answer him: But, cousin, for more than twenty years your story languished in a drawer; you were dead in fact, your life lingered in hardly anyone's memory. And now, because I have used you, more people have read your story than you ever could have dreamed. Cousin, you live, even if you dance to my tune.

How to Insult a Writer

Herbert Gold

"Could you recommend some books to take with me on my two-week Caribbean cruise? I'm a lover of good reading."

The questioner was a man whose locker stood next to mine at a health club. I saw him naked as often as his wife did; occasionally we exchanged manly observations about teams, politics and fitness. Now literature was having its turn. I recommended several books, adding shyly, "And you could read one of mine, a novel or nonfiction, depending on . . ."

He shook his head sternly. "Sorry, but I'm a very busy dermatologist. I only have time to keep up with well-validated books on the best-seller list."

I was sympathetic with his problem. After all, he wouldn't prescribe a pimple remedy that didn't have a large success-ful trial.

Once, on a happier occasion, I was lurking in a bookstore

during a successful run of publication when I spotted an elderly couple picking up my book. I was about to see an actual person, not my mother, actually choosing my novel. They examined it, turned it over, scanned the jacket copy, studied the photo of me as a somewhat more presentable person than I am in real life. "Have we read this one?" the woman asked her spouse. He answered, "I think so, maybe," and they replaced the book on the table.

Every writer hopes the work is memorable. The bibliophilic couple almost remembered mine. I told myself that a book club computer must have shipped it to them unasked on some sort of automatic basis because they had neglected to reject it in advance. Experience in the truth-'n'-beauty jungle out there teaches writers to be skilled injustice collectors. I was determined to be different, just as I was determined to ignore the paranoids beaming their radio signals into the fillings of my teeth.

Alas and alack, life is filled with hurt. A relative in Cleveland telephoned to say that she really loved the beginning of my latest novel. Only the beginning? Well, she was reading it in the bathtub and dropped it, and all the pages got stuck together; a wet, stuck-together text is really icky. My voice turned a bit shrill and piping as I suggested picking up another copy.

Her silence expressed pity. My book had had its chance and muffed it. Of course I could have shipped her one of my own copies, purchased at the wholesale rate from the publisher, but there is something contrary—short of paranoid—in my nature.

Most writers have acquaintances who eat only in classy restaurants, drink only classy wines, sighing and suggesting that books are so expensive, so would you . . . ? My preferred procedure is to write a check on the spot so that the literary gourmet can buy a copy. Since I have a high-I.Q. brand of acquaintance, they usually suspect sarcasm in the gesture as I whip out my checkbook. They look puzzled. They thought the seeker of truth-'n'-beauty (see above) would be past such paltriness.

So I tell them the story of publication of my first novel, back in ancient times, when Richard Laukhoff, a distinguished bookseller in Cleveland who had once employed Hart Crane as a clerk, pulled me to the door of his shop and said: "See that hofbrau? See that Blue Boar cafeteria? If people had lunch in that nice cafeteria instead of that German restaurant, they could afford to buy one of your books every day."

Good idea! I thought. Every single day. But judging from the sales history of most novelists, people really prefer their hofbrau cuisine with all the fine mustards and relishes.

Relatives do it, cuisine-loving lunchers do it, even fellow writers do it. A colleague asked with great sincerity for my honest appraisal of his forthcoming novel. He wanted help; there was time for last revisions. I passed along the suggestions that occurred to me.

Surely shrewd students of human nature will predict the tenor of his reply, but probably you haven't anticipated its elegance. "Well," he said, "your last book didn't send me into empyrean heights of divine bliss, either."

Probably the most stringent denunciation I've ever received was from a well-known novelist of my former acquaintance (name upon request, with payment of my usual fee) who wrote to me that I was a fascist and wrote to the chairman of the English department at the University of California at Berkeley, where I was then teaching, that I should be driven from campus as a corrupter of the young, and also to suggest that he was available to fill my position. He wrote to my publishers that they would withdraw the book if they had any integrity at all. He wrote to potential reviewers and book-review editors to warn them against giving my novel favorable notice.

I enjoyed his campaign (he was moved! he was stirred!) and suggested to my publishers that they use his letters in advertisements. But what do publishers understand about useful publicity?

My most dire experience along the line of serious organic criticism—and here I challenge fellow writers to compete with me in the Indoor Derogation Olympics—came when I picked up one of my books and, seeking to impress the charming young person with whom I was browsing in the bookshop, proposed to buy it for her. (The price was marked down. This appealed to the instinct to save money for my old age or my summer vacation, whichever came first.) But as I carried it to the cash register I noticed—how to explain this with dignity?—that the book gave off an alley reek. I asked the proprietor, What happened?

"Oh, it's nothing personal," he said. "It wasn't a human being or a critic who did that. It was my cat."

I accepted his consolation in the spirit with which it was offered, but sniffed at the book, still suspicious. A pungency, a rancidness. O.K., but I would take his word.

So now, dear readers, you can understand why I prefer either human beings or literary critics to the kind of pussy that thinks it can make summary judgments on my soul's fulfillments, my life's work.

Calming the Inner Critic
and Getting to Work

⟨⟨⟩

Allegra Goodman

They say writing is lonely work. But that's an exaggera-
tion. Even alone at their desks, writers entertain visitors: characters of a novel, famous and not so famous
figures from the past. On good days, all these come to the
table. On bad days, however, only unwelcome visitors appear:
The specter of the third-grade teacher who despaired of your
penmanship. The ghost of the first person who told you that
spelling counts. The voice of reason pointing out that what
you are about to attempt has already been done—and done
far better than you might even hope.

So why bother? Why even begin? It is, after all, abundantly clear that you are not Henry James. Your themes are
hackneyed, your style imitative. As for your emotions,
memories, insights and invented characters, what makes
you think anyone will care? These are the perfectly logical
questions of the famous, petty and implacable inner critic.

What should a writer do when the inner critic comes to

call? How to silence these disparaging whispers? I have no magic cure, but here, from my own experience, is a modest proposal to combat the fiend.

Forget the past. Nothing stops the creative juices like thoughts of the literary tradition. "You'll never be John Donne!" your inner critic shrieks. Or: "'Middlemarch!' Now that was a book!" These thoughts used to fill me with gloom. Then I went to graduate school at Stanford, and I steeped myself in Shakespeare, Wordsworth and Defoe. The experience set me free.

It happened like this. I was sitting in Green Library trying to write a story, and I looked at all the shelves of books around me, and suddenly the obvious occurred to me. All the great Romantic poets and Elizabethan playwrights and Victorian novelists that tower over me—they're dead! Oh, they still cast their shadow, but I'm alive, and they are irrefutably dead. Their language is exquisite, their scenes divine, but what have these writers done lately? Not a damn thing. Think about it. The idea should give you hope. Past masters are done. Their achievements are finite, known, measurable. Present writers, on the other hand, live in possibility. Your masterpiece could be just around the corner. Genius could befall you at any moment.

"Well," your inner critic counters gloomily, "just remember that when you're gone, your books will suffer the same fate as all the rest. They'll be relics at best. More likely, they'll just languish in obscurity." To which I have to say: So what? I won't be around to care.

Carpe diem. Know your literary tradition, savor it, steal from it, but when you sit down to write, forget about worshiping greatness and fetishizing masterpieces. If your inner critic continues to plague you with invidious comparisons, scream, "Ancestor worship!" and leave the building.

Treat writing as a sacred act. Just as the inner critic loves to dwell on the past, she delights in worrying about the future. "Who would want to read this?" she demands. "Nobody is going to publish a book like that!" Such nagging can incapacitate unpublished writers. Published writers, on the other hand, know that terrible books come out all the time. They anguish: "The reviewers are going to crucify me, and nobody will want to publish me after that."

But take a step back. What are you really afraid of here? When you come down to it, this is just a case of the inner critic masquerading as public opinion, and playing on your vanity.

I know only one way out of this trap, which is to concentrate on your writing itself, for itself. Figuring out what the public wants, or even what the public is: that's the job of pollsters and publicists and advertisers. All those people study the marketplace. But the creative artist can change the world. A true writer opens people's ears and eyes, not merely playing to the public, but changing minds and lives. This is sacred work.

Love your material. Nothing frightens the inner critic more than the writer who loves her work. The writer who is enamored of her material forgets all about censoring herself. She doesn't stop to wonder if her book is any good, or who will publish it, or what people will think. She writes in a trance, losing track of time, hearing only her characters in her head.

This is a state of grace possible only when you are truly desperate to tell a story. Suddenly you are so full of voices, ideas and events that it is as if you were rushing from the scene of the crime. How you arrange your sentences or whether a similar tale has been told before: these could not be farther from your mind. It never occurs to you to question whether your characters are well drawn or whether their dialogue is realistic because all these people are pushing and shoving and talking at once, and to your mind they are real, so realism is not much of a problem.

There is nothing better than listening to your characters regale you. I laughed and shook my head at the things Sharon Spiegelman said and did in *Paradise Park*. I was surprised sometimes, as I wrote *Kaaterskill Falls,* by the sweetness of Isaac Shulman and the determination of his wife, Elizabeth, and by the calculating, grieving, uncompromising voice of the old Rav Kirshner. They were all fictional characters, and yet in the writing they were real.

Now you may ask, what if my characters won't talk to me? What if they won't even visit? The only answer is to think and think some more, and then go out and read and look and listen some more. Do not sit and mope. Do not sigh. Do not throw up your hands and give up on the whole project. Do not go back to the drawing board. There is nothing more depressing than an empty drawing board. No, go back to the world, which is where all characters originally come from.

Go back to your library, your forest, your newspapers, your family, your day job, your photos, your music, your maps and jottings of old dreams. All these are teeming with life, and life is the stuff of fiction. There are no guarantees, but if you go out where stories congregate, it's far more likely that characters will come.

Recognize that deep down you love your inner critic.

How sad, how sordid. How cheap. Secretly writers do love the censor within. We say we hate that sanctimonious inner voice, but there is no better excuse for procrastination, lethargy and despair. There is no better excuse for getting nothing done than to lock yourself in battle with the famous inner demons of self-criticism and doubt.

External obstacles have such obvious, prosaic remedies: time can be found, paper purchased. But when it comes to inner obstacles, the difficulty is spiritual, and thus infinite. "I'm blocked!" you moan. Or, "I'm such a perfectionist, I can never finish." Which is to say your inner critic is blocking the way and too busy pointing out mistakes to let you finish. It's terribly depressing but, admit it, also comforting, to hear that you'll never perfect your work, and thus never finish. If you know you'll never finish, then there is no point in trying any longer. And if you don't try, then you can't fail.

This is a safe situation, but not conducive to creative work. If you want to write, or really to create anything, you have to risk falling on your face. How much easier to sit back and snipe at the efforts of yourself and others. How sophisticated you can become, your own contribution unimpeachable, because it does not exist. Sometimes insightful, always acute, the inner critic can become your closest literary friend, the one who tells you the truth, the one who makes you laugh at yourself and punctures your delusions.

This is all to the good. The danger is in identifying so much with your inner critic that you enjoy self-deprecation more than your work itself. Writer, beware! The inner critic is insidious, subversive, always available for depressive episodes. Stay alert. Know the enemy. Know yourself.

Ultimately every writer must choose between safety and invention; between life as a literary couch potato and imaginative exercise. You must decide which you like better, the perfectionist within or the flawed pages at hand.

Perhaps you'd rather hold yourself to the impossibly high standards of writers long dead. Or perhaps you'd rather not waste time writing something that will go unpublished, unnoticed and unread. You have received no encouragement from anyone else, and so you would never think of encouraging yourself. Or you choose to be a realist. You're smart enough to see your talent is limited, your gift too small to pursue. You can convince yourself of all this, or you can listen to your imagination instead. You can fire yourself up with words and voices. You can look out into the world teeming with stories and cast your net.

A Narrator Leaps
Past Journalism

Vivian Gornick

I began my working life in the 1970s as a writer of what
was then called personal journalism, a hybrid term
meaning part personal essay, part social criticism. On the
barricades for radical feminism, it had seemed natural to
me from the minute I approached the typewriter to use
myself—to use my own response to a circumstance or an
event—as a means of making some larger sense of things.

At the time, of course, that was a shared instinct. Many
other writers felt similarly compelled. The personal had
become political, and the headlines metaphoric. Immediate
experience signified. But from the beginning, I saw the dangers of this kind of writing—people rushing into print with
no clear idea of the relation between narrator and subject,
falling quickly into confessionalism or therapy on the page
or naked self-absorption—and I resolved to work hard at
avoiding its pitfalls. The reliable reporter, I vowed, would
keep the narrator trustworthy.

One day a book editor approached me with an idea that struck a note of response. I had confided to her the tale of an intimate friendship I'd made with an Egyptian whose childhood in Cairo had strongly resembled my own in the Bronx, and now I was being invited to go to Egypt to write about middle-class Cairenes. I said yes with easy pleasure, assuming that I would do in Cairo what I had been doing in New York. That is, I'd put myself down in the middle of the city, meet the people, use my own fears and prejudices to let them become themselves, and then I'd write as I always wrote.

But Cairo was not New York, and personal journalism turned out not exactly the right job description. The city—dark, nervous, tender; intelligent, ignorant, fearful—invaded me, and I saw myself swamped by thoughts and feelings I couldn't bring into line. When I had been a working journalist, politics had provided me with a situation, and polemics had given me my story.

Now, in Egypt, I found myself confused by a writing impulse whose requirements I could not penetrate but whose power I felt jerked around by.

What, exactly, was the situation here? And where was the story? Above all, where was my familiar, polemical narrator? I seemed to have lost her without having found a suitable replacement. At the time I didn't understand that it wasn't personal journalism I was trying to write; it was personal narrative. It would be years before I sat down at the desk with sufficient command of the distinction to control the material, to serve the situation and tell the kind of story I now wanted to tell.

A dozen years after Egypt I set out to write a memoir about my mother, myself, and a woman who lived next door to us when I was a child. Here, for the first time, I struggled to isolate the story (the thing I had come to say) from the situation (the plot, the context, the circumstance) and to puzzle out a narrator who would serve.

I soon discovered that if I wanted to speak truthfully in this memoir—that is, without cynicism or sentiment—I had to find a tone of voice normally not mine. The one I habitually lived with wouldn't do at all: it whined, it grated, it accused; above all, it accused. Then there was the matter of syntax: my own ordinary, everyday sentence—fragmented, interjecting, overriding—also wouldn't do; it had to be altered, modified, brought under control.

And then I could see, as soon as I began writing, that I needed to pull back—way back—from these people and these events to find the place where the story could draw a deep breath and take its own measure. In short, a useful point of view, one that would permit greater freedom of association—for that of course is what I have been describing—had to be brought along. What I didn't see, and for a long while, was that this point of view could only emerge from a narrator who was me and at the same time not me.

I began to correct for myself. The process was slow, painful and riddled with self-doubt. But one day I had her. I had a narrator on the page who was telling the story that I alone, in my everyday person, would not have been able to tell. Devotion to this narrator—this persona—became, while I was writing the book, an absorption that in time went unequaled. I longed each day to meet again with her. It was not only that I admired her style, her generosity, her detachment (such a respite from the me that was me); she had become the instrument of my illumination. She could tell the truth as I alone could not.

I reread the greats in the personal essay, the ones we

think of as open, honest, confiding—Montaigne, Hazlitt, Orwell, Didion—and now I saw that it wasn't their confessing voices I was responding to, it was their brilliantly created personae, their persuasive truth-speakers: Orwell's obsessed democrat, Hazlitt's irascible neurotic, Didion's anxiety-ridden Californian.

Each delivers that wholeness of being in a narrator that the reader experiences as reliable; the one we can trust will take us on a journey, make the piece arrive, bring us out into a clearing where the sense of things is larger than it was before.

Living as I now did with the idea of the nonfiction persona, I began to think better than I had before about the commonplace need, alive in all of us, to make large sense of things in the very moment, even as experience is overtaking us. Everywhere I turned in those days, I found an excuse for the observation that we pull from ourselves the narrator who will shape better than we alone can the inchoate flow of events into which we are continually being plunged.

I remember I once went on a rafting trip down the Rio Grande with the man who was then my husband and a friend of ours. The river was hot and wild; sad, brilliant, remote; closed in by canyon walls, desert banks, snakes and flash floods; on one side Texas, the other Mexico. A week after we'd been there, snipers on the Mexico side killed two people also floating on a raft.

Later we each wrote about the trip. My husband focused brightly on the "river rats" who were our guides, our friend soberly on the misery of illegal immigrants, I morbidly on what strangers my husband and I had become. Reading these pieces side by side was in itself an experience. We had all used the river, the heat, the remoteness to frame our stories. Beyond that, how alone each of us had been, sitting there together on that raft, carving out of our separating anxieties the narrator who, in the midst of all that beauty and oppressiveness, would keep us company and tell us what we were living through.

It mimics one of the earliest of narrative impulses, this kind of writing: to pull from one's own boring, agitated self the one who will make large sense of things; the persona—possessed of a tone, a syntax, a perspective not wholly one's own—who will find the story riding the tide that we, in our unmediated state, otherwise drown in.

That is what it means to become interested in one's own existence as a means of transforming event into writing experience.

They Leap from Your Brain Then Take Over Your Heart

Andrew Greeley

"You're working on a story, aren't you, Father Greeley?" one of my teenage water-skiing companions complained.

"How did you know?"

"You're not paying any attention to the way you're driving the boat."

Guilty as charged. But that's the nature of writing stories. You create a world, fill it with characters and set them on a path toward a conclusion of which they are unaware and you but dimly aware. Then they invade your life and take it over.

They babble next to you when you're driving your car. They preoccupy you when you pilot the ski boat. They interrupt your pathetic attempts at prayer. They intrude into your shower. They distract you at Mass. They keep you awake at night. They bother you in your dreams. They demand your constant attention as they struggle for happiness.

You fall in love with them, and that makes their agony and their hope all the more poignant. You struggle mightily to get their actions and their dialogue on paper (hard disk) and to keep up with them as they plunge through their lives. The storyteller is a pale metaphor, I have often thought, for God who creates our world and us, falls in love with his creatures, even obsesses over us because we don't act right, and always reserves the right to say the final word.

Does God really obsess over us? Anyone who claims to be God and doesn't obsess over us (and the birds of the air and the flowers of the field) is a fraud and a phony. As Elie Wiesel remarked somewhere, God made humans because he loves stories, and our lives are the stories he tells.

Where do my people and their worlds come from? They are all fantasy and fairy tales. Fantasy is not merely a distinct genre. All fiction is fantasy, a narrative of a world and people created by the storyteller's imagination. My world and my people leap out of the soup of my preconscious, the ever-flowing, ever-changing reservoir of bits and pieces of memory that my consciousness is always scanning.

I instinctively snatch some of these bits and pieces in an act of bricolage and thus create my people and their lives. I don't develop them subsequently as the story progresses because they are already, Venus-like, fully grown. Rather I come to know them more fully and understand them better.

They are very difficult at times, especially when they realize that I have fallen in love with them. They try to take the story away from me, an experience that the Irish novelist Flann, O'Brien (né Brian O'Nolan) describes vividly in his *At Swim-Two-Birds* (the name of a pub). The characters are so angry at the slow pace of the story that they come off the page, kill the author and finish the story themselves.

John Fowles (also Irish but Orange) in *Mantissa* tells of how a beautiful woman comes to life from the pages of the book, seduces him and then slips away. In a nod to his Green countryman, he gives the names of O'Brien's killers to some of his characters.

None of my people have tried to seduce me, however. Good Irish Catholics that they are, they wouldn't dream of it. Matriarchs or matriarchs in the making, they content themselves with telling me how I should finish the story. If I'm wise, I listen to them.

A young woman, programmed to be a nasty, spoiled late-adolescent brat and one more burden in her poor father's life, rejected my plans for her. She was a junior at Stanford University about to become a senior, just at that point in life when many young women mature almost overnight (or perhaps their parents only grow wise almost overnight). She was determined that she would help her dad find Ciara Kelly, a women who never existed. She did, saving me a lot of trouble.

I have the last word in a story, all right, but I'm smart if I let my characters guide me to it, even speak it. Obviously I don't hallucinate, I don't literally hear and see these people. But that does not mean that they are any less real, any less vivid, any less demanding. Obviously, too, their story is gushing out of my imagination.

Yet the psychological experience of writing for me of listening to and watching these creatures of mine as they work out their salvation is like worrying over recalcitrant parishioners in God's world.

Nor will they leave me alone when the story is finished. I say to my sister that Eileen Ryan Kane, sister of my bishop-detective, is now a federal judge. She's not a real woman, my sister protests. She is in my world, I insist. Now in fact she's the chief judge of the Seventh Circuit.

Why do I put up with such difficult phantoms, fairy tale people who think their fairy tale world and fairy tale problems are real? Because they and their problems are very real. And they are the material of my story.

Why then tell a story? That's the heart of the matter. One tells a story not to educate, not to indoctrinate, not to propagandize, not to show off one's skill with words, but to illuminate. The storyteller invites the members of the audience to enter his world for a brief time, to meet his creatures, to love them, if only just a little, and to learn from them and their lives possibilities for their own lives. Thus it becomes possible that the readers will leave behind the world of the author with a richer understanding of who they are and who they might become. Such illumination is a thin hope perhaps, but it is enough and more than enough to drive a person to storytelling.

What are the illuminations in my story? It is risky to reduce poetry to prose, fiction to nonfiction. But I would like to think that the illumination in my story is that we live in a cosmos that is finally, however oddly, implacably forgiving; that it is never too late to begin again; that there are always second (and more) chances; that it is possible, Ulysses-like, to go home again; that we will all be young again and all laugh again; that love is always and necessarily renewable; and that life is stronger than death. These, I suppose, are standard enough Catholic themes, though Catholics have no monopoly on them.

Given my own cultural background, I present them mostly in Irish Catholic images. Rather, to be more precise, the themes emerge as Catholic images that I then reduce, for the purpose of this article or of self-defense, to nonfiction.

Writing about the people I have created in my own version of the big bang world is exhausting. My creatures are difficult, troublesome, contentious, intrusive, obsessing. But, and I'll probably get in trouble for saying this, I delight in them. Writing about them is fun. Let someone else drive the ski boat.

When Inspiration Stared Stoically from an Old Photograph

∽

Kathryn Harrison

Thirty-five years ago, in suburban Los Angeles, my grandfather showed me a photograph he had taken in Alaska in 1915. It was a picture of a native woman smoking a pipe. He said her name was Six-Mile Mary, and she stood alone in a bleak landscape, somewhere outside the new town of Anchorage. There was no house behind her, no man or child beside her, no dog, no horse, no campsite, no tree.

Her black hair was parted from forehead to crown with a line so exact it struck me as cartographic, necessary and absolute as a division of longitude. Looking at the photograph, I knew that Six-Mile Mary had neither ancestors nor kin but had invented herself, too powerful to consider beauty, and so her beauty surpassed any I had encountered before. Lingerie, lipsticks, bottles of perfume, curlers and talcum powder and Dippity-do: under her gaze the alchemy of my mother's dressing room would collapse into ash.

"Why did she smoke a pipe?" I asked my grandfather,

whose rules for women prohibited the comparatively mild sins of whistling and drinking beer.

"She just did," he said.

"How did you know her?"

"I knew her, that's all."

"What were the six miles?"

He shrugged.

"She was your friend?"

"No, not a friend."

Of course not. Friendship is a human measure; Six-Mile Mary was, I already suspected, an immortal. Years away from the work that would one day consume me—decades away from a novel I titled *The Seal Wife*—I had seen a muse.

During the time that intervened, Six-Mile Mary appeared, often in disguise, but I recognized her. On a bench in a La Jolla, California, park, a blond woman sat smoking a pipe. Twelve years old, I sat next to her. When she got up, I stood, too, and followed her along the path that overlooked the beach, through the picnic area and into the dank public restroom. "Do I know you?" she demanded, and I fled.

In my life as a writer I often remind myself—comfort myself—with what William Faulkner said about *The Sound and the Fury*. The whole novel, he claimed, hung on one image, the glimpse of a little girl's muddy underpants seen from the ground as she climbed a tree. How can an entire world spin off so small and incidental a hub? Can it be possible that Faulkner conceived his masterpiece from this tiny, grubby moment?

I imagine most writers of novels begin with such a fragment, a shard of experience so compelling, so troubling and unavoidable—always there, on the periphery of consciousness—that around it he or she must construct an elaborate world. This world, the novel, is not merely a container or a means of filing the image away but an attempt to make it comprehensible, and to guard its power.

Afflicted with wanderlust, my grandfather, who was born in London in 1890, drifted west and north across the Atlantic, across Canada, until the land gave out and he reached the coast of Alaska. The stories he told me of living on the frozen frontier helped me to assemble, stick by stick, a town in which to put Six-Mile Mary, whose face I can no longer see. The photographs my grandfather took in the north were lost in a move.

When I consider what survived the journey from one to another neighborhood in Los Angeles: chipped china, worn rugs, mismatched sheets—all of these unpacked and then discarded in the critical light of freshly painted rooms—it seems impossible, and inevitable, that the album was mislaid.

Bound in creased, dry leather that left crumbs on my hands, its luminous content was hidden by a shabby disguise and remained, like the magic of fairy tales, outside mortal agendas. Even when I was a child and the image of Six-Mile Mary was in front of me, she eluded perception, an apparition caught by my grandfather's camera, one among others: The silver mirror of an arctic lake, reflecting both moon and sun. My grandfather as a young man with a full head of blond hair, jodhpurs and shotgun. A white cloud stitched to a black sky with needles of ice.

The pictures I remembered, so fragile and so necessary, fragments of a life I could not stand to lose, demanded that I imbed them in a narrative that would ensure their survival. All the corollary and not inconsiderable work of creating characters and plot, as well as a plausible place and time in which to put them, I undertook as the only means I had of preserving my connection to my grandfather. So it is all the more paradoxical, if not exactly surprising, that Six-Mile Mary still seems to me self-created, without human attachment: without the vulnerability, the need for connection, that enslaves me to writing novels.

Bigelow, the main character of *The Seal Wife*, the narrative trap I set for Six-Mile Mary, is a scientist. Sent by the weather bureau to establish a meteorological observatory in the frontier town of Anchorage in 1915, he's obsessed with finding a formula that will let him understand and predict the weather. What Bigelow wants is not just to penetrate the heavens but the mind of God, or whatever force it is that throws us together in families and tears us apart.

Seduced by an Aleut woman who refuses to speak to him, seduced because she won't speak to him, whenever Bigelow is with the Aleut he searches her face for emotion. She is the only woman who has allowed him to watch her as intently, as much and as long as he wants, and the reason for this comes to him one night. She is self-possessed. There is nothing he can take from her by looking.

At the thought, he gets up from the bed and goes to the window; he rests his forehead on its cold pane. She possesses herself. How much more this makes him want her.

He is myself, of course, with the photograph of Six-Mile Mary in my hands. I made him a scientist, but like a writer he loves a woman who is more muse than mortal, so grand and self-sufficient, so complete unto herself that she would never labor over words and commas, tenses and metaphors. Six-Mile Mary's silence, and her solitude, her body that casts no shadow onto the ground: the gods take human form, but something always gives them away.

A Career
Despite Dad's Advice

❧

Michael Holroyd

When readers ask me at festivals and seminars for qualities that go toward the making of a good biographer, I seldom omit recommending stubbornness.

Though he would have stubbornly denied it, I owe this useful quality to my father. I did not simply inherit it from him, but I went on to develop it through prolonged opposition to the many sensible plans he mapped out for my career. Writing biographies was not among these plans.

Owing to some overcautious investments on the stock exchange (and one or two injudicious liaisons in the bedroom), the family fortune was on course to reach me in the form of serious debts. My father explained this while making arrangements for me to specialize at school in physics and chemistry. He had been looking through the lists of job advertisements and had seen how the modern world was moving into a scientific age. He was determined that I should benefit from his foresight.

Having little grasp of mathematics, I grew increasingly worried by the prospect of continuing my scientific education at a university. I was a word person, I told my father, not a number person. I repeated this so often that he accused me of becoming argumentative. Where I had picked up such stubborn eloquence baffled him; he had never noticed this awkward persistence in my mother. But my peculiar talent (if talent it could be called) was well suited, he had heard, to the courtroom, where you got paid even if you lost the argument, as I had lost so many arguments with him.

It took me around eighteen months to prove beyond reasonable doubt that I was not cut out to be a great lawyer. Nor could I alleviate the family's financial crisis. These were still Dickensian days, very far from the world of Ally McBeal. Instead of receiving salaries, clerks paid their employers for work experience. I soon discovered that I was interested only in criminal law, which is essentially an interest in human nature rather than the law itself. I advanced this thesis while losing another argument with my father. He wryly expressed the hope that some lingering knowledge of the law of bankruptcy might one day come to my aid.

Meanwhile I became a soldier. At festivals and seminars I sometimes exhibit my modesty by claiming that leadership on the battlefield is not always a necessary quality for a biographer such as myself. My two years' compulsory national service in the British Army was a surreal experience that these days appears to belong to the pages of Gothic fiction. I pass over the humiliations and inadequacies of those years quickly. I survived. That is all my readers need to know. If I learned anything, it was the art of camouflage: in short, I learned how to make myself invisible. For it is the invisible person who tells the visible world's stories.

While amassing this imposing list of disqualifications as scientist, solicitor and soldier, I was quietly pursuing my alternative career at the public library, which became my university. My father was keen for me to stay in the army until the age of sixty, after which, he explained, I would receive a pension and could safely begin a career in writing. In addition to stubbornness, he accused me of impatience when I replied that I wanted to begin writing a little earlier. He suspected that I had inherited this impatience from my mother. And it was true that her impatience with him had led to their divorce. It was not, my father gravely advised me, a good omen.

It was coming across the biographies of Hesketh Pearson in the library that emboldened me to try biography myself. Between the 1930s and the '50s Pearson was the most popular biographer in Britain, and he built up a good following in the United States, too. His technique as a biographer derived in part from his early years as a stage actor. To some extent he acted his subjects' lives on the page. Though I write a different sort of biography, I gained from him the confidence to follow his example by going my own way.

My own way did not much impress my father. As an untried writer, I proposed as my first book the life of a forgotten author, Hugh Kingsmill, whose essays, novels and biographies exerted a powerful influence on me. What F. R. Leavis was to many writers of my generation, Kingsmill was to me. He was my guide. I never met him; he died in 1949. His books, however, taught me not to make simple differentiations between people by reason of color, sex or politics, but to chart how imagination and will played with our lives and to find a balance between the force of inevitable facts and compelling fantasies.

Kingsmill had been a close friend of Hesketh Pearson, to whom I wrote a letter asking for help. In his reply, he invited me to his home for supper.

He was in his early seventies when we met at the end of the 1950s, and I was in my mid-twenties. But there appeared to be almost no generation gap between us. Pearson was a natural enthusiast, a great encourager with a love of eccentricity and wit, a man who remained young in spirit all his life. He introduced me to his wife, Joyce, who had worked at the local bank. (It was rumored that he had proposed to her while cashing a check.) Then his cat strolled in and demanded to be introduced.

The house was apparently well known to cats, and whenever one died, another would magically present itself and be admitted. Each cat, over the years, would be named after the subject of Hesketh's current biography. Watty had arrived while Hesketh was writing *Walter Scott* (1954), after Dizzy (named after Benjamin Disraeli) had died, he in the mid 1940s having replaced Conny, who had turned up while Hesketh was at work on the life of Sherlock Holmes's creator, Arthur Conan Doyle.

Hesketh liked to gossip about the past as if some literary or historical figure—Tom Paine, Anna Seward, Gilbert and/or Sullivan—might breeze in at any minute. I found his conversation wonderfully invigorating and left that first evening feeling that anything was possible.

It was Hesketh Pearson who placed my feet on the first rungs of the literary ladder. Observing that I was somewhat isolated and certainly impoverished, he would suddenly telephone and invite me to the theater or recommend me as a reviewer to some editor.

Like me, he had never been to a university and wrote his biographies as a quintessential amateur: that is, without any sense of furthering his career but out of passionate interest in his subjects, from Bernard Shaw and Sydney Smith to Whistler and Wilde. For forty years his *Oscar Wilde* was generally considered to be the standard biography, before the publication of Richard Ellmann's, and Hesketh's book remains a fine introduction to Wilde's life and career.

He became a second father to me, and one of whom my own father approved. He had enjoyed several of Pearson's biographies and, with grudging generosity, conceded that I was "wasting my time with the right people." After Hesketh's death in 1964, Joyce Pearson told me that she believed I had replaced her husband's son by his first marriage. He had been killed in the Spanish Civil War, and at their last meeting, they had quarreled. Hesketh was close to suicide for months afterward.

Perhaps his goodness to me was a means of reconciliation with his son. When his autobiography, *Hesketh Pearson by Himself,* was published after his death, I saw that he had dedicated it to me.

My life of Hugh Kingsmill is an immature biography. But like a skater who falls down and picks himself up again and again until he can get across the rink without falling, I used it to learn something about my craft.

Kingsmill also led me to my next subject, Lytton Strachey. Insofar as he wrote biographies, he had been classed as "school of Strachey." While attempting to modify this classification, I grew fascinated by Strachey's work. So began a process in which a significant minor character in one biography evolves into the subject of my next, a process that gives the feeling that they are choosing me rather than that I am choosing them.

To some degree I orphaned myself from my family and was adopted by the friends and families of my biographical subjects. These subjects became the teachers I never had at a university, and I have continued to conduct my education at my readers' (and my publishers') expense. The last of these subjects was Bernard Shaw, whose principal biographer before me was Hesketh Pearson and whose plays I had first seen with Pearson.

My father is dead now. But I like to think that his anxieties would have abated, and looking back at our arguments—his Pyrrhic victories and my paradoxical losses—he might have detected in my marathon efforts some reflection of his own quixotic stamina.

Seeing the Unimaginable Freezes the Imagination

～～

A. M. Homes

I begin the days quietly, preferring to see no one, speak to no one, to get to my desk early, before the "real world" intrudes, seeking to preserve for as long as possible that fertile creative zone that exists somewhere between sleep and waking.

The events of September 11 rip me from that zone, putting me on full alert. The ever-unfolding implications loom so large that for the time my imagination remains stilled.

It starts with a call from a friend, telling me there has been an accident. "Go to the window," she says.

I stand, phone in hand, looking south, witness to tower one in flames. And then I see the second plane; the instant it is in view it's clear this is not an accident. The plane is moving toward the second tower counterintuitively; rather than avoiding the tower, it is determinedly bearing down, picking up speed.

I see the plane, and I see the plane crash into the building. I see the buildings burn, and I see the buildings fall down. I see imagery that until now did not exist in reality, only in the fiction of film. Seeing it with your own eye, in real time—not on a screen, not protected by the frame of the television set, not in the communal darkness of a movie theater—seeing it like this is irreconcilable, like a hallucination, a psychotic break.

In an effort to put an order to things, I take pictures. When I don't know what else to do, I document. I have always taken pictures as though storing what I am seeing, saving it for later when I am myself again.

In the seconds after the second plane hit tower two, I did two things: filled the bathtub with water and pulled out my camera. Zooming in, pulling the burning buildings closer, I begin to feel the disconnect. I take dozens of pictures, clicking faster, more frantically as I feel myself pushing away. When I go to rewind the film, the camera is empty, the pictures are only in my head.

There is a self-preserving fracture that denies in order to stay sane in the moment, a short circuit that prevents this unreality from registering what is fast becoming history. But in this sudden flattening, this absence of affect and emotion there is guilt. I feel bad for being home. I should be down there, doing something.

I spend the afternoon moving back and forth from the window to the television. By late in the day I have the sense that my own imagery, my memory, is all too quickly being replaced by the fresh pictures, the other angle, the unrelenting loop.

I become fearful of my mind's liquidity, my ability to

retain my own images and feelings rather than surrendering to what is almost instantly becoming the collective narrative.

There is no place to put this experience, no folder in the mental hard drive that says "catastrophe." It is not something you want to remember, not something you want to forget.

In an act of the imagination, I begin thinking about the buildings, about the people inside, the passengers on the planes. I am trying on each of the possibilities, what it might be like to be huddled in the back of a plane; to be in an office and catch a half-millisecond glimpse of the plane coming toward you; to be in a stairwell in one of those towers, struggling to get down; to be on the ground, showered with debris; to be home waiting for someone to return.

There is the sound of a plane coming in overhead. No longer innocent, everything is suspect, everything is something we need to protect ourselves from. The plane has become a weapon, a manned missile, a human bomb. I duck. It is a United States warplane, circling.

The phone rings. People call from all over the city, from around the world. Attendance is being taken, and some of us are absent, missing.

"I'm O.K., I'm alive, aren't I? And you?"

"I'm worried I'm not feeling enough, not feeling the right things. I feel like I'm not doing anything. I should be doing something."

"We all saw it," another one says.

I am on the phone when the first building collapses. A quarter mile high, the elevators take you up 110 stories in fifty-eight seconds. It crumbles in less than a minute as though made of sugar cubes. The tower drops from the skyline, a sudden amputation. My eye struggles to replace the building, to paint it in, to fill in the blank.

When the second building goes, when there is just a cloud of smoke, I can no longer stand the strange isolation of being near and so incredibly far. I go outside.

The city is stilled, mute. There are no cars moving, no horns blowing, and for the most part not even any sirens. The occasional person walks by oblivious, en route to the everyday. And among the others there is a perverse sense of festivity, a stress reaction along the lines of those who laugh inappropriately at bad news. Everyone is talking: this is something to be shared, to be gone over, a story to be repeated endlessly until we are empty.

Coming up the West Side Highway is a postapocalyptic exodus, men and women wandering north, walking up the center of the road, following the white lines, one foot in front of the other, mechanized. Behind them is thick black smoke, before them are blue skies, a nearly perfect fall day. They come north gray with dust, with a coating of pulverized concrete. They come in suits, clutching briefcases, walking singly or in small groups. People stand on the sidelines, offering them water, cellphones, applauding them like marathon runners. They are few and far between.

Wind carries smoke uptown as if to keep the disaster fresh in people's minds, somehow begging you to breathe deeper, to be a part of it.

Coming home, I buy flowers, as if to prove I still can, as if to make sure there is still a semblance of the normal.

Those twin towers were my landscape, my navigational points, my night lights. I write staring out the window, depending on the fixedness of the landscape to give me the security to allow my thoughts to wander, my imagination to unfold. Now I am afraid to look out the window, afraid of what I might see. I've been sent somewhere else in time, to a different New York, a different America. Today we are all war correspondents.

Hemingway's Blessing,
Copland's Collaboration

A. E. Hotchner

In 1957 I received a phone call from the producer John Houseman who said he was planning a new live CBS Sunday-afternoon series to be called *The Seven Lively Arts*, a compilation of dance, drama, music and the like. "I saw what you did last year with Hemingway's 'The Battler,'" he said, "and I wondered whether there was a Hemingway you could do for us."

He was referring to my first attempt at dramatization, an hourlong adaptation of Hemingway's ten-page Nick Adams story that featured a little-known Broadway actor named Paul Newman as a battered punch-drunk prizefighter, a performance that landed him in his first big movie, *Somebody Up There Likes Me.*

I told Houseman that there were several of Hemingway's semiautobiographical Nick Adams stories that could be dramatized, but that they were fragmentary, and I suggested that if Hemingway consented, I could attempt to weave several of them into a cohesive hour drama. Ernest had seen a kinescope of "The Battler," which he liked, but I felt insecure about trying to join these stories cohesively, although all of them were autobiographical incidents that nineteen-year-old Nick (Ernest) encountered after he left his Oak Park, Illinois, home on his way to enlist in the Italian ambulance corps.

Ernest readily gave his consent. I asked him if he would read the script when I completed it. "Nope," he said. "I trust you to do a good job."

"But what if I don't get it right?"

"Then I won't trust you anymore," he said.

Not an optimum atmosphere for a neophyte playwright. I chose four stories, "The Battler" included, and bridged them with "Now I Lay Me," which occurs in a silkworm cottage on the Italian front lines, where Nick, now in his Italian uniform and recovering from his war wounds, reflects on what befell him on his journey to this primitive place.

Houseman approved the script, but both he and Robert Mulligan, who was to be the director, felt that it needed a strong musical score to bolster the script's episodic structure. "We need serious music," Houseman warned, "not Hollywood's weeping violins."

Naive about such things, I said I had just heard a piece on the radio that perhaps was the right kind of music, a piece called *Appalachian Spring*. Houseman gave me a look. "Do you know who the composer is?"

"No."

"Well, why don't you give Aaron Copland a ring and ask him how he feels about doing an hour's score for a Sunday afternoon television show." Unaware that he was putting me on, I succeeded in getting a phone number for Copland but was taken aback when, instead of an assistant, Copland himself answered the phone. I stumbled around, telling him the nature of my call, but he gently put me at ease and suggested that we meet the following week at the Harvard Club to discuss the project further.

Aaron Copland was a gracious, soft-spoken, gentle man who over drinks discussed his feelings about Hemingway:

"I've admired Hemingway ever since our early days when we both lived in Paris. There was quite a parallel between us. We were born within a year of each other, both came from middle-class families: my father owned a small department store in Brooklyn, Hemingway's was a small town doctor in the Midwest. We both had decided on our careers when we finished high school.

"I was intent on composing and had no interest in entering my father's business, and Hemingway, determined to be a writer, rejected his mother's attempts to make him follow a musical career as a cellist. When I was twenty-one and he was twenty-two we went to Paris with very little money and no place to stay. Luckily Paris of 1922 was very inexpensive, and we were able to exist. I used to see Hemingway at Sylvia Beach's bookstore, Shakespeare & Company, but he was a big presence surrounded by friends, and I, being quite shy, never mustered the courage to introduce myself.

"He was writing short stories that publishers rejected, and I was composing pieces that were also being rejected. Paris then was a time of originality and innovation, but I suppose we were both a touch too original and innovative. My immediate influences were Stravinsky and Schoenberg, and Hemingway's were Gertrude Stein and James Joyce, and we were both under the spell of those Paris years, André Breton and surrealism, Georges Braque, Max Ernst and the other 'originals' we used to see at the Dôme and Deux Magots.

"I sold my first music to a French publisher for five hundred francs [about twenty dollars] and Hemingway got about the same for his first piece of fiction that was published in a little Paris review."

Copland said that for a long time he had harbored a notion to set music to Hemingway's writing. After he saw the movie of *For Whom the Bell Tolls* in 1943, he had investigated the possibility of turning it into an opera.

Three weeks later Copland phoned to tell me that he had already started on the Nick Adams score, which he completed within a month. I called Ernest to tell him of my coup in getting Copland.

"Who?" he asked.

"Aaron Copland," I said.

There was a lengthy pause. "Is he a starter or out of the bullpen?" he asked. I assured him Copland was in the rotation.

These stories are connected only by the fact that Nick appears in all of them; other than that they are isolated experiences of fear, disillusionment, courage, love, war and loneliness. Each one of them is a glistening shaft sticking in the heart of an emotional experience. But to fuse them and embellish them in a dramatization was a difficult challenge. For an Ernest Hemingway story is constructed, as he himself once described it, like an iceberg, with one-fourth above the surface and the other three-fourths deep in the paper where it does not show.

"The test of a good story," he once said, "is in how much good stuff you can leave out."

Hemingway had a practical leniency toward the metamorphosing process of dramatizing, and his only real concern was that the spirit and intent of his story and people were retained in the dramatized version. This is not as easy as it sounds. For what you get from most Hemingway short stories are the people, the times and a nuance of the emotional problem involved; these ingredients are rich, but beyond them you are on your own.

The confluence of Copland's music and Hemingway's vibrant stories beautifully complemented each other, and the production received widespread acclaim. But my script and Copland's score somehow got lost, and it was only last January that they were found among Copland's effects at the Library of Congress. Looking them over, I thought I might be able to transform the play into a concert piece using the original Copland music and expanding the Nick Adams presence.

I gave my script to Newman with whom, in 1985, I had founded a free-of-charge camp in Connecticut, the Hole in the Wall, for children with cancer and other life-threatening diseases. Now there are four additional camps for seriously afflicted children, in New York, Florida, Ireland and France, and three others being built in North Carolina, California and on the Israel–Jordan border. I suggested to Newman that we stage a benefit for these camps, which had recently been formed into an association, and I asked him to repeat his "Battler" performance of forty-four years ago and to help me with the casting.

He did indeed help me, the two times we performed *The World of Nick Adams*, a searing pastiche of the adventures of young Hemingway on his inquisitive foray into the world beyond his boyhood. The first performance was at Lincoln Center's Avery Fisher Hall in November 2001, the second at the Kodak Theatre in Hollywood a year later, with movie-star casts the like of which I venture to say had never before been assembled on a performing stage. Sixty-seven hundred people saw the two performances and well over three million dollars was raised for the camps.

When I was writing the 1957 *Nick Adams,* Ernest phoned one day from San Francisco de Paula, Cuba, something about his typewriter needing a replacement part, and in the course of the conversation he asked me how the script was going

"All right, I think. It's hard to tell."

"Well, Hotch," he said, "don't forget that old Cherokee saying, 'You pays your money, and you takes your chances.' Just don't play it safe. You haven't, have you?"

"No."

"Then you're all right. Even if it doesn't work, you're all right. The hell with playing it safe."

Returning to the
Character
Who Started It All

⤳

Susan Isaacs

A petite madeleine dipped in a lime-blossom tisane got Proust's narrator started. Sensing that the analogous experience for the protagonist of my as-yet-unwritten first novel would be an encounter with a Hebrew National hot dog, I set aside the notion of an exquisitely observed seven volumes and wrote a whodunit.

Write about what you know: like me in the mid '70s, Judith Singer, the hero of that book, was a suburban house-wife with two young children, a husband who commuted into the grown-up world of Manhattan and a passion for murder mysteries. I merely devoured them, four or five a week, clearly an unwholesome number; Judith, on the other hand, wanted to solve them.

That first book, *Compromising Positions*, told the story of how she tracked down the killer of M. Bruce Fleckstein, the Don Juan of Long Island dentists. Not only did the book get published, it was also so successful that it equaled my most grandiose fantasies—and sitting in the den of my split-level (I'd given Judith the Tudor we couldn't quite afford), I could get fairly grandiose.

There were foreign translations, a dramatic paperback auction, even a movie deal. And because of the book's success, the inevitable question "When can we expect the next Judith Singer?" was asked more than a few times.

Being a mystery devotee, I understood that some series characters—Dorothy L. Sayers's Harriet Vane, for instance— grew in complexity in direct proportion to the number of titles in which they appeared. Nevertheless, I concluded it was time for Judith and me to part company. That novel had been my first attempt at fiction. If my second were a sequel, I could wind up writing my fifteenth *Compromising Positions Goes Hawaiian,* a score of years hence, loathing the character I'd once loved, creating increasingly contrived plots and, ultimately, loathing myself.

And I might never get to try any other kind of fiction. Whodunits, essentially, are about equity. A murder sets the world out of whack. In tracking down the killer, the sleuth helps bring the scales of justice back into balance. Whether crude or literary, nearly all mysteries have a powerful narrative thrust. This sense of urgency can preclude spending much time on the hue and cry of an overhead crow, exploring the psyche of the guy who bags the body, inquiring into social or philosophical issues.

But having left Judith Singer behind, I was confused about how to develop my next protagonist, Marcia Green. I knew Marcia would be, as I'd once been, a political speechwriter working for a candidate in a New York Democratic gubernatorial primary (thus assuring the novel's comic tone).

But I kept thinking about the success of my first novel

and pondering how I could do it again. Women of a certain age (mine) were brought up to please. Add to that the heady feeling of being a best-selling author, of transmogrifying to Most Popular Girl and the concomitant dread of deCinderella-ization.

I liked Judith more than I did Marcia. I found myself fretting over whether Marcia would be reader-friendly enough; she was more vulnerable than Judith, not as warm. This apprehension made me anxious: to work myself up to a genuine froth, I brooded about whom to kill off in order to appease, if not please, the Judith/I-love-a-mystery fans.

After several weeks of ripping pages from my typewriter, crumpling and hurling them across the room, a histrionic gesture I'd picked up from one of those wearisome movies about sensitive artistes, I recalled what had worked for me the first time: writing the novel I was desperate to read. Shelving the homicide, sticking with Marcia's barely midrange charm quotient, I came up with *Close Relations*, a book about politics: democratic, sexual, ethnic and family. (The only death that occurs is accidental, when the patrician governor, appearing in Queens, chokes on an overly enthusiastic bite of knish.)

So I was free of Judith. In the years following, I wrote a saga about private versus public lives, a story about heroism set in World War II, a chronicle about the combination of qualities that makes an American and a novel in which an omniscient narrator keeps cutting off the protagonist to offer facts the latter can't know or won't tell.

I also wrote a few more of my beloved whodunits, one with a first-person narrator who was everything—a half-Catholic, half-Protestant, recovering alcoholic, recovering heroin addict male homicide cop—I was not. In each work,

I was able to experiment with a new method of fictional biography, with plot, voice, social context and structure revealing that stretch of the main character's life that best showed the stuff she or he was made of.

I probably missed Judith more than I realized, because in the mid '80s I jumped at the chance to adapt *Compromising Positions* for a film, although it is possible I merely longed to spring myself from the isolation of my office and have company at lunch. However, I discovered what all adapters of fiction learn: The protagonist of a novel cannot be copied and pasted into another medium. The Judith of the movie *Compromising Positions* was a collaboration not only between me and the director, Frank Perry, and the star, Susan Sarandon, but ultimately with the cinematographer, costume designer, makeup and hair people, and so forth.

Mr. Perry wanted his Judith to be more of an activist in the detecting department, so I transformed her from a former doctoral candidate in American history to a *Newsday* reporter who had retired to raise her children. He kept saying "Visual!" until the novel's numerous kaffeeklatsches became scenes of characters talking while toting laundry, schlepping firewood, preparing dinner, ambling around a duck pond, grabbing french fries at Burger King.

Ms. Sarandon's Judith, meanwhile, seemed to have more of an independent streak than mine, so the love affair between Judith and Nelson Sharpe, the homicide cop in charge of the case, was de-emphasized. Though filmed, it never made it into the final cut. (Additionally, middle-class suburban Methodist Nelson of the novel became the more urbane—or suburbane—Lt. David Suarez when Raul Julia was hired during that autumn of All WASP Actors Filming in Toronto.)

If a novelist is a god creating a universe, then a screen-writer is an architect working with finicky clients and obdurate contractors. While I thought the movie-Judith was swell, she was not my Judith. Ergo, saying good-bye to her was so easy that a couple of months later, when I was offered the chance to write a *Compromising Positions* television series, what a certain producer might have believed to be a frisson of anticipation was, in fact, a shudder.

So there I was, a living American novelist reasonably content with her lot. About three years ago, I sensed it was again time to write about my home, the suburbs. I certainly was aware how my contemporaries—women inspired, unnerved or untouched by the feminist movement—were faring now that they were in their fifties. But I also wanted to take a close look at my younger friends and neighbors, the new generation of thirty-somethings in all those center-hall colonials, the young women staying in promising careers and those leaving them to be full-time mothers. And the only way I could imagine viewing this world was through Judith's eyes.

After a more than twenty-year separation, however, I had to determine how to deal with the facts of her life. Should I leave her as she was in my first book, age thirty-four? Or make her fifty-four, a woman who had experienced the joys of menopause? Could I stick to the material of the novel, Judith a scholar on extended maternity leave, her pal Nancy a free-lance journalist? Or would I be better off using the details of the film—Judith with a Latino admirer/compadre and press credentials, her friend Nancy a ("Visual!") sculptor?

Naturally I chose the facts of my Judith's novel life. Then I waited to be captivated by her voice telling me about Long Island and the world. Well, it sounded familiar and dear to me. But as I began writing, my fingers didn't exactly fly across the keyboard. Her voice had changed. Estrogen depletion, no doubt. But also, life had altered Judith. Her husband had died, her children were grown and out of the house. She'd completed her dissertation and was now teaching history at a college over the border in Queens.

What surprised me was that to find her voice this time, I had to go through the same process I underwent with each new novel. Write, retch, rewrite, grimace, rewrite again and again. Only after two years, when I'd completed a second draft and found myself back at chapter 1, did I get to that blissful state in which writing ceases being work and becomes stenography.

My old friend and I were truly together again. Judith's voice dictated while I typed as fast as I could. I didn't want to miss one word she said, or one second of her companionship. After all, who knows if she and I will ever meet again?

Negotiating the Darkness, Fortified by Poets' Strength

Mary Karr

The events of September 11 nailed home many of my basic convictions, including the notion that lyric poetry dispenses more relief—if not actual salvation—during catastrophic times than perhaps any art form.

After the disaster, we did what perhaps most families did. We prayed in gratitude and fury and desperate petition. We watched hours of news. And we read poetry. I probably faxed more copies of poems—and received more faxes from other devoted readers—in the following weeks than I had in years, though as a professor at Syracuse University, I essentially butter my biscuit with the reading of poetry.

The diverse crowd of readers I swapped poems with encompassed colleagues, secretaries and administrators; but also the *New York Times*'s conservative columnist William Safire; the poet Sharon Olds; my agent, Amanda Urban; my godson's parents in England; neighbors; the novelists

Salman Rushdie and Don DeLillo; and my insurance-selling sister.

The first poems I turned to were those of fury. The political satires the Polish poet Zbigniew Herbert lobbed against Soviet oppression dispensed a particularly warming fire. In "The Monster of Mr. Cogito" (translated by John and Bogdana Carpenter), he poses as a chivalrous figure fighting not a dragon but an invisible enemy, "The shimmering of nothingness." Mr. Cogito's monster very much resembles the one behind the World Trade Center attack:

> *it is difficult to describe*
> *escapes definition*
> *it is like an immense depression*
> *spread out over the country*
> *it can't be pierced*
> *with a pen*
> *with an argument*
> *or a spear.*

We only know the monster by "its suffocating weight/ and the death it sends down." The fury I felt at the invisible enemy was embodied in the hilarious, almost Quixote-esque figure of Mr. Cogito walking out at dawn:

> *carefully equipped*
> *with a long sharp object*
> *he calls to the monster*
> *on the empty streets*
> *he offends the monster*
> *provokes the monster . . .*

he calls—
come out contemptible coward

But just as we still stare helpless into our television screens, hoping for some glimpse of Osama bin Laden and Al Qaeda, so this eager knight peers into fog, seeing only "the huge snout of nothingness."

European poets like Herbert who endured war have resounded the loudest and longest in these months. Asked to read for the *New Yorker*'s benefit shortly after the attacks, I struggled with whether or not to include the Holocaust survivor Paul Celan's agonized poem about the digging in mass graves (translated from German by Michael Hamburger). It was somber and furious with the God whose universe contained the graves' possibility:

There was earth inside them, and
they dug.
They dug and they dug, so their day
went by for them, their night. And they did not praise God,
who, so they heard, wanted all this,
who, so they heard, knew all this.
They dug and heard nothing more;
they did not grow wise, invented no song,
thought up for themselves no language.
They dug.

The cadence of the poem drummed out the relentless dirge of a people's grief, but was it perhaps too dark? The digging at ground zero was only blocks away, and perhaps the poem would fall on the audience like another blow.

The editor of the *New Yorker*, David Remnick, ultimately persuaded me to read it. He reminded me that its conclusion suggests not just digging toward the lost, but also a collective digging into history, how one person in despair and loneliness digs toward the salvation of someone else. The poem concludes with a moment of awakening, the sound of a ring striking metal as one human being reaches another.

> *On one, o none, o no one, o you:*
> *Where did the way lead when it led nowhere?*
> *O you dig, and I dig, and I dig towards you,*
> *and on our finger the ring awakes.*

Poetry is about such instantaneous connection—one person groping from a dark place to meet with another in an instant that strikes fire.

After the benefit, strangers wrote in gratitude for the Celan poem, though I regretted not being able to include Whitman's long passage from "I Sing the Body Electric," which describes the body in its various attitudes of beauty and in this section winds up with firefighters, whose recent courage we as a country have been so star-struck by.

> *But the expression of a well-made man appears not only*
> *in his face,*
> *It is in his limbs and joints also, it is curiously in the*
> *joints of his hips and wrists,*
> *It is in his walk, the carriage of his neck, the flex of his*
> *waist and knees, dress does not hide him . . .*
> *The march of firemen in their own costumes, the play of*
> *masculine muscle through clean-setting trousers and*
> *waist-straps,*

The slow return from the fire, the pause when the bell
   strikes suddenly again, and the listening on the alert,
The natural, perfect, varied attitudes, the bent head, the
   curved neck and the counting . . .
Swim with the swimmers, wrestle with the wrestlers,
   march in line with the firemen, and pause, listen,
   count.

Memoir has permitted me to relay to readers the yards of intricate information I could never roll into a lyric poem, but prose never works in a reader's mind with poetry's instant infusion of feeling.

Poetry is economical. And for the gravely pained, swift relief is of the essence. A poem's brevity touches most readers when the mental focus required by a lengthy prose work just won't do. The poet Philip Larkin once wrote that the reader puts the penny of attention into the poem's slot and immediately gets a feeling as payoff.

A short poem is also, arguably, the most portable art form. Maybe pianists can recall whole concertos note by note, or painters can evoke in their minds the most subtle brush strokes. From a great novel a few sentences might linger, a character or scene. But those are abbreviations, not the novel itself.

Only lyric poetry yields the artwork in its entirety, anytime, anywhere. And it arrives in common language—the same tool we use to get gas pumped into a dry tank. While standing in a bank teller's long line, I can rerun a whole sonnet in my head and enjoy a rush of tenderness that sometimes disperses my impatience as if a wand had been waved. The act plugs me into the great invisible company of Shakespeare or Dickinson.

It's strange that an act so solitary—reciting a silent poem—can invoke that sense of being drawn into the human community. Long works of prose are rabbit holes that let me vanish from this world into alternate realms. But lyric poetry's alchemy yields for me a strange and sudden kinship with the actual world and its citizens.

Since the bombings, I've turned perhaps most often to the work of the ninety-year-old Polish exile and Nobel laureate Czeslaw Milosz. In "On Prayer," translated here by former poet laureate Robert Hass, Mr. Milosz bestows a way to pray onto even the most faithless.

You ask me how to pray to someone who is not.
All I know is that prayer constructs a velvet bridge
And walking it we are aloft, as on a springboard,
Above landscapes the color of ripe gold
Transformed by a magic stopping of the sun.
That bridge leads to the shore of Reversal
Where everything is just the opposite and the word is
Unveils a meaning we hardly envisioned.
Notice: I say we; there, every one, separately,
Feels compassion for those tangled in the flesh
And knows that if there is no other shore
We will walk that aerial bridge all the same.

James Joyce once said that everyone starts out as a poet, then realizes it's too hard. For those of us with the hubris to keep writing verses that will seldom reach the exalted status the great works do (much less buy dinner or cover a mortgage), there's a great joy in the absurdity of one's enterprise. It's the joy derived from true wonder at poetry's redemptive quality, like taking your Little League slugger bat into the cathedral of Yankee Stadium.

Here I stand, bat cocked, ready for whatever impossible pitch history flings. It may be a presumptuously comic posture, but the cathedral itself offers me the constant consolations of magnificence.

Hometown Boy
Makes Waves

⟡

William Kennedy

O ne of the most inspirational lines I ever heard relating
to the creation of fiction was spoken by a longtime
mayor of Albany, a politician who was a maestro of evasion,
half-truths, hidden truths, untruths and antitruths: a political achiever and deceiver of cosmic reach. His line was, "I
try to tell the truth whenever I can." It was his comic effort
at the whole truth; but of course he was deceiving himself.
He had below-zero interest in the truth.

Deceit as a way of life is ubiquitous. Animals hide, mimic,
change color, play dead to avoid predators; people disguise
themselves, hallucinate, dream, forget and lie to avoid reality, but unlike animals they also lie to themselves. That writers are liars is a commonplace, but the truly achieved
writers (or artists) are the ones who deceive themselves so
well that they can pursue a lie that becomes true in spite of
its implacable falsity: Picasso's revisionist version of the

human face; Joyce's belief in the incomprehensible dream language in *Finnegan's Wake* and so on.

I came to this gradually when I began forty years ago to think about writing the novel about Albany politics that has just been published as *Roscoe*. Everything appeared deceitful or even fraudulent about the politicians—Democrats all—who ran the city and county. They were either beefy philistines or suave hypocrites or truculent con men, all wizards at controlling public opinion and winning elections.

I could not understand the complacency of the voters, their lack of self-interest, their indifference to manipulation of public money, and especially the overwhelming pluralities they gave the machine at every election. Nobody could beat its candidates, and after a while nobody tried. The bosses did allow a few suburban Republican enclaves, but that was a humanitarian decision, like permitting leper colonies in the Congo.

The machine, chiefly Irish-Catholic but with an indispensable WASP partnership, took over Albany in 1921 and runs it still. The present mayor, Gerald D. Jennings, an ex-teacher, is a progressive and of a different breed; yet he's Irish, Catholic, Democratic and as usual unbeatable. His landslide reelection last November amounts to eighty-plus, going on eighty-four, uninterrupted years in power for the Democrats, which I suggest is a national, perhaps planetary, endurance record.

The mayor I mentioned at the outset, Erastus Corning II, had held office for eleven consecutive terms, or forty-three years (longer than Franco, Stalin, Napoleon, Henry VIII or Ethelred II) when he went out horizontally, the only definitive way to get rid of an Albany Democrat. The boss of the machine, Dan O'Connell, was thirty-six when the Democrats took city hall in 1921, and he died at ninety-two in 1977, still the boss, saying his rosary and maligning the newspapers.

These were compelling political figures, and they insinuated themselves into my imagination years before I realized how deeply rooted they had become. The more I learned about them, the more I felt I should write about them. By the late 1920s, after only a few years in power, their machine owned not only city hall but also the city and county legislatures, the police, the district attorney—and therefore the jury system; it owned the election board—and therefore all close election decisions; it sent its own men to Congress and to the state legislature; it elected or helped choose all judges, including some on the state's highest court; it controlled the very substantial city, county and education budgets; and of course it managed a vast patronage.

It sometimes registered more voters than existed in Albany, and collected more votes than voters it registered. Mario M. Cuomo once told of the time O'Connell was stranded on a desert island with another man and all they had to eat was one coconut. They decided to vote on who would eat it, and Dan won, 110 to 1.

When I tried to write a novel about this almost forty years ago, I found I could not; for I had no clue as to how Albany politics really operated from the inside. I was a reporter on the *Albany Times-Union* and at psychic and moral odds with the machine. My family was solidly Democratic, and a dozen of my relatives owed their jobs to Dan O'Connell, including my father. But when I was twenty-one, I registered as an independent. As I grew into journalism and watched the corrupt manipulation of power, I viewed the pols as the benighted enemy; and they took a comparable view of me.

During the civil rights era, when I was muckraking in the slums for the newspaper, I found myself barred from covering local government meetings, though my editor was allowed in; and when I showed up at one gathering, the mayor left the room. In time I quit daily journalism to focus on fiction, and I briefly reconsidered writing that political novel; for I had gotten to know the machine better.

But this knowledge had come chiefly through adversarial eyes, still not good enough; and so I wrote three other novels. In the third one, *Billy Phelan's Greatest Game*, I managed to write with modest insight and an unexpected degree of sympathy about the boss, whom I called Patsy McCall, and how he found it important to monitor a lowly pool hustler like Billy Phelan and punish him for his insolent behavior.

I also published at that time a piece about why I wrote about Albany, and soon thereafter I had a call from Mayor Corning, the same mayor who had left the room when I arrived. He said he liked my Albany piece, and did I want to write his biography? We never got around to making that happen, but I did a few interviews with him, and not only did I learn a great deal, but I got to like him, and we became casual friends.

I was discovering that if I was really interested in writing fiction about the machine, then my political alienation was self-defeating. I needed to talk to the people who ran it and find out precisely how they did it. So I interviewed Dan, who could have been my uncle, and we talked for a couple of hours in his home, which could've been my uncle's home, and after that I had access to his lawyers, his judges, his hangers-on, and *Roscoe* started slouching toward creation.

I set my novel in the years between the world wars,

which is when the machine consolidated its control. On a morning after a Franklin D. Roosevelt presidential landslide and the election of a Democratic governor, Roscoe tells a fellow Democrat: "We own the city, the county, the state and the nation. Things could be worse."

Roscoe, the novel, dwells on these phenomenal political realities, but it also treats of the public and private life of Roscoe the politician and his prismatic love story, from which politics is inseparable. I first tried using Patsy, the boss, as my central figure, then I tried his wealthy Protestant political partner, then the chief of police; all based in Albany reality, all inadequate narrators for the complex reality my story demanded.

The need to achieve realism in the novel is so important that the infusion of actual experience becomes addictive: a cultivation of historical event and biography with painstaking exactitude, without which it feels like cheating. But even as you try for exactitude, you know that you're betraying yourself; that enormous distinctions exist between what is exact historically and what is authentic for the work; and that without a metamorphosis of the experience, you are working journalistically, which can be fatal. Fiction demands the necessary falsity, the essential lie that the imagination knows is truer than what your rational self thinks is true about your experience.

And so, because my real figures were inadequate to the narration, Roscoe Owen Conway appeared, demanding to be invented. With his life having no counterpart in actual history, he invaded my imagination in the freewheeling way he and his pals (and his father, a three-time Albany mayor, before him) invaded city hall. What Roscoe had that the others lacked was a self-critical wit and an intelligence that Henry James said was the principal element of any serious novel's center of consciousness.

James, who seems to have something to say about everything that is literarily significant, also summed up, in an essay on Hawthorne, what I came to feel about forty years of studying the machine and trying to create from it what might pass as a work of art: that "art blooms only where the soil is deep, that it takes a great deal of history to produce a little literature, that it needs a complex social machinery to set a writer in motion."

Roscoe is the No. 2 man in my complex machine, content to be behind the scenes but privy to, and part of, every aspect of power and decision making. Yet at the book's outset he also wants to quit politics and can't, and wonders why he went into it in the first place. He knows he's a lifelong fraud (with a magnificent success record), and he says so frequently, although no one believes him. Life keeps him in politics against his will, and he must use his considerable wiles to protect his loved ones, to fend off the governor, who is trying to destroy the machine and to shield himself from conspiracies by reformers, his ex-wife and the always capricious unknown.

Roscoe sanitizes his deceit in order to live with himself. He deeply opts to avoid the truth. He believes his own lies are truest, and he then bets on the impossible. This is not rational behavior; and yet there are partisans, other than I, for Roscoe's method.

Eduardo Giannetti da Fonseca, a Brazilian writer, described such behavior as a definition of hope, and wrote of the value of self-deceit for a writer, "Much of the strength of a creative artist who can continue his work, despite all frustrations, may come from . . . a belief with very low chances of becoming true." And he concluded, "Thus, the false ex ante can become true ex post, or, as William Blake observed in his "Proverbs of Hell": 'If the fool would persist in his folly he would become wise.'"

Roscoe's perverse behavior makes an honest man, more or less, out of a career deceiver. He moves into the future, wholly created from his own lies, capturing the elusive reality as he goes, reinventing it to suit himself, and triumphing, in a Rosconian sort of way. He is propelled by a political idea that he absorbed at his daddy's knee in the city hall of yore: that righteousness doesn't stand a chance against the imagination. And this maxim I have contemplated with some profit, for I find in it parallel resonance as literary dogma.

I long ago came to think that, with a bit of an early shove in a different direction, Roscoe, my lying politician, might instead have thrived as a lying literatus, which is to say, a novelist, in whom the truth is not.

As Her Son Creates His Story, a Mother Waits for the Ending

Beth Kephart

My son is on the hunt for a surprise ending. He trails up and down the hallway, sighs, goes outside, paces the yard. It is late autumn, the leaves have lately rained down from the trees, and as I watch him through the window, I feel the melancholy of the season, the melancholy of a twelve-year-old boy whose own story cruelly eludes him.

I can do little to help; I've already tried. We have sat with the sprawl of his long first draft between us, charting the story's terrain, hypothesizing plot. We have analyzed characters, settings, coincidences, motivations, the frissons between so many telling details; we have sketched out what-ifs with words and symbols. For weeks he has worried his mystery along with a seriousness that has become its own brand of worry, with a singleness of artistic mind that has made me wonder what I was thinking when I first seduced him toward writing.

At what price, writing? Outside, in the Chardonnay light

of late fall, my son kicks at the leaves as he paces and grimly paces, while at this window I stand and consider all I've failed to warn him about stories and their making. What kind of love is that, I ask myself, leading my only child into the lair of writing without equipping him for its demoralizing hazards?

Language is stingy, I should have said. Plots don't always yield. You can learn the rules of framing, form and voice, but rules do not make stories. And you can love your characters as you love your friends, but that doesn't mean that they'll return the kindness. And you can deny yourself the noise of life, but don't assume that silence leaches language. Stories are inside us, but they are also just beyond us, too, so that whatever you write, no matter how rare or good or true, will be subject to the scars of so much searching.

Jeremy wants, he says, to shock his readers with his ending. He wants a Harry Potter-style aha! in a book that festers with nefarious adults, white-collar crime. He'll use conspiracy theories and lurking twin brothers and multiple locales, if he has to. But he won't be satisfied unless he hears, in his mind's ear, the collective gasp of his someday readers.

"I want to surprise them." This has been Jeremy's refrain for the past month at least, and the more he has dissected his own complex mystery, looking for leverage and clues, the less willing he has been to call himself a writer.

"The dialogue doesn't sound like people talking," he'll say of his own work. "I'm better at creating characters than I am at creating scenes. The plot is not as interesting as it used to be, at least to me."

Across the love seat in my office he has thrown himself like a fragile analysand, reading his story aloud to me so that I can type it and print it and read it back to him with new suggestive intonations.

I know what he is feeling. I know how desperate-making writing is, how it marches one out to the edge of one's capacity, which is never big, deep, wide or, frankly, generous enough. I know what it is to be denied: not to hear the plaint in a character's voice, not to feel the wind on the opposite side of the wall, not to see the history in a garden plot, not to anticipate the future. Not to write well, or to write too well, obscuring the larger purpose, which is the story.

We are only as good as our own imaginations; the question becomes: How do we take our dreaming further? How do we improve on who we are and how we think so that the stories we conjure will somehow please us? We want to write exhilarating stories. We want to surprise ourselves.

Reading other people's work is a partial cure, of course. This Jeremy already knows, has taken to heart. Above his bed is a shelf, and on that shelf are books he loves: *The Phantom Tollbooth, The Call of the Wild*, the Lemony Snickets, the Harry Potters, the Roald Dahls, the Wayside Schools. And in those books are his own fat circles around sentences that thrilled him, characters he rooted for, plot twists that surprised him, strokes of genius. My son understands that story rises out of story, that we stand on shoulders and stretch up. He understands that to be a writer one must, first and always, acknowledge those who write for us.

But beyond reading, how does one grow, how does one light the lamps in writing's lair? Even after all this time I am struggling for an answer. Struggling to know what to do for my son, who is outside disturbing the leaves like the anti-hero Charlie Brown, while inside his mystery tarries: on note cards, on torn scraps, under his bed, beside the canister of flour, on my computer.

He doesn't want to be suggested to. He doesn't want to borrow. He will not compromise. He is the only one alive who can write his story's ending, who can finally pronounce who stole the race car and why and how severe will be the consequences.

"Mom," Jeremy said to me, before he went outside, "I hope I don't always want to write. It is too painful. It is just too hard." Closing the door before I could find an answer; leaving me here at the window, watching him.

Yes, writing is almost always too hard; it can feel like a curse, a condemnation. It can feel like a room without windows or doors, or like a tree without its leaves, exposed to weather. It can feel like nothing, endless nothing, a stoppered life, a broken dream.

Yes, writing is almost always too hard, except for those breathtaking times when it isn't, except for those almost ineluctable moments of deliverance when the lair's lamps burn bright, and the air carries a scent, and through the silence one hears the chitterings of language. Writing is almost always too hard, except when the story blows in.

The Glory
of a First Book

Brad Leithauser

Publication's purest joys belong to the first-time author. Whether you're a novelist, a poet or a nonfiction writer, initially there's something giddy and unreckonable to that process by which an untidy manuscript is converted into the neat, durable-looking, hinged rectangle of a book. Magic alone, seemingly, could account for such a transformation.

Most writers I've talked to retain vivid memories of their first books. They recall precisely where they were when they learned their manuscript had been accepted or first spotted themselves on a bookstore shelf. With nine books behind me, I have only muddy memories—if any at all—of where I was and what I was doing when most of them materialized. But memories of the arrival of my first book, a volume of poetry, remain crystalline.

It was 1982, and I was working in Kyoto, Japan, at a legal research institute. A box from my publisher arrived. Only two of us, a Japanese secretary and I, happened to be in the office. She knew that I'd been, day by day, awaiting this package. I began hacking at it with a kitchen knife, but she, seeing my clumsiness and sensing the gravity of the occasion, took the blade from me and opened the box with the delicacy a sushi chef shows a tuna's belly. Ceremoniously, she handed me my first book.

Some writers seem capable of perpetuating such feelings of enchantment. I know somebody whose every new book—and he's prolific—inspires him to a sort of stunned bedazzlement at having managed once again to surpass his every previous achievement. Since he held a high opinion of himself at the outset, I suppose by now he must have overtaken Thomas Hardy, Victor Hugo, Herman Melville. (Actually, his self-regard inspires less resentment than entertainment among his writer friends, who, knowing what a morale-lacerating business it is—this business of erecting a shelf of books—view his boastfulness as a flamboyant, almost charming, defense mechanism.)

For those writers who lack this sense that they are steadily retooling the definition of literary excellence, publication's purest joys eventually give way to other, mixed pleasures, in an ebb and flow that feels like maturation. As some of the sheer enchantment wears off, your realization grows that any finished book is, predictably, a falling short.

Out there in the distance, brightly, it leaps and dances, that unnamed and still uncaptured creature, that elusive and most excellent beast that was the book's beguiling genesis. Over time you begin to understand better how Tolstoy ultimately could have doubted the value of *Anna Karenina*. Sure, he'd written one of the world's great novels, but how wan and specious it must have appeared when set beside the golden visions in his leonine head!

One pleasure, however, seems as pure and imperishable as ever: the satisfaction to be taken in a book's looks. Here is something both intimately related to your book—nothing less than the clothing it will wear on library shelves into perpetuity—and yet detached from it. You can crow about a book's appearance with an abandon that would, for most of us, feel unseemly if devoted to the contents themselves.

If your text never will be perfect (I'm reminded of Randall Jarrell's wry, nifty definition of a novel as "a prose narrative of some length that has something wrong with it"), its physical guise can come pretty close. As you're thumbing through some coffee-table collection of paintings or photographs, perhaps you will suddenly—aha!—come upon it: the ideal dust jacket image for your next book. For this is a hunt in which you can actually seize your quarry.

Some of my happiest literary memories are linked to the quest for a handsome book. As an ignorant but obdurate quality inspector, I've sometimes visited the printing plants where my dust jackets were being run. Occasionally scenes arose that belonged in a Preston Sturges film. I remember standing before an absolutely enormous, futuristic press (in my memory it stretches like an ocean liner), with thousands, perhaps millions of dials and knobs. At the end of it stand two inky men who, having run off a trial dust jacket, are conferring.

"You think maybe it needs a bit more red?" one is saying.

"I dunno," the other replies. "Maybe a little yella."

When my first novel was accepted, back in 1984, I wanted to make sure that it would have, like my first book of poetry, a full-cloth binding, rather than the slightly cheaper three-piece binding (cloth spine, cardboard composite boards) then favored by my publisher. When my request was turned down, I asked my puzzled agent to rewrite the contract, reducing my advance in order to cover the additional cost, at which point the amused editor in chief, declaring, "Writers rarely volunteer to pay for anything," generously agreed to swallow the cost.

Largesse of this sort hasn't always been extended, and I've often gone into my own pocket to ensure that each book was bound the way I wanted. Such decisions can turn faintly comical when you're dealing with something as non-commercial as a book of poetry, since you can blow most of your modest advance on a cover that will never be seen by those book buyers who fail to peer under the dust jacket.

Many writers don't seem to fret too much about how their books look. Some years ago I was one of the judges for a major fiction prize, and copies of some two hundred new books were shipped to me. I didn't know where to put them all. They sat in piles on my dining-room floor.

When I'd first agreed to this formidable task, my naive hope was that I would figure out where we as a literary nation were collectively heading. Or at the very least I would find myself in possession of all sorts of incisive, singular judgments, like "Today America's best novels are being written by octogenarians," or "Albuquerque is currently the hub of a national literary renaissance." But as I contemplated the two hundred books on my floor, the only clear conclusion I arrived at was that most of them were ugly.

This was ugliness, obviously, for which the writers couldn't always be held accountable. Many were first-time authors or struggling mid-list authors who naturally felt lucky to be published at all. But there were also plenty of best-selling writers whose books' shoddiness—in terms of design, fonts, paper, dust jackets, bindings—bespoke a simple indifference as to appearances. And this struck me as not just lamentable but inexplicable. In a world in which reviews are so chancy, why would you fail to avail yourself of the deep and dependable comfort that comes of holding in your hands a good-looking book?

Like most professions, the writer's is surrounded by truisms and ready analogies, among them the common notion that books are an author's children. As such analogies go, this one strikes me as pretty solid. My reluctance to play favorites among my books feels quite similar to my hesitation, as the father of two teenage daughters, to praise one of them at the other's expense.

Many writers doubtless share my feeling that when you meet the worst sort of dismissive review—one that seems not merely obtuse but intentionally cruel—your grievance runs deeper than if the cruelty had been directed at you personally. Seeing your book bullied is like seeing your kid bullied: there's more than mere pain involved. Our books, like our flesh-and-blood children, are more vulnerable than we are.

I'd extend the analogy to clothing. If as a conscientious parent you wouldn't send your child out into a blizzard wearing a skimpy jacket, why release your novel into a possible blizzard of icy reviews wearing an inadequate dust jacket? Yet here the analogy breaks down. For there are plenty of days—the balmy days of spring—when your children can go outside dressed any way they please.

That's not quite true of books. The climate in Bookland is different. Perhaps the weather will be gorgeous. But even when skies looks favorable, you can't discount the possibility of sudden chilly winds, obliterating fogs, hailstones the size of golf balls. Potentially it's always a very cold world out there. And there's enormous comfort to be had in the assurance that against such storms you've dressed your book as warmly—lovingly—as you could.

Easy on the Adverbs, Exclamation Points and Especially Hooptedoodle

∽

Elmore Leonard

These are rules I've picked up along the way to help me remain invisible when I'm writing a book, to help me show rather than tell what's taking place in the story. If you have a facility for language and imagery and the sound of your voice pleases you, invisibility is not what you are after, and you can skip the rules. Still, you might look them over.

1. Never open a book with weather.

If it's only to create atmosphere, and not a character's reaction to the weather, you don't want to go on too long. The reader is apt to leaf ahead looking for people. There are exceptions. If you happen to be Barry Lopez, who has more ways to describe ice and snow than an Eskimo, you can do all the weather reporting you want.

2. Avoid prologues.

They can be annoying, especially a prologue following an introduction that comes after a foreword. But these are ordinarily found in nonfiction. A prologue in a novel is backstory, and you can drop it in anywhere you want.

There is a prologue in John Steinbeck's *Sweet Thursday,* but it's O.K. because a character in the book makes the point of what my rules are all about. He says: "I like a lot of talk in a book and I don't like to have nobody tell me what the guy that's talking looks like. I want to figure out what he looks like from the way he talks. . . . figure out what the guy's thinking from what he says. I like some description but not too much of that. . . . Sometimes I want a book to break loose with a bunch of hooptedoodle. . . . Spin up some pretty words maybe or sing a little song with language. That's nice. But I wish it was set aside so I don't have to read it. I don't want hooptedoodle to get mixed up with the story."

3. Never use a verb other than "said" to carry dialogue.

The line of dialogue belongs to the character; the verb is the writer sticking his nose in. But said is far less intrusive than grumbled, gasped, cautioned, lied. I once noticed Mary McCarthy ending a line of dialogue with "she asseverated," and had to stop reading to get the dictionary.

4. Never use an adverb to modify the verb "said" . . .

. . . he admonished gravely. To use an adverb this way (or almost any way) is a mortal sin. The writer is now exposing himself in earnest, using a word that distracts and can interrupt the rhythm of the exchange. I have a character in one of my books tell how she used to write historical romances "full of rape and adverbs."

5. Keep your exclamation points under control.

You are allowed no more than two or three per hundred thousand words of prose. If you have the knack of playing with exclaimers the way Tom Wolfe does, you can throw them in by the handful.

6. Never use the words "suddenly" or "all hell broke loose."

This rule doesn't require an explanation. I have noticed that writers who use "suddenly" tend to exercise less control in the application of exclamation points.

7. Use regional dialect, patois, sparingly.

Once you start spelling words in dialogue phonetically and loading the page with apostrophes, you won't be able to stop. Notice the way Annie Proulx captures the flavor of Wyoming voices in her book of short stories, *Close Range.*

8. Avoid detailed descriptions of characters.

Which Steinbeck covered. In Ernest Hemingway's "Hills like White Elephants" what do the "American and the girl with him" look like? "She had taken off her hat and put it on the table." That's the only reference to a physical description in the story, and yet we see the couple and know them by their tones of voice, with not one adverb in sight.

9. Don't go into great detail describing places and things.

Unless you're Margaret Atwood and can paint scenes with language or write landscapes in the style of Jim Harrison. But even if you're good at it, you don't want descriptions that bring the action, the flow of the story, to a standstill.

And finally:

10. Try to leave out the part that readers tend to skip.

A rule that came to mind in 1983. Think of what you skip reading a novel: thick paragraphs of prose you can see have too many words in them. What the writer is doing, he's writing, perpetrating hooptedoodle, perhaps taking another shot at the weather, or has gone into the character's head, and the reader either knows what the guy's thinking or doesn't care. I'll bet you don't skip dialogue.

My most important rule is one that sums up the ten.

If it sounds like writing, I rewrite it.

Or, if proper usage gets in the way, it may have to go. I can't allow what we learned in English composition to disrupt the sound and rhythm of the narrative. It's my attempt to remain invisible, not distract the reader from the story with obvious writing. (Joseph Conrad said something about words getting in the way of what you want to say.)

If I write in scenes and always from the point of view of a particular character—the one whose view best brings the scene to life—I'm able to concentrate on the voices of the characters telling you who they are and how they feel about what they see and what's going on, and I'm nowhere in sight.

What Steinbeck did in *Sweet Thursday* was title his chapters as an indication, though obscure, of what they cover. "Whom the Gods Love They Drive Nuts" is one, "Lousy Wednesday" another. The third chapter is titled "Hooptedoodle 1" and the thirty-eighth chapter "Hooptedoodle 2" as warnings to the reader, as if Steinbeck is saying: "Here's where you'll see me taking flights of fancy with my writing, and it won't get in the way of the story. Skip them if you want."

Sweet Thursday came out in 1954, when I was just beginning to be published, and I've never forgotten that prologue.

Did I read the hooptedoodle chapters? Every word.

A Famous Author Says: "Swell Book! Loved It!"

Elinor Lipman

In the spring of 1986 my editor sent bound galleys of my first book, a story collection, to six authors, soliciting endorsements (a.k.a. blurbs) for the back of the jacket. The first turndown came from an extant Lost Generation novelist, apparently irked by a lofty editorial assertion. "If I wanted to read Dorothy Parker, I'd read Dorothy Parker," she grumbled.

"Nothing to worry about," my editor said.

Eventually kind words arrived from a short-story wunderkind who'd once shared a cubicle with my editor, from a novelist I'd met at a party and from a writer published by Viking, which was also publishing me. My fondest hope, a comedy-of-manners top dog, didn't answer. On one hand, I understood. Wouldn't everyone want her anointment? On the other hand, I knew she had worked in publishing. How could a former solicitor of blurbs not send a collegial turndown? My heart didn't break, but it hardened. The final no arrived from a short-story starlet, pleading overwork but wishing "Ms. Lipman well." What a mensch, I thought. What a gifted and sensitive soul.

The first time an editor asked me for a blurb, I put my work aside and sat down with the manuscript. It stank. I wrote a full-page apology explaining how flattered I was, how disloyal I felt to my brother author and to my imprint, but that I couldn't lie. When the editor didn't respond, I called him.

Huh? Oh, that. Don't give it a second thought. He certainly hadn't; he'd sent it to every living author on his list. And by the way, some rather big fish loved it.

My policy—no compromises and no dutiful blurbs—was codified after a minor moral dilemma. A prizewinning author, who had praised my first novel in private and my second in public, suggested I might have something kind to say about his new work. I called my editor for advice. She cut me off as soon as she heard the problem: that I hated most of it. "Don't do it," she said firmly. "He won't remember who was sent the book versus who came through. Never blurb something you don't like."

"I won't," I promised. (P.S. End of friendship.)

Nonfeasance is the norm in blurbing. Publishers expect little. Several galleys per week arrive at my door. I always open the envelope, and I always read the editor's letter. I like the personal, the flattering, the imploring: "In so many ways this book reminds me of yours, Ellie—." (Heartwarming adjectives follow the dash.) Or, "I would be in your debt— more in your debt, that is, than I already am for having your wonderful books to enjoy, if only . . ." Am I truly this novelist's favorite author? Did her book group really do *The Inn at*

Lake Devine? Maybe not, but what gratifying editorial unc-
tuousness.

Cover-letter scholarship has made me didactic. When a
dear friend's novel was being sent to her A-list, I stepped in
to preach. The cover letters needed to be enlivened, person-
alized, grovelized. Mention the deserving author's worship-
ful admiration for the recipient of this letter. No form
letters. No lifeless "I think you will agree that . . ."

Will I blurb a book because its editor implores me
charmingly? No. Will I take a stab at it? Yes. When do I
decide? I read until something stops me: Clunky sentences.
No life. No story. Too much story. Too many italics. Too
earnest or pretentious or writerly.

I generally give the promising stuff, the big-name stuff,
and the friend of a friend's stuff a fifty-page trial. That's
enough. If a few chapters don't set my matchmaking anten-
nae aquiver, if I'm not thinking, "I can't wait to send this to
————. She'll love it. Maybe she'll blurb it, too," I put it
down.

A manila file folder labeled "To blurb or not?" holds the
galleys' cover letters, which I always mean to answer. Mostly
I do; I e-mail the editor and make my excuse: Thank you,
but I'm judging a contest and therefore have cartons of
novels to read over the next three months. I'm on deadline.
I'm leaving soon for a book tour. And the truest of all, "My
name is on so many books this upcoming season that I fear
it will render those endorsements meaningless." (My computer stores this document under "blurb moratorium tem-
plate.")

"I saw your name on a book," people say. "Did you really
like it, or were you being nice?"

"I'm never nice," I answer. "I never write something out of obligation." The specter of the old "Logrolling" column in *Spy* magazine is a helpful tool. "Can't," I say. "She reviewed my third novel in the *Berkshire Eagle*, and we quoted it in the front matter with full attribution."

I appreciate the sociology and transparency of blurbs: heads of M.F.A. programs praising their darlings, editors turned novelists praising authors turned girlfriends. I will see a mentor thanked in the acknowledgments for his support, his faith, his in-law apartment. Then I turn to the back cover and see the acknowledgee declaring the book "huge, important, dazzling, incandescent."

I don't think I've ever bought a book specifically because of a blurb, but I've returned a few to the shelf because of an overwrought rave from a pretentious jackass with whom I've had the misfortune to serve on a panel. Similarly, I've been put off by bombast, declaring this author the best of his generation, the heir apparent to . . . , the greatest living practitioner of . . .

Not that I haven't offered up a few overstatements in my day. I have gone on record predicting intimations of immortality and major prizes for books that were stillborn. On the other hand, I've been dropped from the jackets of second editions once the book hit the big time, and I've dismissed novels that Oprah went on to bless.

Modesty and reason make me wonder if anyone will notice "Elinor Lipman" on four books or eight or ten in one year anyway. Just when I think it's vainglorious to worry about overexposure, I receive something like reinforcement. "I saw your name on so-and-so's advanced reader's copy," a bookseller will write me. "We're recommending it in our newsletter."

Perhaps I am too full of myself. When I feel a blurb coming on, I alert the editor that my seal of approval is on its way, as if it's an emergency; as if she's the answering service, and I am five centimeters dilated. Male editors are businesslike in their gratitude; female editors are more apt to be ebullient. One confided turning cartwheels in the corridors of Alfred A. Knopf. Can I believe them? I want to. And still better: hearing from the object of my admiration. This winter I received a hand-written note that brought tears to my eyes. "For as long as I live," an author wrote, "I will never forget that you went out of your way to help my first novel."

What's in it for me? Just that. If the system works, a shiny new hardcover will be turned over by a logical fan who thinks: "I like her. She loves this book. Therefore I'll love it, too."

Word gets around in editorial circles, so blurb ubiquity begets more padded envelopes. I screen their contents because it's something I can do. In sports-announcer parlance, I am giving back. Critics have been described as people who go into the street after battle and shoot the wounded. No blurb can be a bullet-proof vest, but in my own experience it can put a square inch of Kevlar over a worried writer's heart.

Hearing the Notes
That Aren't Played

David Mamet

M y piano lessons began fifty years ago, in September 1951. My teacher was an Austrian martinet—Isadore Buchalter. He told my family that he had hopes for me, that I was somewhat musical, but that I couldn't learn to read.

I realized, forty-plus years later, that I wasn't cursed with indolence, but that I couldn't see the notes. I was hopelessly myopic. I got my first eyeglasses when I was eight, but by then I had quit the piano.

Around 1963 my lessons continued when I had the great fortune to meet Louise Gould. She sat me down and had me playing triads, and triads with the octave, both hands, up and down the keyboard. She used this simple exercise to show me the cycle of fifths, and its additions, subtractions, alterations, inversions, which are the foundations of music theory. I realized that my toddler piano lessons had taught me to play without reading, to fake it, to play by ear.

I played four hands one afternoon with Randy Newman.

I apologized for rushing. I said I was such a musical doofus that I almost felt as if I had to "count." He stopped and looked at me a bit in incomprehension and said, "Everyone counts." He also taught me to hear the passing tone, to listen for it, as it was driving the music.

Joel Silver produced several of my wife's records, and I got a priceless tip from him: "Leave out the third—we hear it anyway."

The passing tone and the excised third opened up a new world to me. I began to get (timorously) bold, to eschew the first inversion and the keys of F and C major.

The Stoics cautioned us to keep our philosophical precepts few and simple, as we might have to refer to them at a moment's notice. These tips became my philosophical principles, and they forced me to slow down and think.

I remember Bensinger's pool hall in Chicago, in the '60s, and the hustler-instructor who taught: if you can see more, don't shoot. Same idea.

People say the great genius of Nat Cole was his ability to accompany himself on the piano, that he understood that most delicate and intricate duet and its demand for spaciousness, for elegance. "We hear it anyway."

This is the genius of Bach, and the overwhelming demand of dramaturgy—this understanding, or its lack, divides those who can write from those who can really write: How much can one remove, and still have the composition be intelligible?

Chekhov removed the plot. Pinter, elaborating, removed the history, the narration; Beckett, the characterization. We hear it anyway.

It is in our nature to elaborate, estimate, predict—to run before the event. This is the meaning of consciousness; anything else is instinct. Bach allows us to run before, and his resolutions, as per Aristotle, are as inevitable (as they must be, given the strictures of Western compositional form) and surprising as his elaborate genius. We are thus delighted and instructed, as per Freud, in a nonverbal way, as to the varieties of perception, possibility, completion—we are made better. Our consciousness, listening to Bach, has been rewarded, refreshed, chastised, soothed—in Bach and Sophocles both, the burden of consciousness has momentarily been laid down.

Both legitimate modern drama (Pirandello, Ionesco) and the trash of performance art build on the revelation that omission is a form of creation—that we hear the third anyway—that the audience will supply the plot.

But our experience of such can be, at best, a smug joy.

We listen to some concert pianist improvise waterfall arpeggios for an hour, or view puerile performances and, though we may leave the theater smiling, we are left poorer, for we celebrated not the divine but the ability of the uninspired to ape the divine. This is idolatry.

We rejoice both in the familiar and the surprising. Music, drama, circus, the creation of all the performing arts proceeds from researched or intuited understanding of the nature of human perception, thesis-antithesis-synthesis: I can fly from one trapeze to another. But can I do a triple somersault? Yes. No. Yes.

Much modern art is either a slavish reiteration of the form (musical comedy) or its slavish rejection (action painting). Yes, it is true that life would be better if we were all a little kinder, and it is true that paint spattered in the air will fall to the ground. Both are true, but who would have suspected that they were notable?

The commandments are the same: leave out the third, concentrate on the missing tone. Yes, we know that in the key of G a C chord would like to resolve to G. How does it get there? The ardor to address this question accounts for the genius of Beckett and also of Vernon Duke, Prokofiev, Kurt Weill. The fascinating question of Art: What is between A and B?

Heroism in Trying Times

⟨⎯⎯⟩

Patrick McGrath

Some years ago, having written several novels in succession about insanity and obsessive sexual love, I decided that the next would be a story about the American Revolution. Instead of wild delusions, ungovernable passions, bad decisions and flawed perceptions there would be horses and muskets and sailing ships and thunderstorms. There would be sacrifice, treachery and bloodshed. Tyranny would be overthrown, a nation born. It was a chancy venture, but every author will recognize the impulse to travel down strange roads, if only for one book.

Why the Revolution? There was of course its sheer romanticism, this band of farmers challenging the greatest army in the world, with the wilderness landscapes of colonial America as a backdrop and the idea of Liberty shimmering at the heart of it all. But there was a more personal motive involved. I had grown up in England, and after various rebellions and failures fled the place, eventually settling in New York, where I became a writer. That was twenty years ago. My feelings for this country are like those of many immigrants: powerful, affectionate, grateful but somehow never easy to articulate without resort to large vague abstractions.

Virginia Woolf, contrasting the English and American peoples, wrote that "while we have shadows that stalk behind us, they have a light that dances in front of them. That is what makes them the most interesting people in the world—they face the future, not the past." It occurred to me that if I turned the other way, and faced America's past—in particular, her overthrow of British imperial power and the invention of a new form of republican government—then I might discover in an early, legible form just what it is about this country that inspires such patriotic fervor in its people, including uprooted Europeans like myself.

It is not a project for the faint of heart, the writing of a historical novel. The research alone absorbed years of my life, and there were no shortcuts possible: one has to be able to feel, breathe and even smell the air of the period being portrayed, and when that period is the eighteenth century those smells can be pretty ripe. This turned out to be a large part of the joy of the thing, however, and during the endless trawling through the history and fiction of the time, I read no prose more pungent—perhaps with the exception of Smollett's—than that of Thomas Paine, the best-selling author of the eighteenth century and also the man who saved the republic with a pamphlet.

Some novels declare their design and intentions to their author only gradually, as characters and themes emerge through the creative process. The writer of such a book will be wise to hold only lightly to his first ideas, so as to abandon them without a pang when seemingly of its own accord the story veers off in a new direction. Other novels require certain firm commitments to be made up front. My novel of the Revolution seemed to be of this second type. It was clear to me it would have to address the themes of, first, history and its claims to truth; then of power, both personal and political; and thirdly of parenting, inasmuch as the relation of a king to his colony was in those days often represented as that of a parent to a child.

Tom Paine was helpful here. He loathed kings with a passion, and none more so than George III, whom he called "a sottish, stupid, stubborn, worthless, brutish man." He described him as a pimp who prostituted his own children. He compared him to Saturn, who ate his own children. He wrote that "even brutes do not devour their young, nor savages make war upon their families." In short, to quote a French revolutionary sentiment from the National Convention of 1792, "kings are in the moral order what monsters are in the physical."

What I required, then, was a monster, who was also a father, to stand for imperial Britain and her king; and a child, grown strong enough to claim her independence, to stand for the colonies. The child defies her monstrous parent and achieves autonomy, and there we have it. But that of course is absurdly simplistic. Plans for novels generally turn out to be inadequate, and my crude schematic equations soon became the faintest part of the design: characters outgrow their function if they have any vitality at all. But as my story came to life, so, oddly, in its growing complexity, did the human dimension come to mirror the political.

The child in question, an English girl called Martha Peake, loves her father dearly, and it is only when he begins to behave badly, having become besotted with cheap gin, that she is forced to distance herself from him. She attempts a reconciliation, but he is too far gone. Nothing will do but that they separate, and in the fall of 1774 she takes ship for Boston. It grieves her bitterly to do this, for she and her father have lived together happily for many years. But he gives her no choice. So did the colonies, more in sadness, at first, than in anger, recognize that they could no longer tolerate the imperial relationship; their father, the king, insisted on imposing unjust taxes and stifling their ability to trade.

But having decided they must fight, the colonists did so with dogged courage, and also, it became apparent, with a canny eye to the public relations aspect of the conflict. As early as 1770 the use of propaganda had proved effective for the patriot cause. The Boston Massacre—when British soldiers occupying the town fired into an angry crowd, killing five—won international sympathy for the people of Massachusetts largely because, with the help of an engraving by Paul Revere, they got their account of the event across the Atlantic first.

Viewed from this perspective—that is, in terms not merely of how the war was fought but also of how it was perceived—the significance for the Revolution of Tom Paine's writings comes into sharp focus. He it was who, when the Americans were filled with despair and irresolution in the winter of 1776, rallied them so successfully with his pamphlet "The Crisis" that the revolutionary cause did not collapse but was, rather, reinvigorated. His closing battle cry, as one historian put it, "might almost have startled slain patriots from their new graves under the frozen clods."

The struggle, then, was not merely one of arms, but of

meanings—and it seemed to me vital that this idea be woven into the fabric of the novel. So it was arranged that Martha Peake, an English girl adrift in war-torn Massachusetts, pregnant and unwed to boot, is riven by conflicting loyalties, not only nationalistic but filial and sexual as well. And that as a result of these conflicts she is provoked into an action that will turn her into a heroine, and her story into a legend, despite the fact that she feels none of the elevated sentiments attributed to her when she performs the heroic deed, being driven by quite other emotions.

The cause is served not by truth but rather by the rhetorical inflation of an event whose meaning is fiercely contested. My own first naively romantic image of the Revolution had come to seem similarly distorted—and unreliable historical narration became a central feature of the novel's design. As for the project helping me understand why I love America, I still find that difficult to articulate properly, although hating kings has a lot to do with it.

But I do know now why I love Tom Paine. He may have been smelly and not always sober, but by the power of his fiery prose he kept the Revolution alive and with it the fledgling republic. I have done what I can for him, even giving him a small cameo late in the novel, where he terrifies a child just by looking at it. I would propose him as the patron saint of writers everywhere, had he not been a godless atheist.

Shattering the Silence,
Illuminating the Hatred

❧

Arthur Miller

Focus sprang off the streets of New York in the '30s and '40s. With no money for college, I had spent three years driving trucks, pushing carts in the garment district and working as a parts clerk in a warehouse. I knew what I knew, what I had seen and heard, and too often it didn't match what I was reading in the papers and hearing on the radio. Especially the Big Secret—the city was pulsing with hatred. Perhaps not always but on certain days, yes. On certain days Hitler was rising, but not only in Germany.

With the abject failure of my first Broadway play, *The Man Who Had All the Luck,* I resolved never to write another play but to give novelistic form this time to the assault, figurative and sometimes literal, that was coming at me from the streets.

It's all a long, long time ago. Only now, after nearly sixty years, does some of the feel of that time begin to return. The color and tone of an era are harder to convey the closer one is to it. Dickens's London comes more vividly to mind than the New York of the early '40s.

Pearl Harbor hadn't yet been attacked; the city like the nation was split in a lot of different ways as to how involved we ought to be in Europe's never-ending woes. Franco's destruction of the Spanish Republic was met by a mute, official America. Maybe the silence helped create the craziness, as when the American Legion and the Communists found themselves on the same side for a while, both opposing our involvement: the Left because the Russians, incredibly, were suddenly allied with Hitler; the Legion because veterans were generally opposed to a replay of World War I.

And if the ranks of the British Army were filled with Irishmen, their brothers here didn't at all mind the British being in trouble now. And besides, a lot of veterans were Irish or Catholic or both, and the Church had its concordat with Hitler and was generally perceived to be less than perturbed by Fascism. It was all no less confusing then than it seems now.

Wherever one looked, the straight lines went crooked. World War II was several wars, not one. The South was gung ho, Britain having supported the Confederacy in the other century, and southerners like shooting anyway. The most racist part of the country hated Hitler, who dared raise the swastika over church altars, but of course they were not exactly pro-Semitic down there either. It was like a dropped vase, cracked in all directions; touch it and it might shatter.

And the silence inevitably covered the Jews and their fate. More Jews than not were on the left side of the political spectrum, but here was the Soviet Union lying down with the Jew-hunting Nazi. And Roosevelt, friend of Jews, had denied landing privileges to the *St. Louis,* the ship carrying a couple of hundred of the Jews allowed to leave by the Germans. The ship's captain first tried landing in Cuba and, turned away, headed back to Germany. There were not many protests within or outside the Jewish ranks. In fact, that ship disappeared over the horizon going east in a bubble of silence, probably the largest crowd to leave the Statue of Liberty behind.

Along with a lot of others, what I made of the silence was that everybody, not excluding myself, was afraid of an outbreak of open anti-Semitism in America should that shipload of refugees be allowed to disembark. (This was a fairly prosperous, middle-class group of people and not what "refugee" seemed to connote, but even that seemed not to count.) Meantime one of the biggest radio audiences in the United States waited eagerly every Sunday for Father Coughlin's harangue against Jews on a national network.

The writing of *Focus* was an attempt to break through the silence; just putting the words down was a relief. But I had no idea whether the subject itself would make publication unlikely, and so it indeed appeared from the moment it was offered to publishers. No one I talked to could think of any fiction on the subject, although the widespread existence of anti-Semitism, from the universities on down through the large corporations and professions, was of course known to everyone. It was like some sort of shameful illness that was not to be mentioned in polite society, not by gentiles and not by Jews.

But I was lucky. Reynal & Hitchcock, a new gentile publisher, had opened only a year or so earlier, and Frank Taylor, an associate of my wife who worked at a medical publisher, had just been hired to get new authors for their virgin list. Taylor was swinging his lasso all over the city and had looped in a number of exciting young talents.

That the book was already making some people very nervous only enhanced its value at Reynal & Hitchcock. If there was no explosion once it appeared, I thought it was quite possibly because *Gentleman's Agreement* had beat it out by a month or two and helped break the ice. But when the left-wing Book Find Club adopted *Focus*, some of its members did object on the ground that the book repeated anti-Semitic slurs, as of course it had to when some of its characters hated Jews.

But even recalling all this doesn't quite revive the feel of that time, more than a half century ago. Rather, I can recall my own amazement that the story was to be published at all, so accustomed was I to the fearful silence surrounding the issue. But I do very clearly remember the day I was supposed to come to the publisher's offices to have my picture taken for the book jacket. I had totally forgotten the appointment until my wife walked in and was surprised to find me in Brooklyn when I had this important appointment on Madison Avenue.

I rushed about getting into decent clothes and walked straight into the edge of a partially open closet door and by the time I arrived at Reynal & Hitchcock's had a nice black eye. This is why I am in profile on the jacket. That long-ago photo, of a young man with hair, looking confidently into the distance, brings back some of the excitement of the imminent publication date and, for all anyone knew, outraged public condemnation.

Some sixty years later a movie has been made of *Focus*, so its relevance has apparently not disappeared. The cur-

rent attacks on people for their appearance—Middle East-
erners this time—runs right down the middle of the book's
theme. This time around, however, silence is out of fashion,
and a lot of us find ourselves struggling very consciously
with our fears.

Overcome by Intensity, Redeemed by Effort

Honor Moore

W hen I started to write seriously in my twenties, I took a trip to see my grandmother, Margarett Sargent. She had been an artist when she was young, her paintings and sculpture prominently exhibited in New York, Boston and Chicago during the 1920s and '30s. Now she was a flamboyant, magisterial Bostonian in her eighties, no longer an artist but still living in her vast, dark house, near Prides Crossing on the North Shore.

Though I saw very little of Margarett when I was growing up, I had once stayed with her as a small child, long enough to become enchanted by her elegant suits, her dark lipstick and the extraordinary paintings and sculpture—by Gauguin, Degas and Calder among others—vividly placed in the vaulted, skylighted living room that had once been her studio.

Margarett fed my fascination all through my childhood, responding to the "brilliance" of drawings and stories I sent her. Now I was an adult embarking on an artistic career, and I wanted her blessing.

She didn't have much to say, but after lunch, from her wheelchair, she directed me to a small windowless room. There, neatly stacked, was an uncountable number of canvases, many unfinished or encrusted with grime and, on the floor beside them, a carton of palettes enameled with swirls of hardened paint.

When Margarett and I had our next exchange about her creative life, I was a published poet, and she was living in an apartment above the Boston Common. I remember a nurse escorting me to the door of her room. The sheets were bright yellow, and a bouquet of blown pink peonies leaned from the night table. Wearing a fuchsia bed jacket, Margarett sat on her hospital bed surrounded by open scrapbooks from which spilled crumbling clippings, reviews of her exhibitions. "These were good," she said, wide-eyed with astonishment and confusion. "Why did I stop?"

Finally she was going to tell me about her painting. "Why did you stop?" I asked. She didn't want to talk about it.

"For twenty years I worked," she said slowly, speech blurred by the effects of repeated strokes, "and then it got too intense."

That was all she said, but I thought I could understand what she meant. There were times when the intensity of my feeling fueled my poems, times when I could imagine no greater pleasure than writing. But there were also mornings when my words lacked any dimension of the magical, hours I sat blank before the page or began a sentence only to fall asleep. Whole days passed when I rose from my desk every half hour to make a cup of tea; days when, not writing, I felt empty, depressed, despondent. I was always afraid I would stop.

I began to visit Margarett more often, thinking that eventually she would offer some wisdom I could make use of. But she didn't, and so, after she died in 1978, I decided to write her biography. If she wouldn't tell me her story, I would discover it.

I had always been told I took after her: I coveted her beauty and glamor but not the precipitous ending of decades of creative work, the years of mental hospitals, shock treatment and bedridden sadness. I thought that if I wrote her life, I would not have to live it. I did not imagine that my worst fear would come true, that in the process of writing about Margarett's art, I would abandon my own.

Before I began to research *The White Blackbird*, as if to inure myself, I wrote a long poem, the most ambitious I'd ever attempted. A few years later, when my first collection was published, I believed I had triumphed over my grandmother's fate. But my confidence was short-lived. What I was writing about Margarett's life was stiff on the screen. If I was a poet, why did my language read like an encyclopedia entry? Margarett Sargent was an artist. Her biography should have the audacity, color and angularity of her paintings.

From my present perspective it seems that I was struggling with an ordinary writing problem. I spent my days of necessity scrutinizing Margarett's shopping lists and sketchbooks, analyzing her love affairs and friendships, keeping track of her career. Between interviews and research trips I tried to return to poems, but the images that came to me, even my dreams, spoke of Margarett's existence, not my own. Years were passing, and poets of my generation were publishing and growing. Worse, I felt peculiarly dull, as if part of me was no longer alive. The redemptive jolt of inspiration came from an unlikely quarter—Margarett herself.

On impulse one morning I set up a slide projector next to my computer and tacked an old window shade to the wall. Color flashed, and after a while these phrases came: "A shiver of magenta vibrates a yellow aureole of wall . . . dark eyes, scraped at by the stick end of a brush, asymmetrical."

Another day I sat down with one of Margarett's sketchbooks. Soon I had written a narrative that seemed to bring her act of drawing to life, and I was on familiar ground. What I was doing had the feel of working on poems: the attention to music, image and juxtaposition that gives each word dramatic valance.

I wrote and published a short piece, somewhere between a poem and an essay, that had nothing to do with Margarett. Perhaps, I thought, I was more suited to imagistic prose. Perhaps I would never write poems again.

I told myself I was relieved, but the truth was that as time went on, I felt like a child shut out of the playground. For years I had told my students that poetry was a calling, not a career. Was I going to turn away, in middle age, from the great dead poets with whom I always conversed when I struggled with a sapphic or a sestina? Would I never again enter the exploration of rhythm, the rigor of distillation, the pleasure of making a line that teetered, dipped, then finally balanced?

The day I finished *The White Blackbird* was a sunny June Friday. I wandered the house in a haze of tears, surprised that having written Margarett's death, I myself remained alive. Now that the book was finished, what would I do with myself? When an invitation arrived to spend two weeks in Cuba, I accepted. It was 1994.

My first dusk in Havana I spent walking the Paseo, a boulevard whose promenade was shaded with old glossy-leaved trees and lined with park benches. Most of the time what remained of a bench were its cast-iron ends, floral patterned shapes standing upright, emptiness instead of a seat. The occasional finned Cadillac, the ghost of prerevolutionary times, cruised slowly past, and the chatter of families filtered from the balconies or stoops of apartments partitioned from what had once been the mansions of the elite.

At the end of my walk, I stood at the Malecón, the great sea wall at the city's ocean's edge. As waves driven south from Key West sheared up and pulled back, crashing against the sweeping curve of stone, I felt myself reenter my imaginative life. Suddenly this romantic city stripped of the contemporary was an embodiment of the place in my psyche where past and present collide, dream and dread coexist, from which the only release is some kind of making.

When I got home from Cuba, I came down with bronchitis, and one day in bed, a blizzard raging outdoors, I began to jot images. Here was a voice I didn't recognize. I was making a poem whose landscape was a curious blend of Havana and the snowy forest outside my icy window, putting language together in the way that "writing" Margarett's paintings had taught me.

Some time later, returning to poems I'd attempted and abandoned while writing *The White Blackbird*, I leafed through page after page, astonished. I'd written about a Havana cemetery, dry white human bones visible beneath a shattered gravestone, the tomb of La Milagrosa, where you knock at stone to arouse the mercy of the dead. In those fragmentary lines I saw hints of what came to fruition in the poem I'd written during the snowstorm.

Perhaps the canvases in Margarett's storeroom might have been, for another woman, a way station rather than a final destination. Perhaps in returning to her abandoned work, that other woman might have found, as I did, the beginnings of something new.

A Novelist's Life
Is Altered
by Her Alter Ego

Marcia Muller

Thirty years ago, in the fall of 1971, a woman took up residence with me in my small San Francisco apartment. Granted, she didn't fill much space and was not visible to the eye, but she was a powerful force to be reckoned with. This was the beginning of my long association with my series detective, Sharon McCone, and as I—endlessly, it seemed—contemplated a career as a novelist, she developed a persona all her own.

She was taller, thinner and braver than I. She had a job, while I had no prospects of one. She commanded an amazing variety of skills—marksmanship, judo, bread-baking, automotive repair—while I could barely type. She would go anywhere, safe or dangerous, and ask anyone questions, while I had been known to become nervous when dialing the phone for the correct time.

Fiercely independent, that was McCone, a state toward which I was only beginning to struggle. Many of her traits were intentional on my part of course. We writers of series fiction tend to idealize ourselves in our characters, giving them attributes we wish we possessed and ever more interesting lives. As I sat in a small room constructing what seemed to me awkward sentences and paragraphs, McCone was out having exciting adventures.

It was not until sometime after her first full-length case, *Edwin of the Iron Shoes*, saw print in 1977 that I realized I'd crossed a line and was out there with her in spirit, also having an exciting time. Then our differences gradually began to disappear.

I didn't grow taller, but I did lose weight and become braver. Not to the point of facing down criminals with a .38 or subduing them with judo, but I was definitely more confident. In the course of my research for subsequent novels, I would learn to walk into places safe and dangerous and ask anyone questions. Finally I'd declared my own independence.

Over the course of our partnership in crime McCone has changed, too. She's taken on a number of my own characteristics: a somewhat cynical worldview, an unconventional sense of humor, an intolerance for the criminal and sympathy for the victim. As my horizons have widened, so have hers. Initially she worked for a '70s-rooted poverty law firm peopled by shadowy characters whom I neglected to give names; now she owns a successful agency staffed by complex people, all of whom have names and lives of their own.

About ten years ago, in an effort to gain a better grasp on McCone's world, I took up the hobby of building fully electrified scale models, first of the legal cooperative where she started out and then of her own brown-shingled cottage, a pursuit that the more tactful of my friends label unusual, and that the more blunt refer to as obsessive. Later, through the misguided notion that writing about flying was easy, I had McCone become a pilot. When I learned that research in books wasn't enough, I forced myself to take lessons.

Most of my friends called that a devotion to my work bordering on insanity. While roaring down a rapidly shrinking runway at ninety miles per hour in a contraption that resembled nothing so much as a matchbox with wings eventually became commonplace, my airborne experiences were such that I determined never to allow McCone to take up skydiving.

The twenty-first novel in the series, *Listen to the Silence*, was an emotionally draining exercise for both McCone and me, and it seemed time for her to take a vacation and for me to try something different, a stand-alone novel. When I started *Point Deception*, I had a single vision, that of a young woman standing beside a disabled car on the California coast highway. Three characters followed: a female deputy sheriff in a small seaside community, a successful male journalist from New York City and the young woman, a murder victim.

Although the deputy would be very good at her work, under the surface she would be haunted by past mistakes and damaged by loss; the same would be true of the journalist. And the young victim, heard from in flashback, would be a product of both financial and emotional poverty.

A solid enough starting point, but I had misgivings. Could I convincingly write such characters? They were so unlike McCone and her associates, so unlike me. And it had been such a long time since I'd lived within the mind and soul of anyone other than her. Besides, McCone seemed to be constantly looking over my shoulder, her voice intruding on those of the new characters. Was she insecure? Worried about her future existence? I began to wish she'd go away.

McCone persisted, however. Oddly enough, she had no adverse effect upon the two characters I'd been most concerned about: the male journalist and the victim. In spite of the oft-stated claim that it's difficult to write from the viewpoint of a character not of one's sex, I had no problem identifying with my hero and allowing him to develop as he saw fit.

The victim, a hardened and cynical nineteen-year-old, was her own person from the first word she uttered. But the female deputy seemed a lesser McCone, speaking in Sharon's vernacular and acting as she would but without the individual spark that authenticates a character. At first she only irritated me. Then I began to hate her. And finally I began to blame McCone for interfering.

The only way to remedy the situation of course was to banish my longtime companion for a while. I indulged her need for a vacation, imagined her in a bikini on a sunwashed beach and sent her packing.

Now my new heroine no longer seemed alien to me. As McCone had, she revealed hidden facets of herself. As with McCone, those facets came from within me: the mistakes and losses and deprivations that make up the dark side of the human mind. The character's milieu also began to come alive, and I was able to create fictional Soledad County, California, an amalgam of various coastal counties both there and in the Pacific Northwest. Its character, too, derives from dark places that the tourist brochures fail to mention.

It's been a long journey back from Soledad County. I've had to disconnect with my people there and reconnect with McCone for her next outing. We've gradually been getting to know each other and San Francisco again. Internal conversations during visits to her old and new haunts help. (Fortunately I manage those without moving my lips in public.) And there's the occasional argument to keep the relationship lively. (These are conducted in my office, where I'm free to rant out loud.)

Vacations are great, but so is coming home again.

Computers Invite
a Tangled Web
of Complications

∽

P. J. O'Rourke

For reasons of high aesthetic principle, I do not write on a computer. Writing on a computer makes saving what's been written too easy. Pretentious lead sentences are kept, not tossed. Instead of sitting surrounded by crumpled paper, the computerized writer has his mistakes neatly stored in digital memory.

All writers know how hard it is to practice tough love on the children of our verbiage. Kick the silly, labored metaphor out of the house. But with a computer, that metaphor is back by dinner time, claiming a rightful place in the family of the final draft. A result is a thematic disorganization and a meandering prolixity that, for example, will interrupt an essay on a writer's own technique with a meditation on the popular press of the Elizabethan era.

We can count ourselves lucky that in the late sixteenth century the "feature story" had not developed to the point where Shakespeare was holding forth about the relative merits of duck vs. goose quills and whether to grind ink himself or outsource the grinding to the kid who played Silvia in *Two Gentlemen of Verona*.

Writing without the aid of a computer, I am not tempted into such snares. I also believe that writing owes much of its artistic power to the portability of the craft. Other creative types have string sections, naked artist's models and opera scenery that they must lug with them everywhere they go. Writers can grab the stub of a pencil and the back of an envelope and dash off "Lines Composed a Few Miles Above Tintern Abbey" any time Tintern Abbey happens to be a few miles away. Even the most compact laptop would be an encumbrance on a walk through the Lake District. And where would Wordsworth have plugged his battery recharger?

I view this portability with approval, even though I view it out a small window in a cramped guest room where I keep the forty-pound IBM Selectric that I'm compositionally helpless without. In the guest room I also keep two other IBM Selectrics (given to me by writer friends who bought PCs), because it isn't easy to get a Selectric repaired anymore, plus boxes of felt-tip pens in the three colors of ink that are necessary for really thoughtful scribbling in second-draft margins, and a used Encyclopaedia Britannica missing the T and P volumes. All of this could be replaced by a tidy little LCD screen and some software, but then I'd get distracted.

With a complete Britannica on the Web, I'd be able to look up "Tintern Abbey," and next thing I'd be in the Lake Poets chat room discussing what kind of pencil stub Wordsworth used. Or I'd become a compulsive video solitaire player. I'm sure video solitaire is more addictive than the deck of real cards that are spread on my desk at the moment. Darn that six of diamonds. And e-mail would be more distracting than the telephone I use to call everyone I know, when I'm blocked.

A fellow blocked writer, with whom I just got off the phone, says he looked up "pencils" on the Internet. They were invented in the late sixteenth century, which may moot the whole Shakespeare duck-goose quill question. Fortunately I don't have a computer and can't get onto the Antique Writing Instrument electronic bulletin board to find out.

Or I might not get distracted enough by the computer. I might use it to write too much too fast. Excessive speed and quantity are, like chattiness and digression, besetting sins of cyber-assisted authorship. *Slate* generates a remarkable amount of thoughtful material with astonishing rapidity, thus driving the reading public to *Maxim* and *Us*.

I once saw an interview with a famous writer of too many horror novels who lamented that he hadn't gotten a computer sooner. He is a talented writer, but he's notorious for his hurried characterizations and the hasty lack of internal logic in his plots. "I could have written much more if I'd had a computer," said the famous horror writer, or something like that.

No! Slow down and consider objective correlative and tragic stasis when the giant rabid dog traps the psychic child in the compact car.

Then there's the famous writer of legal thrillers who seems to have a computer program that automatically generates courtroom dialogue and the famous writer of international intrigues who gets his story lines on-line from intriguetogo.com. To write too much too fast is . . .

My wife (bringing me a fresh box of multicolored felt-tip pens) has just leaned over my shoulder and muttered, "You wish."

I suppose marrying a writer seemed more romantic than it turned out to be. Lack of romance is my real objection to writing on a computer.

I decided to be a writer when Hemingway and Faulkner (and Mickey Spillane) were still lighting the literary sky. I was going to be a hard-drinking guy, tough but sensitive, in my old tweed jacket, pounding out truths on the Royal portable that I'd dragged through Normandy (or Yaddo anyhow).

I can't picture myself fiddling with wires and transistors and geeky *Popular Electronics* hobby stuff like somebody who belonged to Ham Radio Club in high school. I became a writer to have a cape buffalo head on my wall, not a mouse on my plastic laminated Scooby-Do pad.

And how did those old-time writers get their tweed jackets to wear out only at the elbows so they could have cool leather patches? My tweed jackets wear out because I spill ketchup on them. Also, tweed jackets ride up on the back of my neck when I'm writing and itch. Which brings me to the honest confession of why I don't use a computer. Like the tweed jacket, I can't get it to work.

I'm too tough and sensitive to have to have some pubescent twerp with his mom's earring in his tongue, who combs his hair with Redi-Whip and has an Ani DiFranco tattoo on his shin, come show me how a computer works. What does the twerp know about Wordsworth and *Two Gentlemen of Verona* and shooting a cape buffalo?

For that matter, what do I know? If I were Web savvy, I could find out. And easy access to facts is one more terrible thing about writing with computers. There's nothing worse than getting a hard fact stuck in the Royal portable (or IBM Selectric) when you're trying to pound out truths. Imagine *Gulliver's Travels* if Jonathan Swift had known what was on the other side of the world.

Give me facts, and I'd turn into one of those dreadful information technology-type writers—probably writing for *Maxim* or *Us*—who tracks down any piece of information no matter how obscure and can explain everything. Then I'd have to explain how I can make a living as a writer when I don't know how to use a computer.

Saluting All the
King's Mentors

⤳

Jay Parini

Writers, perhaps like anyone trying to learn a craft, look anxiously around them for mentors. There is, in fact, a long and fascinating history of literary apprenticeship. One thinks of young Samuel Beckett sitting at the feet of Joyce, or of Joyce himself learning Norwegian so that he could correspond with his hero Ibsen.

Any number of would-be novelists, like Sinclair Lewis, Ernest Hemingway and William Faulkner, put themselves in the tutelage of Sherwood Anderson, who gave them advice and moral support. A few decades later, Robert Lowell pitched a tent on the lawn of John Crowe Ransom, making himself into a determined apprentice of that magnanimous poet and critic, who played a similar role in the lives of many writers, including Robert Penn Warren, Peter Taylor, and Randall Jarrell.

Today young writers often attach themselves to graduate programs in creative writing, where they pay good money to find mentors. This can of course be effective; one has seen any number of fine writers emerge from M.F.A. programs. But there is always an element of chance here. The chemistry between the young and older writer in the end has to work; it cannot be feigned. It can certainly not be purchased.

I was, myself, lucky in my mentors. In 1968 I headed for Scotland, to the University of St. Andrews, where I would spend seven years as a student. One day my history tutor, an eccentric woman named Anne Wright, asked me about my interests, and I told her I wanted to write poetry.

She said, "Ah, then you must meet Alastair." She referred to Alastair Reid, the Scottish poet, essayist and translator, who lived in a stone cottage overlooking the North Sea, with its endless throaty rumble. She made a phone call, and Alastair agreed to meet me at a local pub. "Bring a poem," he said.

I did, and continued to do so. Most afternoons I would put a poem into my knapsack and pedal out to his cottage, making my way through an elm rookery to his front door. We would sit together at his kitchen table, drinking tea as he "corrected" my poems, crossing out words and adding others, rearranging stanzas, cutting lines with a deft editorial stroke of his fountain pen. I learned a prodigious amount by sitting next to him, watching closely, saying little.

Sometimes we would read poems by other poets: Yeats, Hopkins, Neruda. I still recall a vivid paraphrase of "Among School Children" that was triggered by my confession that I didn't understand a word of Yeats's poem and couldn't see why anyone considered it great. That poem has remained a touchstone of my emotional life.

Alastair himself had learned to write while sitting beside Robert Graves on the island of Majorca. He had gone there as a young man seeking a mentor, and Graves had given him an assignment: to make a rough translation of *Lives of the Caesars* by Suetonius. (Alastair of course was a Latinist.) Proud of his prose, he put his not-so-rough translation before Graves, then watched as Graves adroitly "corrected" his work: superfluous adverbs were swallowed into stronger verbs; adjectives disappeared, as nouns became more particular, more precise. Graves rearranged the syntax of sentences, transforming passive into active constructions. Everything became tighter and stronger.

My relationship with Alastair continues to this day. He just spent a month with me in Vermont, and our long conversations about literature reminded me of those days when I was just waking into my own voice, getting a sense of myself as a writer. It's almost impossible to recapture the thrill of those times, but I recall a little of what that felt like.

When I returned to the United States in 1975 and began mixing poetry with prose, I happened into a friendship with Robert Penn Warren, whose novels and poems I'd been reading since high school. He spent summers and holidays near me, in a rustic house in West Wardsboro, Vermont, and I took to visiting him there, often with a manuscript in hand.

I'd grown used to the attention that Alastair Reid gave to my work, and Warren—he was known as Red to his friends—seemed more than willing to help. He was, in fact, quite ruthless with his pen and could be harsh with his critiques of a poem or piece of fiction. But he was generous, too, and understood that praise and censure have to be carefully meted out so that the younger writer doesn't lose hope. It is just so miserably easy to lose hope.

Once, on a long hike through the woods near Mount Stratton, Red asked why I hadn't shown him anything in a long time, and I explained that my life had become over-wrought. I had been unable to complete a poem or story for months. Everything I wrote seemed secondhand, boring and impossibly crude. He looked at me sternly and said, "You must cultivate leisure."

I knew instantly what he meant: I had neglected my own essential laziness, that mental place where you have to spend, or to waste, a lot of time. For a writer there is no such thing as wasted time. It doesn't work that way.

Red Warren himself moved easily between poetry and fiction, and he loved teaching as well. I was able to use him as a model, to see how the pieces of his life's puzzle had been fitted neatly together.

"Poetry is the great schoolhouse of fiction," he said to me one evening, over a glass of bourbon. He talked of Hardy and Lawrence, Goethe and Hugo. "This literary specialization in America has actually hurt our literature," he said. I believed him, and while I have kept poetry at the center of my writing and reading life, I have found useful expression in various prose forms, including the novel and the critical essay.

It's gratifying now when younger writers come to me with their manuscripts, their questions and their hopes. If the chemistry is right, amazing conversations will ensue. There is so much to talk about. And I often feel as though I'm taking part in a much larger conversation, one that reaches back as far as Athens and has kept the lamp burning in many windows down the centuries, wherever young writers have gone for advice, for inspiration, for "correction" and—of course—for love.

Why Not Put Off Till Tomorrow the Novel You Could Begin Today?

Ann Patchett

M y life is a series of ranked priorities. At the top of the list is the thing I do not wish to do the very most, and beneath that is everything else. There is vague order to the everything else, but it scarcely matters. The thing I really don't want to do is start my fifth novel, and the rest of my life is little more than a series of stalling techniques to help me achieve my goal.

This essay, for example, which I asked to write because all of the other essays I have thought of are now finished, will easily kill a day. I have already restored my oven to the level of showroom-floor cleanliness, written a small hill of thank-you notes (some of them completely indiscriminate: "Thank you for sending me the list of typographical errors you found in my last novel"), walked the dog to the point of the dog's collapse. I've read most of the books I've been meaning to read since high school.

The sad part is, when there is something I very much

don't want to do, I become incredibly fast about shooting through everything else. This week I have cleaned out my sister's closets. And then my mother's.

For a long time before I start to write a novel, anywhere from one year to two, I make it up. This is the happiest time I have with my books. The novel in my imagination travels with me like a small lavender moth making loopy circles around my head. It is a truly gorgeous thing, its unpredictable flight patterns, the amethyst light on its wings. I think of my characters as I wander through the grocery store. I write out their names like a teenage girl dreaming of marriage.

In these early pre-text days my story has more promise, more beauty, than I have ever seen in any novel ever written, because, sadly, this novel is not written. Then the time comes when I have to begin to translate ideas into words, a process akin to reaching into the air, grabbing my little friend (crushing its wings slightly in my thick hand), holding it down on a cork board and running it though with a pin. It is there that the lovely thing in my head dies.

I take some comfort that I've done this before, that eventually, perhaps even today, I will write the opening pages. Somewhere around page 80 I will accept that I am neither smart enough nor talented enough to put all the light and movement and beauty I had hoped for onto paper, and so I will have to settle for what I am capable of pulling off. But the question then becomes: On what day do you format a new file on the computer and type that first sentence? I don't actually sell the book until I've finished writing it, so I don't have a deadline to compel me. And if I'm careful with the money I've got, it could last me for a while.

Suddenly, five novels seems ungainly. The thought of it

convinces me how boring I've become, and I start to wonder why I never went to medical school. I imagine Elizabeth Taylor choosing a dress in which to marry Richard Burton. Did she believe that this time everything would be different? That this time she would be true until death did them part? I marvel at such hopefulness.

Starting a novel isn't so different from starting a marriage. The dreams you pin on these people are enormous. You are diving into the lives of your characters, knowing that you will fall in love with all of them, knowing (as surely Elizabeth Taylor knew) that in the end the love will finish and turn you out on the street alone.

From the vantage point of a novelist trying to get inside the novel, it makes the most sense to me to shoot for something along the lines of *A Man Without Qualities* or *Remembrance of Things Past,* a genuine tome that will keep me busy for the next thirty years or so. But that doesn't work either, because as soon as I'm comfortably inside my book I inevitably long to get out. The farther into the story I get, the harder and faster I write. In short, I become a malcontent dog, either scratching to get in or scratching to get out.

It should be noted that there are two blissful things about writing novels: making them up and seeing them finished. The days I spend in either of these two states are so sweet, they easily make the rest of the process bearable. The novel in my head is all mapped out and ready to go, but in these final minutes before departure I feel the rocking waves of doubt.

In trying to start a novel, I dream about the novels I wish I had written, the ideas I should have had. A book about a boy in a boat with a Bengal tiger? Surely I would have come up with that one had Yann Martel not written *Life of Pi.* Surely with a little more time I would have come up with something as important and beautiful as Carol Shields's *Unless*. And yet, the books I most long to plagiarize are my own.

Every time I start a new novel, I think what a comfort it would be to crawl back into the broken-in softness of the old one. Would it be completely unreasonable to write another book about opera and South America? Would reviewers say I was in a rut? Honestly, how often do reviewers actually read the preceding novels? Of course when I was starting *Bel Canto*, I was longing for just one more book about a gay magician, and so on, backward.

Despite the hand-wringing, housekeeping and the overdrive of unnecessary productivity, there will come a point very soon when I will begin, if for no other reason than the stress of not beginning will finally overwhelm me. That, and I'll want to see how the whole thing ends. Sometimes if there's a book you really want to read, you have to write it yourself.

The Eye of the Reporter, the Heart of the Novelist

Anna Quindlen

There's always a notebook in my purse. I learned my lesson one day many years ago when I found myself at the scene of a crime, taking notes on the back of checking account deposit slips. Before I was a novelist, I was a columnist; and before I was a columnist, I was a reporter; and the reporter is always there, jumbled amid the Altoids, the keys and the lipstick, there forever in the notebook.

The connection between the two incarnations, between the newspaper and the novel, is clear to me but confusing to readers. Here is the question they ask most often, the one that underlines the covertly snobbish way in which we delineate the professions from the so-called arts: How did you manage to make the leap from journalism to fiction?

I used to answer flatly that there's not much difference between the two, that good writing is good writing wherever you find it. But that answer really threw people into a swivet, speaking to their deepest suspicions about both lines of work. It turned out that when I was writing about the people I actually met and the places I actually went, the enterprise was enshadowed by reader suspicion that we reporters made everything up. But when I made things up as a novelist, readers always suspected I was presenting a thinly disguised version of the facts of my own life.

So the facts were assumed to be fiction, and the fiction fact. Go figure, as the guys at Katz's delicatessen used to say. The quotation is somewhere in one of my old notebooks; I know it's true.

The truth is that the best preparation I could have had for a life as a novelist was life as a reporter. At a time when more impressionistic renderings of events were beginning to creep into the news pages, I learned to look always for the telling detail: the Yankees cap, the neon sign in the club window, the striped towel on the deserted beach. Those things that, taken incrementally, make a convincing picture of real life, and maybe get you onto page 1, too.

I learned to distinguish between those details that simply existed and those that revealed. Those telling details are the essence of fiction that feels real. The command of those details explains why Charles Dickens, a onetime reporter, has a byline for the ages.

I learned, from decades of writing down their words verbatim in notebooks, how real people talk. I learned that syntax and rhythm were almost as individual as a fingerprint, and that one quotation, precisely transcribed and intentionally untidied, could delineate a character in a way that pages of exposition never could.

All of us in journalism know of the times we've read a neat little quotation that seemed to sum up the entire point of a story, and we thought, almost reflexively, "It's piped," reporter's jargon for "It's invented." It's just too pat, too flat, too homogenized, too perfect at one level, too impersonal at another. That happens in fiction, too, the line of dialogue that sounds like a speech or a stage direction or a maxim instead of a sentence. You can hear the fake with a reporter's ear.

I learned in newspapers to make every word count. All those years of being given twelve hundred words, of having the twelve hundred pared to nine hundred at three o'clock, of having to take out another hundred to shoehorn it into the hole in the layout: it teaches you to make the distinction between what is necessary and illuminating and what is simply you in love with the sound of your own voice.

A novelist doesn't write to space, of course; eighty thousand words, a hundred thousand, it's up to the writer to say when the story is done. Some have a harder time than others. The most common shortcoming I find in good novels nowadays is excess; many of them should be fifty pages shorter than they are. I learned how to cut where cutting is commonplace, swift and draconian.

In that same place, crowded and noisy and redolent of adrenaline in the late afternoons, I learned about writer's block, too. People have writer's block not because they can't write, but because they despair of writing eloquently. That's not the way it works, and one of the best places to learn that is a newspaper, which in its instant obsolescence is infinitely forgiving.

Some days you plod, some days you soar, but always you churn out copy on demand, whether you feel the muse or not. (Where is the muse, by the way? Does she ever show up?) Occasionally you hit it, grinning behind the nominal privacy of your partition like a Mardi Gras mask.

Jacques Barzun once wrote: "Convince yourself that you

are working in clay, not marble, on paper, not eternal bronze: let that first sentence be as stupid as it wishes. No one will rush out and print it as it stands." Journalism is the professional embodiment of that soothing sentiment.

Of course, it is also the professional embodiment of fact-finding, and that, more than anything else, is why a switch to fiction by a journalist perplexes readers and even colleagues. "I could never make it up," one of the very best reporters I've ever known said to me a little accusingly. But that notion of untrammeled invention becomes illusory after a while, even in the most freewheeling novel. (Although, as a former reporter, I undoubtedly find a thrill in being able to take a name that is unwieldy and simply to change it, poof!)

If you manage to build characters from the ground up carefully, make them really real, your ability to invent decreases as their verisimilitude grows. Certain people will only behave in certain ways; certain behaviors will only lead to certain other behaviors. The entire range of possible events decreases as characters choose one road, not another. Plot is like a perspective drawing, its possible permutations growing narrower and narrower, until it reaches a fixed point in the distance. That point is the ending. Life is like that. Fiction is like life, at least if it is good.

I always wanted to write fiction. It said in my high school prophecy, "Ambition: to write the great American novel." (I'm just reporting the facts here, mortifying as they may be.) I only went into the newspaper business to pay the rent. And then I discovered that, for a Catholic girl with napkin-on-the-lap manners, the professional obligation to go places I was not welcome and ask questions that were intrusive and even rude was as exhilarating as work could be.

I drank bourbon at noon in the police shack and got spit on at town meetings by folks who couldn't inveigh without expectorating. I rode in a search-and-rescue plane in a snowstorm, and I rode in a limo with the mayor in high dudgeon. Geez, what a deal.

I taught myself a shorthand of my own invention, and I use it still. But now, memory being what it is, or more often isn't, my notes are the ideas for a new novel that occur to me as real life eddies around me. "Rd hr," means one character will be a redhead, and "Viet Wr?" means another may have fought in that conflict. It's just that the scene I see is not, as in my past life, in Flatbush or on Fifth Avenue.

The story, the people, the neighborhood: they're all in my own mind. But the notebook still helps to keep the details fresh and true, to hold the quotations clear as consonants, to provide those little touchstones that will rescue me from the slough of writer's despondency. I am a reporter of invented stories now, but no less a reporter because of that.

A Retreat
from the World
Can Be a Perilous Journey

~~~

Jonathan Rosen

The Jewish mystics believed that God, in order to create the world, had to make himself smaller. I consoled myself with this notion when my daughter was born and I had to move my office out of the large spare bedroom and into the maid's room.

Long before my move, I'd been keenly aware of the weird expansions and contractions necessitated by creative life, particularly the painful paradox that to write about the world, you have to retreat from it. Not completely, of course. I like the way Walt Whitman described himself: "Both in and out of the game, and watching and wondering at it."

Even with that credo in mind, writing is lonely work. For Virginia Woolf it wasn't glorious travels or vast experience but a room of one's own that the writer needs most. She knew you can only advance by retreating. Of course her maid's room probably had a maid in it, which no doubt took the edge off the solitude.

But all writers wind up metaphorically in the servants' quarters. When you write, you're taking orders from somewhere—a higher (or at least a lower) power—and the work isn't always pretty. I was appalled to discover that my first novel, *Eve's Apple*, was about a woman starving herself and a man madly in love with her and morbidly fascinated by her illness. It is not the novel I thought I would write, not how I wished to enter the world. But I was forced to say, like Prospero pointing at Caliban, "This thing of darkness I acknowledge mine."

The inner journey is often a perilous one. Even the divine contraction was fraught with danger. The mystics concluded that because God had to shrink in order to make room for the world, he was no longer all-powerful. The vessels intended to receive his glory broke, scattering divine sparks all over the place and introducing imperfection into the world, presumably explaining why the world is full of flawed characters and horrific plot twists. All I had to do was install a second phone line.

But even if I do not have to worry about my superabundant energy overflowing inadequate containers (if only I did!), stepping out of life can be disorienting. It can even seem a little humiliating, especially in New York City, with the busy world streaming past my windows. I became keenly aware of this when, along with our daughter, my household acquired a nanny. She only works three days a week, but her presence has made me awkwardly aware of just what my writing day looks like.

Our nanny's husband is a welder and works outdoors in all kinds of weather. What does she think when she sees me, a grown man who goes to work in his bedroom slippers? Or when I wander out of my little room at midday, while my daughter is taking a nap, to lie on the couch with a book? Or if I sit by the window staring out for a while? Or if the need to figure out a certain scene or a certain sentence—or the need to escape from a certain scene or a certain sentence— drives me from my desk over to, say, a box of cereal for a late-morning snack.

Keats referred to the poet's "diligent Indolence," a state of suspended activity necessary for creativity. On days when I'm really diligent, I might even take a nap, not unlike my daughter who, after twelve hours at night, still needs a little supplementary sleep to feel refreshed. Play, after all, is hard work; Anna Freud called play the work of children. And perhaps of writers, too.

Play is work; inside is outside; indolence is activity. One might add that the imaginary is real, and introspection is actually a form of social research. No wonder I have to take a nap from time to time. Eventually one must put aside the paradoxes and the explanations and simply write.

But even then I find that the paradoxes make their way into the writing. *The Talmud and the Internet*, my most recent book, despite its title and subject, wound up having at its core a description of my two grandmothers. In a book about harmonizing unlikely elements, nothing challenged me more than my own contradictory inheritance: one of my grandmothers lived a long and prosperous American life; my other grandmother was murdered by Nazis.

Each life and death pointed to radically different conclusions about the nature of the world, of human conduct. The best I could do was put them side by side and, in the manner of the Talmud, let them each stand as point and counterpoint, neither dissolving into the other. I let my grandmothers take their place alongside all the famous figures in my book, Talmud sages and great writers and historical figures, because without that personal element my public speculations seemed weirdly abstract. There's always a piece of writing that for me must be close to home, the string that binds the balloon to the earth.

I was at some level as embarrassed to find myself writing about my grandmothers as I was to find myself writing about a self-starving woman. Where was the grand picaresque American adventure I had always imagined I would create? What were my grandmothers doing in the middle of everything, calling me home? The wonderful thing about writing is that it forces you to confront yourself in a way you don't usually have to. That is, needless to say, also the terrible thing.

I used to waste my energy envying an earlier generation of Jewish writers, children of immigrants who seemed umbilically linked to authentic experience I was born too late for. They were fueled by a world-conquering hunger that made their protagonists born-again Don Quixotes. Well, as Jorge Luis Borges wrote, "The world, unfortunately, is real; I, unfortunately, am Borges." This is a universal problem, not a literary one. Everybody has to find his own voice, whether or not he is a writer.

This is why all the arcane things a writer discovers about his craft aren't really arcane. Everybody has to make the inner descent into himself, everybody needs metaphors to live by and everybody has to order the chaos of experience into some kind of narrative, if only in the depths of dream-fashioning sleep. In that regard, the writer who stays home is really a kind of everyman. There should be more novels about him.

He is also something of an immigrant himself, exploring the world and groping for the words that will help him master it. And staying at home has taught me something else: my daughter is a kind of immigrant, too. I hear her as I write this; she is in her highchair in the kitchen, just outside my door, being fed her lunch. She is learning to say brief truncated words: "nana" for banana; "mih" for milk. Soon enough she will know my language so well that the physical world she is on such intimate terms with may seem abstract, reaching her through a muffling amnion of mediating words.

Inevitably my home is becoming a sort of melting pot for my daughter. She cannot go through life yanking the phone off the hook, pointing at things and screaming if she doesn't get them. She cannot (very important) push open the door of my maid's room whenever she wants.

And though this process of assimilation is necessary, it has a small element of sadness in it for me. Because I so love her untutored, marveling attitude to the world. I love her deep attachment to sunlight, the way she pokes the water in her bathtub to test its properties, the way she gapes at the mystery of a face, laughing in amazement.

"Not in entire forgetfulness and not in utter nakedness but trailing clouds of glory do we come," Wordsworth wrote. For him God himself was "our home," the Old Country where we all once lived and for which we all secretly pine. On earth we learn a new language. But if we manage to keep the trace of an accent from the mysterious place we once inhabited, so much the better for us.

Certainly all my favorite writers have retained their attitude of wonder. And I think this matters to me most about writing, beyond history and politics, plot and structure, the literal and symbolic. Of course one wants all those things, too. But there is something much more primitive and simple and elusive that lies at the core of writing that has to do with the sheer mystery of the created world. For me it is what links a cave painting to a page of *Ulysses*.

Perhaps it is the need to approach this mystery that explains why I am a grown man who stays home with the nanny when other people are going to work. And why, as I sit in the maid's room proudly overhearing my daughter speak her first words in my language, I find myself hoping I will capture a few forgotten elements of hers.

After Six Novels
in Twelve Years, a
Character Just Moves On

⌒

James Sallis

S ome years back, when I took my seat on the bus, this
guy sat down beside me and started talking.

The trip was unplanned. I thought I was writing a short
story. Now here it is twelve years and six novels later, Karyn
and I have hauled boxes and lives from Texas to New
Orleans to Phoenix to Brooklyn and back, and that voice
has been in my ear the whole time.

Now the voice is fading. *Ghost of a Flea,* the final novel of
six, comes out next month. Through the bus's rear window
as it pulls away I watch my friend. He lifts a hand in farewell.

I recall those last days. Endlessly revising, throwing out
pages, feinting and dodging and second-guessing my way
into books, I always write slowly at first. Then, as time goes
on, momentum develops; with each novel there's a point I
can never quite grasp, when the story takes over and I find
myself stumbling along behind, trying to keep up.

I had told Karyn that I expected to finish *Flea* in a couple of weeks, but those last chapters came, as they do so often, in a tumble. On a Tuesday evening, tears streaming down my face, I met her at the door when she got home from work. She took one look and said, "You finished it." I had, moments before. We sat on the porch with glasses of wine looking across at palm trees as day let go its hold and bands of bright ribbon blew out on the sky.

Twelve years past, in a garage apartment in Texas, I had written:

"And now I must come to some sort of conclusion, I suppose.

"I can't imagine what it should be. . . .

"And so, another book. But not about my Cajun this time. About someone I've named Lew Griffin, a man I know both very well and not at all. And I had only to end it now by writing: I went back into the house and wrote.

"It is midnight. The rain beats at the windows.

"It is not midnight. It is not raining."

Another book.

The way I've measured out my life.

That was *The Long-Legged Fly,* "what might have resulted if Raymond Chandler and Samuel Beckett had collaborated on a detective novel," I remarked in one interview—completed in a single amazing month that saw as well half a dozen new short stories, a brace of poems, six or eight book reviews and the beginnings of my novel *Renderings.* Each morning I'd stumble from makeshift bed to makeshift desk and draw the Selectric close to begin writing. Cup after cup of tea steamed alongside as, across the street, cars delivered children to day care. Mothers pulled away applying makeup in rear-view mirrors. I'd still be there writing at the end of the day, apart and looking on, when they returned.

That summer Lew Griffin set up camp in my imagination—took his seat on the bus beside me—as a failed private detective, failed husband and father, a black man trying to live in the white man's world where rules keep changing and the rug always gets pulled out from under. Together we recalled his boyhood in rural Arkansas, his enrapture by books, his first days in the great gumbo city that's New Orleans. By the second novel, *Moth*, he'd moved up from camping in my imagination to renting out a front room. I went through beatings and a hundred hangovers with him. I watched him become a writer, mourned with him the disappearance of his son, was there beside him through the loss of the many women who loved him.

In *Black Hornet*, sixties ferment becomes real for Lew when a white woman he meets at a black club, a journalist, falls to a sniper's bullet as they leave.

In *Bluebottle*—a mirror image of *Black Hornet*, dealing with white supremacy in much the same manner as the earlier book did Black Power movements—Lew himself falls to sniper's fire, loses a year of his life and tries to piece together the lost year from his own halting memory and what friends are able to tell him of it, dumping in shovelfuls of imagination as landfill. The very novel you are reading is that reconstruction, that cobbling together.

Why Lew?

Why does a white southerner choose to write about a black man in American society? Why does he think he can get away with that?

Why, for that matter, mysteries, after years upon years of publishing literary fiction, science fiction and fantasy, poetry, personal essays, musicology, translations?

Complex questions. The facile response is that I didn't

choose to write about Lew, that he chose me. I'd been reading a lot of Chester Himes, his novels, his autobiographies, and began writing *The Long-Legged Fly* from a single persistent image, lowering myself Archimedes-like into the story, looking to see what might be in there. When the Eureka! came, forty or so pages along, I knew my protagonist was African-American. I knew, too, that I'd been given the perfect window to write about American society in the late twentieth century.

I went back to work.

Mysteries?

What better crucible in which to fire up the reagents of contemporary urban life? Crime novels give access to every level of society, taking on the city in its entirety. The privileged, the impoverished, the invisible. When in the 1980s I began writing in the field, it seemed to me that much of the most interesting work was being done in the crime novel. A whole army of writers, people like Jim Burke, Stephen Greenleaf and Daniel Woodrell, had decamped from "literary" fiction and set up down by the river. They wanted to write serious novels, and they wanted people to read them, and they didn't feel those two desires had to be exclusive.

I dropped my knapsack and unrolled my sleeping bag beside them.

From the first, I knew that Lew's story could only take place in New Orleans. In its unique history and collage of cultures, New Orleans is at once the most and least American of our great cities. "We've moved to the third world," Karyn said a week or so after our relocation there. It was her first time, my fifth, and New Orleans is the closest thing I have to a home. I'd gone there, at seventeen, to attend

Tulane, keep circling back to this brutal, graceful, ugly, beautiful, sophisticated, crude city.

And finally, why end the series? I could easily, as a friend pointed out, go on writing books set in Lew's world year in and year out. But the novels, more or less as predicated in *The Long-Legged Fly* with its four sections set in four decades, form an arc, a concerted movement toward something, in many ways a single long story, and with *Ghost of a Flea* the story's completely told. As musician friends would say, I played the melody, jammed my way through five more books and came back home.

Time to put down the horn and say good-bye to Lew.

Fiction and Fact Collide, with Unexpected Consequences

⟵⟶

John Sedgwick

After three nonfiction books and countless magazine articles, I developed the conviction that novels contained the real writing, in which the author didn't just take the world as he found it but actually imposed his own vision upon it. With each nonfiction book, I found myself creeping farther down the diving board toward fiction, as my journalistic accounts relied increasingly on narrative, setting and character. Finally, about ten years ago, I took the plunge.

I labored for some time on a coming-of-age novel that never did work out. (It was only after I got deeper into the fiction business that I realized that novels are like waffles: you have to toss the first one.) But then, inspired by some experiences I'd had on surveillance with the private eye who was the subject of my first nonfiction book, I hit on the idea of writing a novel about a man who has the unusual hobby of following people in his car, and happily that book clicked, emerging almost two years ago as a psychological thriller, *The Dark House.*

I tend to regard each new book as the antidote to the previous one, and I started in on a new novel, *The Education of Mrs. Bemis,* that would investigate fresh, albeit more challenging, psychological terrain. The thriller had been tense and noirish, and I wanted the new one to be more true to life, with greater emotional range.

In publishing terms, it would ascend from the commercial to the literary, freed from the constraints and security of genre fiction. But as it turned out, such a move entailed hazards I hadn't foreseen. *Mrs. Bemis* was about the unexpected relationship between a Boston dowager who has come to a mental hospital after she is found curled up, nearly catatonic, on a bed at Filene's department store and the young female psychiatrist who treats her, becoming deeply involved in her life. A grisly murder hovers over the tale, but mostly it's about the two of them, often face-to-face in therapy, trying to understand each other.

This may sound like a tidy plot, but the novel was brought on by the experience of placing my aging mother in McLean Hospital, near Boston, for depression in the long, sorry aftermath of my father's death. That was, needless to say, a difficult time for both of us. Yet as it was happening, all I could think was that it was a fine setup for a piece of fiction. The hospital was obviously highly atmospheric, with a rich social history that has since been chronicled in Alex Beam's *Gracefully Insane* and a tragic air stemming from the many grand buildings of the hospital's heyday that were now boarded up, as if they, like the patients they once sheltered, had closed down in the face of an unbearable reality.

Perhaps you sense a determination on my part to maintain some emotional distance here, walling myself off from the pain of delivering my mother to a locked ward. Honestly, I didn't. It was all material to me. And as I started in on the novel, I quickly moved away from my mother's circumstances and personality, transforming her into a grander, more imperious and more romantic character, the Mrs. Bemis of the title.

In my eagerness to escape the last vestiges of the central truth I was addressing, I actually brought in a gangster to liven things up. I might as well have imported a trained bear or a magic show. My editor put a stop to that: my tale, he reminded me, was about the depressed lady. So I settled down and told that story, employing expansive recollections of Mrs. Bemis's youth and early adulthood, while relying on the young psychiatrist, who turned out to have troubles of her own, to uncover the origins of her patient's plight.

Despite the difference in style and setting, this turned out to be a familiar theme for me. As may befit books set in Boston, this most historical of cities, where secrets are buried everywhere, the protagonist of the previous novel, too, proved to be a Brahmin heir searching for the truth about his past. But while he pursues his quest largely in the solitary, male fashion, the high-born heroine of the new book seeks her understanding in the relational style I associate with women. Either way, I found myself pondering what lay back there not just in them, but in me. As the product of a long ancestral past, I began to worry about my own dark history.

As much as I wanted to will it away, the source of Mrs. Bemis's depression remained the book's deep subject. And as

I dwelled on this daily at my computer, while the brightness of summer dimmed with the fall, I found a blackness creeping over me.

Writers are often isolated, mildly crotchety types anyway, but I became unusually withdrawn and morose, especially for me, as I soldiered on with the book. Even my dog looked at me strangely. I gradually turned sleepless, then panicky, imprisoned in a kind of mental hospital of my own imagining. At my wife's urging, I saw a psychologist, who referred me to a psychopharmacologist, who delivered the grim diagnosis. I was experiencing a major depression.

Many are the sources of depression, and I wouldn't want to suggest that the cause of mine was exclusively literary. Surely there were genetic factors at work, and my mother's sorrow obviously weighed on me, since we have always been so close. But all the same I think that one of the basic problems was that I was too drawn in to my fiction. I was living it.

I thought about it as I fell asleep, dreamed it and jumped to it the moment I awoke. On legal pad after legal pad, I obsessively scribbled out plot developments, not realizing that each one would take an entire book to resolve. More disturbing, I began to feel the chilly hands of the elegant, distraught Mrs. Bemis reaching for me. And I began to think those hands resembled my own.

Coming from journalism, I was unprepared to live with my characters quite so intimately. Yes, a prisoner I'd written about once threatened me from jail, and I spent many hours in the car with my private eye. Still, for the most part my journalistic subjects were safely removed from me. But as products of my imagination, my fictional characters were me. How could they not intrude?

It took nearly six months, plenty of therapy and some expensive pharmaceuticals to climb out of the pit I'd dug for myself. Actually what helped most of all was to continue on with the book, torturous as that sometimes seemed, and to see it through to Mrs. Bemis's gradual recovery and final release from her own illness. Her cure became mine.

Now that the book is finished, and it has made its way out into the world, I'm glad to feel liberated from the torment it has evoked. Aren't novels intended for catharsis? But I have gotten something out of my woe. I have come to appreciate far better what my mother and countless others like her—the many Mrs. Bemises of the world—have gone through. For I haven't just imagined their plight; I've lived it. And now I've told the tale.

Confession Begets Connection

∽

David Shields

M any writers pretend that they don't read reviews of
their books, and that, in particular, life is too short to
subject themselves to reading bad reviews. Kingsley Amis
said that a bad review might spoil your breakfast, but you
shouldn't allow it to spoil your lunch. Jean Cocteau suggested: "Listen carefully to first criticisms of your work.
Note carefully just what it is about your work that the critics don't like—then cultivate it. That's the part of your work
that's individual and worth keeping."

Sane advice; I don't follow it. I read all my reviews,
though not necessarily every word of every one. The really
positive ones are boring after a while—your own most generous self-appraisal quoted back to you—but I must admit I
find bad reviews fascinating. They're like the proverbial
train wreck, only you're in the train; will all those mangled
bodies at the bottom of the ravine tell you something unexpected about yourself?

Recently—as an experiment, I suppose, in psychic survival—I reread every horrific review I've ever received, to
see what I would learn. This is what I learned: I'm right.
They're wrong. (Smiley face.) It was a genuinely odd and in
a way a riveting experience, the hour or so it took me to
read bad reviews of five books. I felt as if I were locked in
a room, getting worked over by a dozen supposedly well-
meaning guidance counselors. Suddenly my body felt as if it
had gotten filled with liquid cement.

One otherwise fairly positive review of my novel *Dead
Languages* concluded, "The novel as a whole doesn't quite
uncurl from its fetal position, doesn't open out from self-
consciousness toward reconciliation." A reviewer of my collection of linked stories, *A Handbook for Drowning*, said
about the book's protagonist: "The smudged eye turns into
the eye that smudges what it sees. Clinging to the child role
of bearing witness to itself, it doesn't undertake the adult
role of bearing witness to everything else. Cramped, Walter
tells a cramped story. The glimpses we see, varied and subtle as they may be, are all gray. It is the grayness of life seen
through a caul that has never been shed."

My first reaction when I reread these reviews was to
think: "You know, they're right. I must figure out how to
open out from self-consciousness toward reconciliation. I
must undertake the adult role of bearing witness to everything else." But then I realized that I don't do reconciliation;
I don't do witness to everything else. Sorry.

Nabokov said: "I do not know if it has ever been noted
before that one of the main characteristics of life is dis-
creteness. Unless a film of flesh envelops us, we die. Man
exists only insofar as he is separated from his surroundings.
The cranium is a space traveler's helmet. Stay inside or you

perish. Death is divestment, death is communion. It may be wonderful to mix with the landscape, but to do so is the end of the tender ego." I think of my work as being relentlessly loyal to this existential truth, whereas one reviewer of my most recent book, *Black Planet,* called it the "wretched musings of one white guy with a panicky ego, a pitiable heart, and too much time on his hands."

"Pitiable heart" interests me, as does this judgment about the same book: "At least it should make some white readers feel good about themselves. They may be screwed up about race, but they're not as annoyingly screwed up as David Shields."

The impulse on reviewers' part to use me to get well—to brandish their own more evolved morality, psyche, humanity—flies in the face of what is to me an essential assumption of the compact between reader and writer, especially between the reader and writer of autobiography: Doesn't everybody have a pitiable heart? Aren't we all bozos on this bus?

Robert Dana explains it like this:

"Was Keats a confessional poet? When he talks about youth that grows 'pale and spectre-thin, and dies,' he's talking about his kid brother, Tom, who died of tuberculosis. But he's talking about more than that. The word 'confessional' implies the need to purge oneself and go receive forgiveness for one's life. I don't think that's what confessional poetry is about at all. I think it's a poetry that comes out of the stuff of the poet's personal life, but he's trying to render this experience in more general and inclusive, or what used to be called 'universal,' terms. He's presenting himself as a representative human being. He's saying, 'This is what happens to us because we're human beings in this human world, this flawed and difficult world where joy is rare.'

"Sylvia Plath is certainly one of the outstanding 'confessional' poets, but when she entitles a poem 'Lady Lazarus,' she's trying to connect herself to the whole tradition of pain and death and resurrection. She's not presenting herself as Sylvia Plath, but as a part of a larger pattern. A more grotesque manifestation of it."

My shtick, exactly. When I present myself as a "tube boob" (one review) in *Remote* or as a "pathetically guilty white liberal" (another review) in *Black Planet*, I mean for "David Shields" to be a highly stylized representative through whom cultural energies and all manner of mad human needs flow.

One reviewer said about *Remote*, "The futuristically formless nature of the collection gets irritating; it's an ambivalent comment on bookmaking, and before long it's got us feeling ambivalent, too." Another reviewer said about the same book, "The danger, of course, in writing about fluff and modern life is that you spend too much time thinking about fluff and modern life, until you resemble not a little the prostitutes in 'You'll Never Make Love in This Town Again,' trapped, mired, in it."

I understand these comments are meant as dispraise, but if you're feeling ambivalent about it, that's a good thing; if I seem to you to be trapped, mired in it, that's the point. Theodor Adorno says that a "successful work is not one which resolves objective contradictions in a spurious harmony, but one which expresses the idea of harmony negatively by embodying the contradictions, pure and uncompromised, in its innermost structure." This is what I'm always seeking to do: embody the contradictions.

A reviewer of *Remote* said, "Shields wouldn't thank anyone who suggested, on the basis of the material presented in this book, that as the child of 'Jewish liberal activists,' he might have chosen passivism as the subtlest form of rebellion." Why would the reviewer think I included this information, unless I wanted readers to make precisely this kind of connection?

If via my pitiable heart the reader intuits something about his own, that, to me, is a worthwhile trade-off. What a guy, what a guy. This *Remote* reviewer concluded by mentioning a relatively minor misdeed I acknowledged committing, and then said, "Presumably, by now we're past the stage of being expected to say, 'Hell, we've all done that.'" Not done that—imagined that. Goethe said, "I've never heard of a crime which I could not imagine committing myself."

To me, it's almost unfathomable that a reviewer would say, as one did about *Black Planet,* "The author escapes the morass of self-doubt as so many others do—by vicarious identification with a professional athlete; Shields idolizes Sonics player Gary Payton to the point of unnerving fixation," and then not figure that I'm up to something other than chronicling my own fandom. Another reviewer of *Black Planet* asked: "Do we really need to know what David Shields is fantasizing about when he's having sex? Does he imagine his foibles are our own?"

I'm certain my foibles are your own, if only you're willing to acknowledge them. "A man's life of any worth is a continual allegory," said Keats, who should know.

A Storyteller
Finds Comfort in a
Cloak of Anonymity

∽

Susan Richards Shreve

In the late 1990s I wrote a book from the point of view of a young black woman who has barricaded herself in her college dorm room pursued by a man, either real or imagined, who finally materializes as the father she has never known. What I was searching for, what I'm always after, is understanding character and in this case the mind of a young woman who has slipped into the fog of adolescence.

For a number of reasons, including the political danger of a white writer taking on the voice of a black woman, my longtime editor turned the book down. At the time I hadn't considered going into hiding. But I had grown to love and believe in this troubled girl, and I was not about to set the novel aside, so I took on a pseudonym.

An editor at a different house bought the book assuming initially that she had read an autobiographical novel by a young African-American woman who out of shyness or

other misgivings refused to have her picture on the jacket or
to do any publicity.

And so began the deep pleasure of anonymity.

As a child I was an observer, a listener for the stories of
grown-ups. I led a quiet, solitary life with my mother, inter-
rupted in the evenings by the arrival of my father who preferred to live in a state of emergency. As I got older, I wanted
at least a minor part on my father's stage, which was usually
the kitchen. I invented people in crisis.

Walking home from school on a hot afternoon, I'd pass,
let's say, a young woman with bright red hair and a winter
coat, who seemed to be crying. She was definitely crying.

The image of the woman expanded in my mind from a
single gesture, a glance, the way she slipped her hand in the
pocket of her winter coat. And by the time I got home, I
would have imagined a whole life for her—abandoned at
twelve by her mother with nothing but a winter coat, pregnant by a sometime criminal at eighteen, wandering the
streets in search of her lost child—a tale completed just in
time to hush the conversation at dinner for a few moments
before my father's own exaggerated stories took over. Writing began for me on those brief occasions of my family's
silence when I was able to create for them the imagined
world of a character's life.

Anonymity took me back to those evenings. The pure,
uncomplicated, unself-conscious delight in telling a story.
As the writer of a pseudonymous book, I gave up my own
accumulated history as a novelist and became what I had
been as a child: unnamed, unidentified, unacknowledged.
Invisible. In a very real sense, what I hope for in the process
of imagining a book is to disappear.

Like the actor playing the same role night after night,

creating the illusion "as if for the first time," I recaptured the sense of freedom I'd had in writing my first book, that feeling of wonder, abandon, faith and—yes—innocence. So much of memory comes from the beginning of our lives when we know the world for the first time with a kind of clarity. It is that discovery of the past in the present on which a writer depends again and again as if our lost childhoods, like the surprising cyclamen plant, are forever opening new blossoms.

Write out of your own experience, we're told in school. Write what you know. Disarmed, we know a lot about one another. When I imagine a story, I hope to create a bond of trust with the reader as I give away a character's secrets one after the other until the reader knows them all, knows the character inside out. And the life of my story—perhaps that of a physician or a fortune-teller or a comedy troupe— becomes part of the reader's own experience.

Fiction is a glimpse at our common humanity, a reminder of it, a generous engagement between the reader and the imagined world of a book. So much of what we do as writers, no matter how grounded in the particular a story might be, is a leap of faith.

What I found myself thinking about, disappearing into the mind and heart of my young black protagonist, was the process of discovery, even self-discovery in writing outside of my own experience. Here is this young woman with no sense of who she is racially, sexually, no capacity for telling the truth, sinking toward madness. It is the reader who first knows the truth about this young woman's experience and in that recognition comes, I hope, as I did, to love her.

Initially I did not give a lot of thought to what might happen when a story in the first person is published by an unknown, presumably first-time author. I was curious in the way I used to be, relieved to be anonymous, free from accountability, a kind of literary masked bandit.

As it happened, the book was reviewed by African-American critics, shelved in the African-American section of the bookstore, and I confess I was pleased that readers believed the voice in the story. But I also began to worry that I was an imposter, or worse—if unmasked, I would be considered an imposter—allowing, even inviting the reader to believe that the character in the story and the author of it were the same. I told myself that I chose to use a pseudonym not because I was ashamed but on the contrary because I was proud of this book and would have been happy to have my own name on it.

So I forgave the imposter. After all, there had been this insistent young woman locked in her room, starving herself, duping her family, full of delusions, breaking my heart. I had to do something, limited as I was by the boundaries of this particular cultural climate, to set her loose.

When Eudora Welty died recently, I was in the process of writing about "Where Is the Voice Coming From?," a story she wrote in a dead heat in June 1963, taking on the voice of the killer of civil rights activist Medgar Evers. She imagined this story before the killer, Byron De La Beckwith, was caught, and it was so powerfully kin to reality that the *New Yorker*, which was publishing the story in its next issue, had to ask Miss Welty to change some of the details because her invented murderer was too close to the real one.

Such is the genius of Eudora Welty and her extraordinary capacity to see and reveal even a psychotic stranger thus giving voice to the deeply disturbing reality of racial hatred. The range of fiction is astonishing; in no small way so, too, is our human capacity to know one another.

I'm not an athlete, but I do understand what it means to push against your own sense of endurance until a rush of energy takes you just beyond what you thought possible. Writing is like that, especially writing outside the lines.

Not always, not often, but when the rush comes, we are taken to a place at once strange and familiar, a place we didn't know we knew.

Autumnal Accounting
Endangers Happiness

Richard Stern

Aging, people often draw their lives up around them like blankets against the oncoming chill, a psychological equivalent of the theological bookkeeping supposedly done when the earthly package is delivered to heaven's gate for its ultimate disposition. For those of us who are writers, such autumnal accounting is often but another installment of a long professional self-regard, one that differs from that of haberdashers and geologists or even that of historians and literary critics. Writers, far more commonly than nonwriters, not only organize what happens to them into stories but throughout their writing lives seek out sometimes perilous experience that may make good ones. Like Mailer they enlist in the wartime infantry, or like Hemingway take risks in jungles or bullfight rings, not only to test themselves but to observe their feelings and reactions as they're being tested. Not a few have serial affairs or marriages.

Even cautious writers like me find ourselves risking not

only our own happiness but that of those we love. I will not degrade this risk taking by saying that it serves our ambitions or careers. It is, I believe, the closest thing some of us have to vocation, an almost irrational commitment to the accurate, powerful depiction of what we've felt, seen, believed, conceived and imagined. That the vocational call is almost surely a domestic rather than a long-distance one doesn't matter. Nor does it matter that the one called is also the caller.

Several times in my life I have found myself prolonging a painful situation because describing it became more important to me than eliminating the pain. (The original impulse to write about it was a way of controlling or defanging the pain. "Woe weeps out her Division when she sings," was Ben Jonson's version of this.)

Very recently, to my immense relief and happiness, a very painful separation from dear ones ended. A few hours later, along with the relief and happiness, I found myself feeling oddly hollow and anxious. What was going on? It didn't take long to realize what had happened. The hollowness and anxiety came from awareness that the novel about the separation, on which I'd been working for two years, had been deflated. I'd begun writing it in order to control or defang the pain. That worked for me as psychoanalysis or prayer, abusive fury and outrage work for others. Now the pain was gone.

In the novel my protagonist, not a writer but a retired lawyer, has thought about what I'd been thinking about. He deliberates—as I did—about the advantages of holding on to pain. In a book of Emily Dickinson's poems, given to him—and this is invention—by the loved one from whom he was separated, he finds his situation expressed in these remarkable lines:

Rehearsal to Ourselves
Of a Withdrawn Delight—
Affords a Bliss like Murder—
Omnipotent—Acute—
We will not drop the Dirk—
Because we love the Wound
The Dirk Commemorates—Itself
Reminds Us that we died.

A bliss like murder? Because we love the wound?

Astonishing insights, he thinks and wonders about what went on in the head of that spectral Amherst spinster, and then about the meaning of his own confusion and savagery. How many like my protagonist and myself not only adjust to the resentment or hatred of those who they think have wronged them (or whom they've wronged) but flourish in it? Yet of this many, it is only the writers whose love of and perhaps need for the wound involves a professional opportunity and makes dropping the dirk a difficult decision.

I can't remember who said something like "Happiness is white and doesn't stain the page," but of course almost all stories are about such forms of unhappiness as disturbance, derangement and disorder. These may be comic, may be imaginary, but they initiate storytelling.

In my case, two days after happiness whitened out my subject, or, as I said, deflated it, I received a peculiar, indeed uniquely harsh letter from an old writer friend about something I'd published. Amidst the puzzlement, anger and dismay it aroused, I spotted a gleam of light: the possibility of translating this new schism into an equivalent of the one that had been whitened out. A further complication: the letter writer may well have been contemplating or even writing a work that needed to be fueled by a couple of his longtime themes, broken loyalty and estrangement from those close to him. I wrote him that I understood that.

Another coincidence: the day on which my subject whitened out was December 9, 2000, and the city in which it occurred was Washington. That morning a friend had driven me to the street in front of Vice President Al Gore's house, where Bush-Cheney picketers were disconsolately waving their placards, disconsolately because the Florida Supreme Court had, the day before, ordered the vote recount in Miami-Dade and other counties that looked as if it would reverse what they regarded as the certain election of their candidates.

Late that afternoon, as my personal situation was transformed, the United States Supreme Court ordered that the recount be stopped. The political reversal—a blow to me—fused with the happy personal reversal. This confluence, this coincidence, was the sort of enrichment novelists not only look for but expect.

Writers of my sort are so habitually alert to coincidence that the word itself seems inadequate. In novels in which the coincidences show up, they will usually be described and read not as haphazard coincidence but as devastating or farcical destiny.

From the time of Hesiod and Sappho, Catullus and Li Po, lovers of literature as well as writers have known about and felt the interfusion of life and art. Some writers have been embarrassed to acknowledge it. Like Henry James they burn their papers; like T. S. Eliot they forbid biographies and deprecate their celebrated work as little more than lyrical grouses.

If they descend from Olympian detachment, they hunt for odd excuses like the one Thomas Mann used to explain the origins of *The Magic Mountain:* it's due, he wrote, to "the healthy and sympathetic attitude of the American mind toward the personal, the anecdotal and the intimately human." The intimately human is of more or less intimate interest to almost everyone, including those who despise the stoking of ego furnaces and, like Michel Foucault, dismiss the authority, if not the very idea, of authorship.

The chief social role of writers may well be the extension, complication and enrichment of human intimacy. It is exercised through story, the oldest and most pleasurable way of organizing experience. The primacy of story wasn't first declared by Oscar Wilde or Stéphane Mallarmé, James Joyce or Marcel Proust. It's older than Genesis.

Homer's *Odyssey* offers one of the most remarkable versions of it. This comes near the end of Book 8, in which King Alcinous tells the disguised Odysseus to stop weeping at the song the blind bard Demodocus is singing about him and his fellow Hellenic heroes. After all, Alcinous tells him, the gods "measured the life thread of these men so that their fate might become a poem sung for unborn generations."

No wonder writers in this long tradition can sometimes feel that we've been conscripted for work that, though it may rip up a portion—or much—of our lives, is of imperative, if not uniquely redemptive, importance.

Family Ghosts Hoard Secrets That Bewitch the Living

Amy Tan

In the last week of her life, my three half sisters, my younger brother and I gathered around the easy chair in which our mother lay floating between this world and the next.

"Nyah-Nyah," she moaned in Shanghainese and waved to an apparition on the ceiling. Then she motioned to me. "Invite Nyah-Nyah to sit down. Bring her tea, and quick, fetch her my mink coat."

Indulging my mother these wishes, I began to write her obituary, with the help of my siblings. It was a task that kept our minds focused, unified us, made us feel helpful instead of helpless. That was how I learned for the first time what my mother's birth name was.

"Li Bingzi," my sister from Shanghai told me. My God, to think I had never known the name given to her by her own mother. "Born Li Bingzi," I duly put down, "daughter of Li

Jingmei . . ." And another sister chided: "No, no, Grandma's last name was not Li. It was Gu. Gu Jingmei."

I sensed the ghost of my grandmother in the room. "Ai-ya! What a stupid girl," I could hear her saying. "This is what happens when you let them become Americans." I imagined other wispy-edged relatives, more frowning and head shaking.

As my sisters and I chatted, we exchanged further notes. Our mother, one sister revealed, received a different name, Tu Lian Zen, when she was adopted after her mother's death. Then she chose a school name, Tu Ching, which she kept after she married an abusive man named Wang. Whether she ever legally divorced this man is not clear. Nonetheless, she fled the marriage, left behind three daughters and came to America under the name Ching Tu, then married my father, who christened her Daisy after a song about being half-crazy in love on a bicycle built for two.

My mother, I realized, never told my sisters about the name Daisy Tan Chan, which she took when she married for the third time in her seventies. A year later she had the marriage annulled and reverted to Daisy C. Tan. As to T. C. Lee, the dapper gentlemen whom our family in Beijing met when he and our mother honeymooned there, well, the truth was, she and T. C. had simply lived together without the benefit of marriage. My sisters guffawed.

My mother's many names were vestiges of her many selves, lives I have been excavating most of my own adult life. At times I have dreaded that I might stumble across evidence of additional siblings, husbands and lovers, more secrets, ghosts and shame. I had once thought I was the only daughter, the middle child, a position I took to have great psychological significance. I then discovered I was actually the youngest of five girls, that one had died at birth. There were three brothers as well, including one I didn't know about; he died at age two in 1939. With all taken into account, I was demoted to No. 7 of eight children.

There was also confusion about my mother's age. She had one birth date based on the Chinese calendar of ancient lunar cycles and the method of considering a baby one year old the day it is born.

In determining her younger Western age, she miscalculated the year and date, thus writing that she was born on May 8, 1917, instead of May 9, 1916. When she was about to turn sixty-four, she told me she was really almost sixty-five. She knew this for sure, she insisted, because she was born in a Dragon Year, 1916, just as I was born in a Dragon Year thirty-six years later. There was absolutely no way she could confuse this. Thereafter, she fretted day after day, until my husband untangled bureaucratic knots and set the record straight in time for her to retire in the right year and collect Social Security.

But that was not the end to her questionable age. My sisters and I found out that for her obituary the international Chinese-language newspaper wanted to report her as eighty-six instead of eighty-three, to account for the bonus years she had earned for living a long life. All the confusion about her age, her three marriages, her many names and the order in which her children, living and dead, should be listed led us to nix the idea of a Chinese obituary. It would not look proper if we told the truth.

In writing a simple obituary, I realized there was still much that I did not know about my mother. Though I had written three novels informed by her life, she remained a source of revelation and surprise. Of course I longed to know more about her. Her past had shaped me: her sense of danger, her regrets, the mistakes she vowed never to repeat. What I know about myself is related to what I know about her, her secrets, or in some cases fragments of them. I found the pieces both by deliberate effort and by accident, and with each discovery I had to reconfigure the growing whole.

"Nyah-Nyah," my mother kept calling in the last days of her life.

I finally thought to ask what Nyah-Nyah meant.

"A Shanghainese nickname for 'Grandmother,'" my oldest sister, Yuhang, replied. And then I remembered a story my mother once told me, of her being four years old, delirious and near death as she called to her grandmother to stop the pain. My mother had been horribly injured when a pot of boiling oil fell across her neck. Nyah-Nyah had sat by her bedside, day and night, telling her that her funeral clothes had already been made but were very plain because she had not lived long enough to deserve anything more elaborate.

She told the little girl that everyone would soon forget her because she had lived too short a time for them to remember much. That was how Nyah-Nyah, who loved my mother very much, scared her back to life. Now my mother was calling for Nyah-Nyah once again. This time I think Nyah-Nyah was telling my mother that her funeral clothes had already been made, and not to worry, they were fancy beyond belief.

For four days my mother's breathing kept me in suspense. She would take three breaths, then nothing would follow for forty-five seconds, sometimes longer. It was like watching the tidal wash in anticipation of a tidal wave. At night I lay next to her, sleepless, staring at the pulse bobbing in the cove of her throat, my own heart pounding to this steady yet uncertain rhythm. Later I put a pearl in the hollow so I could more easily see this proof of life. Though I dreaded that she would stop breathing, I was relieved that she would die of natural causes and not from suicide.

For as long as I can remember, my mother talked of killing herself. The threats came at least once a month, sometimes day after day. She would utter them in front of me, my brothers, anyone within earshot. On a few occasions she made an attempt. I remember seeing her lean out an open door as our car sped down the highway, and we, her mute children, sat in the back. Several times she ran into busy lanes of traffic with flailing arms.

In my memories of adolescence there are also flashes of a knife, a cleaver, a pair of scissors. The reasons my mother wanted to die were many. It could have been something my father did or didn't do. It was often something I said or didn't say. Whatever it was, we were supposed to make amends before it was too late. Once I refused to say I was sorry. Then I was really sorry.

I didn't realize until I was in my thirties that her suicidal impulses most likely started when she saw her own mother kill herself. She was only nine when this happened. And thereafter some part of her would always remain the nine-year-old who believed that the only escape from any kind of unhappiness was the route her mother took, an immediate departure from this world to a heavenly form of China. As long as she was alive, her mother's death was an everlasting punishment to her. Whenever bad luck visited us, she asked aloud whether her mother was angry at her. Was this a curse?

Though my grandmother killed herself in 1925, she was a presence in my young life, a ghostly presence. Ever since I

was four, my mother had believed I could see my grandmother. That was because like most children I had complained
about a bogeyman under my bed. Instead of reassuring me
that this was only my imagination, my mother asked me to
pass along messages. She was convinced my grandmother
had taken me as her confidante.

I soon learned not to mention what scared me, and my
mother did not press too much for me to talk to the ghost.
That was because my father, an engineer, was also by avo-
cation a Baptist minister, and the only ghost he believed we
should talk to was the Holy Ghost.

But when I was fifteen, my father and brother died, both
of brain tumors, and my mother began urging me often to
ask their ghosts why this had happened. She had me sit
before a Ouija board, then noted when the room grew cold,
when telltale pings and creaks signaled that the spirits had
arrived. She was always hoping for one last good-bye, one
more message of love.

Pragmatic woman that my mother was, she would also
seek their advice on the stock market. With our fingers
poised over the planchette, she would ask, "Should I buy
IBM or U.S. Steel?" I would push it to whichever answer
was the shortest, a method of stock trading that, by the way,
proved quite successful in my mother's portfolio.

For our mother's memorial card, our family selected the
photos that captured her best: Grinning as she cooked with
a gigantic wok. Smiling shyly for my father in the early days
of their courtship. Staring solemnly as an eight-year-old
adorned in mourning clothes for her grandmother, Nyah-
Nyah.

My mother had always been a natural Shanghainese
beauty and quite vain and snobby as a result. She bragged

how spoiled she was as a child because she was "pretty beyond belief." She used to lament openly that I had not inherited any of her good Shanghainese features, that I resembled my father, a Cantonese. My nose was too broad, my skin too dark, my lips too coarse. I had long recovered from the wounds of those remarks when Alzheimer's began to erode her logic and memory. One day, my mother announced that I looked just like her. It was not too late to hear such praise.

As I studied the photos with my sisters, I saw that I did indeed resemble her. She and I had the same crimped chin, the wrinkling caused by holding back what we felt but could not say. In her case, it was secrets and hopes. In mine, it was protests and desires. For many years we had been unable to say "I love you" to each other.

During the last hour of her life, our family murmured to our mother that we loved her very much and were sad to see her go. We whispered to her all the things we would miss: her dumplings, her advice, her humor. To myself I mourned: Who else would worry about me so much? Who else would describe in explosive detail what might happen to parts of my body if I was careless? Who would be frank enough to warn that my husband might exchange me for a younger woman unless I forced him to buy me jewels so expensive it would be impossible for him to leave both me and the gems behind?

My mother did not speak during those last four days, but with her final breath, a long release of an exhalation, she uttered a faint sound, a single sustained note. I had to bend my ear to her mouth to hear. I was the only one who heard it, but I don't think it was my imagination. To me, she sounded surprised.

After my mother died, I began to rewrite the novel I had been working on for the past five years. I wrote with the steadfastness of grief. My editor and dear friend, the great Faith Sale, would have called that grief "finding the real heart of the story." My mentor, Molly Giles, said the bones were there, I just had to reassemble them in a new way. To find that heart and repair the bones, I had to break them into pieces, then start to dig.

And so I rewrote, remembering what scared me: the ghost, the threats, the curse. I wrote of wrong birth dates, secret marriages, the changing place one has in a family, the names that were nearly forgotten. I wrote of pain that reaches from the past, how it can grab you, how it can also heal itself like a broken bone. And with the help of my ghostwriters, I found in memory and imagination what I had lost in grief.

A Bedeviling Question in the Cadence of English

Shashi Tharoor

As an Indian writer living in New York, I find myself constantly asked a question with which my American confreres never have to contend: "But whom do you write for?"

In my case the question is complicated by both geography and language. I live in the United States (because of my work at the United Nations) and write about India; and I do so in English, a language mastered, if the last census is to be believed, by only 2 percent of the Indian population. There is an unspoken accusation implicit in the question: Am I not guilty of the terrible sin of inauthenticity, of writing about my country for foreigners?

This question has, for many years, bedeviled the work of the growing tribe of writers of what used to be called Indo-Anglian fiction and is now termed, more respectfully, Indian writing in English. This is ironic, because few developments in world literature have been more remarkable than the emergence, over the last two decades, of a new generation of Indian writers in English.

Beginning with Salman Rushdie's *Midnight's Children* in 1981, they have expanded the boundaries of their craft and their nation's literary heritage, enriching English with the rhythms of ancient legends and the larger-than-life complexities of another civilization, while reinventing India in the confident cadences of English prose. Of the many unintended consequences of empire, it is hard to imagine one of greater value to both colonizers and colonized.

The new Indian writers dip into a deep well of memory and experience far removed from those of their fellow novelists in the English language. But whereas Americans or Englishmen or Australians have also set their fictions in distant lands, Indians write of India without exoticism, their insights undimmed by the dislocations of foreignness. And they do so in an English they have both learned and lived, an English of freshness and vigor, a language that is as natural to them as their quarrels at the school playground or the surreptitious notes they slipped each other in their classrooms.

Yet Indian critics still suggest that there is something artificial and un-Indian about an Indian writing in English. One critic disparagingly declared that the acid test ought to be, "Could this have been written only by an Indian?" I have never been much of a literary theoretician—I always felt that for a writer to study literature at university would be like learning about girls at medical school—but for most, though not all, of my own writing, I would answer that my works could not only have been written only by an Indian, but only by an Indian in English.

I write for anyone who will read me, but first of all for Indians like myself, Indians who have grown up speaking, writing, playing, wooing and quarreling in English, all over India. (No writer really chooses a language: the circumstances of his upbringing ensure that the language chooses him.)

Members of this class have entered the groves of academe and condemned themselves in terms of bitter self-reproach: one Indian scholar, Harish Trivedi, has asserted (in English) that Indian writers in that language are "cut off from the experiential mainstream and from that common cultural matrix . . . shared with writers of all other Indian languages." Dr. Trivedi metaphorically cites the fictional English-medium school in an R. K. Narayan story where the students must first rub off the sandalwood-paste caste marks from their foreheads before they enter its portals: "For this golden gate is only for the déraciné to pass through, for those who have erased their antecedents."

It's an evocative image, even though I thought the secular Indian state was supposed to encourage the erasure of casteism from the classroom. But the more important point is that writers like myself do share a "common cultural matrix," albeit one devoid of helpfully identifying caste marks. It is one that consists of an urban upbringing and a pan-national outlook on the Indian reality. I do not think this is any less authentically "Indian" than the world-views of writers in other Indian languages. Why should the rural peasant or the small-town schoolteacher with his sandalwood-smeared forehead be considered more quintessentially Indian than the punning collegian or the Bombay socialite, who are as much a part of the Indian reality?

India is a vast and complex country; in Whitman's phrase,

it contains multitudes. I write of an India of multiple truths and multiple realities, an India that is greater than the sum of its parts. English expresses that diversity better than any Indian language precisely because it is not rooted in any one region of my vast country. At the same time, as an Indian, I remain conscious of, and connected to, my pre-urban and non-Anglophone antecedents: my novels reflect an intellectual heritage that embraces the ancient epic the *Mahabharata*, the Kerala folk dance called the *ottamthullal* (of which my father was a gifted practitioner) and the Hindi B-movies of Bollywood, as well as Shakespeare, Wodehouse and the Beatles.

As a first-generation urbanite myself, I keep returning to the Kerala villages of my parents, in my life as in my writing. Yet I have grown up in Bombay, Calcutta and Delhi, Indian cities a thousand miles apart from one another; the mother of my children is half-Kashmiri, half-Bengali; and my own mother now lives in the southern town of Coimbatore. This may be a wider cultural matrix than the good Dr. Trivedi imagined, but it draws from a rather broad range of Indian experience. And English is the language that brings those various threads of my India together, the language in which my wife could speak to her mother-in-law, the language that enables a Calcuttan to function in Coimbatore, the language that serves to express the complexity of that polyphonous Indian experience better than any other language I know.

As a novelist, I believe in distracting in order to instruct— my novels are, to some degree, didactic works masquerading as entertainments. Like Molière I believe that you have to entertain in order to edify. But the entertainment, and the edification, might strike different readers differently.

My first novel, *The Great Indian Novel,* as a satirical rein-
vention of the *Mahabharata* inevitably touches Indians in a
way that most foreigners will not fully appreciate. But my
publishers in the West enjoyed its stories and the risks it
took with narrative form. My second, *Show Business,* did
extremely well with American reviewers and readers, who
enjoyed the way I tried to portray the lives and stories of
Bollywood as a metaphor for Indian society. With *India:
From Midnight to the Millennium,* an attempt to look back at
the last fifty years of India's history, I found an additional
audience of Indian-Americans seeking to rediscover their
roots; their interest has helped the American edition outsell
the Indian one.

In my new novel, *Riot,* for the first time I have major
non-Indian characters, Americans as it happens, and that is
bound to influence the way the book is perceived both in the
United States and in India. Inevitably the English language
fundamentally affects the content of each book, but it does
not determine the audience of the writer; as long as translations exist, language is a vehicle, not a destination.

Of course, there is no shame in acknowledging that English is a legacy of the colonial connection, but one no less
useful and valid than the railways, the telegraphs or the law
courts that were also left behind by the British. Historically,
English helped us find our Indian voice: that great Indian
nationalist Jawaharlal Nehru wrote *The Discovery of India*
in English. But the eclipse of that dreadful phrase "the
Indo-Anglian novel" has occurred precisely because Indian
writers have evolved well beyond the British connection to
their native land.

The days when Indians wrote novels in English either to
flatter or rail against their colonial masters are well behind

us. Now we have Indians in India writing as naturally about themselves in English as Australians or South Africans do, and their tribe has been supplemented by India's rich diaspora in the United States, which has already produced a distinctive crop of impressive novelists, with Pulitzer Prizes and National Book Awards to their names.

Their addresses don't matter, because writers really live inside their heads and on the page, and geography is merely a circumstance. They write secure of themselves in their heritage of diversity, and they write free of the anxiety of audience, for theirs are narratives that appeal as easily to Americans as to Indians—and indeed to readers irrespective of ethnicity.

Surely that's the whole point about literature—that for a body of fiction to constitute a literature it must rise above its origins, its setting, even its language, to render accessible to a reader anywhere some insight into the human condition. Read my books and those of other Indian writers not because we're Indian, not necessarily because you are interested in India, but because they are worth reading in and of themselves. And dear reader, whoever you are, if you pick up one of my books, ask not for whom I write: I write for you.

Still Replying to Grandma's Persistent "And Then?"

Frederic Tuten

She was a thin woman without much fantasy. In her dress, I mean. Black from head to toe, in the Sicilian manner. She was a Sicilian, in fact, and she was my grandmother. She spoke little, and to my humiliation—I wanted to be like the other American kids in the Bronx—in Sicilian. And then, too, we were at the tail end of the war with Italy. So that in the street and other public places I answered her in English to distance myself.

Not that my Sicilian was great. But at eight or nine I managed to tell her what she wanted to know about my world at school and to conduct her from butcher to grocer and order for her and to check the scales when she thought they were tipping high. Unless we walked some distance to Arthur Avenue, where she did not require my help because you could—and probably still can—spend your life there speaking only Italian. But then we would have had to spend the nickel bus fare to carry back the shopping all that distance home, so we mostly stayed in the neighborhood, and I watched the scales.

She also thought, in the Sicilian fashion, never to ask directions of a policeman because it was not wise to approach the law for whatever reason. Just out of perversity, because we were greenhorns, he might point us the wrong way.

I also, and more importantly, served as her translator for the American news on the radio and for the American movies. There were plenty of Italian-American shows on the radio, especially the soap operas that she loved, but she did not trust the news, as reported in her language, because she believed the wartime censorship was greater for the Italian audience. At the movies is where I shined best, interpreting for her most of the dialogue she missed, which was most of the dialogue. Sometimes I myself didn't understand what was happening on the screen, the love scenes especially, when suddenly the couple stopped speaking, while the music rose and the camera cut away to a train going through a tunnel or to a horse rearing in its stable. "Che cosa è successo?" What's happening? she'd ask me in a whisper too loud for those about us. Or in English: "What he say?" More humiliation for me. But at least it was suffered in the dark. At those times when I lost the film's thread I invented the story just to keep her happy, hoping she would not notice the discrepancy between the action on the screen and my childish interpretation. "He's tired, and he wants to go to sleep," I explained, as the lead walked into his girlfriend's bedroom.

My mother was the firstborn in America, and, while she could read and write, she had to help support the family and left high school at fifteen, and she went to work in the

Manhattan garment district. My grandfather never learned to speak English. He died longing for Sicily, where he could speak his language everywhere, even in the streets. My mother was reared in an all-Italian-speaking household. And except when my father—whose family was in America before the Revolution—on the increasingly rare occasion came home, I was, too.

My mother read romances alone in the bedroom, and I read in the living room I shared with my grandmother, a screen separating the two cots across the room. My mother never told us about the novels she was reading, going to her bed, book in hand, exhausted after dinner and after a long day at work as a draper more than a hour and a half away in Manhattan. I was fascinated by what she was reading, by what kept her so absorbed as to keep her from me. Romances were her special fare: pirate and historical novels with sizzling jackets, books she rented for pennies a day from the stationery store near her subway station. Books I was yearning to read and one day would. But for the moment, in that living room or at the kitchen table, I was buried in my own books of the far away: *Kidnapped, Ali Baba and the Forty Thieves, The Adventures of Tom Sawyer*, the Hardy Boys series, picture books of exotic travel into deserts and jungles and, maybe when I was ten, H. Rider Haggard's *She*, a travel adventure with its mysterious story of a beautiful woman who stayed young a thousand years to wait for her lover to return.

My grandmother did not read. She claimed she could not see the print because of cataracts, which in those days and at her old age were difficult to remove. But I suspect she was illiterate, never having gone to school in Sicily, where she was married at fifteen and where she bore four children, two of whom died of measles. I read for her. Not in the conventional way of translating word for word my childhood books, but by telling her—with my own editing and inventions—the stories in my reading.

From me she learned how an American boy and a slave fled home on a raft on a river a thousand times bigger than the Bronx River running through the Botanical Garden not far away from us, and how a man discovered the secret word to opening a cave in Arabia where outlaws hid their "loot"—I used the English word for that—of gold and jewelry in huge barrels, like the ones heaping with olives and dried sardines in the markets of Arthur Avenue. I was a great storyteller, she said, emboldening me to further inventions and reconstructions of these children's classics. My only rivals for her entertainment, I believe, were her radio soaps and the movies, where I also wielded some narrative power.

I knew one storytelling device that always worked. I would reach a crucial point in my tale—"He was in the outlaws' cave bathing himself in gold coins when he heard a loud noise behind him"—and then I would pause.

"E poi?" And then? she would invariably ask.

The same "and then"—I later read in E. M. Forster's *Aspects of the Novel*—that is the fulcrum of all fiction, going back to the earliest time our ancestors sat about the communal fire spellbound by tales; the "and then" that moves the narrative forward and, most of all, keeps the reader or the listener hooked on yearning to know more of the story.

"And then, Grandma," I said, "he turned and saw the heavy cave door shut behind him." That narrative device, that pause and withholding of information, I had learned from her when she told me her own stories, no less wonderful to me than the ones I had been reading and reinventing.

Her husband had been a policeman, one of the few carabinier in her village, where they had a home and a small vineyard in the hills. Rich grapes to make golden muscatel.

"E poi?" I asked.

He went after some bandits in the mountains. They had been robbing people in the village. The bandits sent word to leave them alone or they would hurt his family. He went after them still. That was his stubborn way.

"E poi?"

They burned the vineyard and they said they would burn the house next, and then they would kill the children.

"E poi, Grandma?"

"Then they burned the house. And then we left for America."

We sat, we two, in the Bronx, telling stories in a darkish room, safely away from the frightening world outside the window, where the police gave misdirections and the butcher tipped the scales.

Stories. Like air, like food, like hope. I read them, I told them, and later I wrote them, stories about men and women seeking the far away in revolutions, in art and in the dreamy search for love, but by that time she, Francesca, my first muse, was gone.

A Pseudonym Returns from an Alter-Ego Trip, with New Tales to Tell

Donald E. Westlake

I've just completed another few months being Richard Stark, and a very pleasant time it was. Richard Stark is the name I write under when I'm not writing under the name above, which is the name I was born with, and these days it is doubly pleasant for me to visit with Stark, because for twenty-three years he wouldn't answer my calls.

The relationship between a writer and his pseudonym is a complex one, and never more so than when the alter ego refuses to appear. I became Richard Stark in the first place, forty years ago, for both of the usual reasons. As a young writer, effervescent with ideas, I was turning out far too much work to ship to the publishers under just one name. Also, being a writer who worked in a variety of styles, I thought it a good idea to offer brand-name definition. West-lake does this, Stark does that.

For fourteen years, from 1960 to 1974, Stark did a whole bunch of that, being sixteen novels about a cold-blooded thief named Parker and four novels about an associate of Parker's named Grofield. By the late 1960s, Stark was better known and better paid than Westlake, which felt a little odd. But after all, we were both me, so there was no reason for jealousy. In 1967 the first Stark novel was made into one of the seminal American movies, *Point Blank* with Lee Marvin (remade recently as *Payback* with Mel Gibson), and half a dozen other Stark novels were also filmed, including one in France directed by Jean-Luc Godard.

But then, in 1974, Richard Stark just up and disappeared. He did a fade. Periodically, in the ensuing years, I tried to summon that persona, to write like him, to be him for just a while, but every single time I failed. What appeared on the paper was stiff, full of lumps, a poor imitation, a pastiche. Though successful, though well liked and well paid, Richard Stark had simply downed tools. For, I thought, ever.

It seems strange to say that for those years I could no longer write like myself, since Richard Stark had always been, naturally, me. But he was gone, and when I say he was gone, I mean his voice was gone, erased clean out of my head.

Which leads to the question I am most frequently asked about Richard Stark when I'm at a book signing or on an author panel somewhere. Are you, people want to know, a different person, with different attitudes and character traits, when you're writing as Richard Stark? Are you sometimes Dr. Jekyll, sometimes Mr. Hyde? (My wife is asked this question about me, too, and her answer is to roll her eyes.)

The real answer, of course, is no. I'm not schizophrenic, I know who's sitting at that desk. But the other answer is, if we really want to get down to it, well, yes.

In the most basic way, writers are defined not by the stories they tell, or their politics, or their gender, or their race, but by the words they use. Writing begins with language, and it is in that initial choosing, as one sifts through the wayward lushness of our wonderful mongrel English, that choice of vocabulary and grammar and tone, the selection on the palette, that determines who's sitting at that desk. Language creates the writer's attitude toward the particular story he's decided to tell. But more than that, language is a part of the creation of the characters in the story, in the setting and in the sense of movement. Stark and Westlake use language very differently. To some extent they're mirror images. Westlake is allusive, indirect, referential, a bit rococo. Stark strips his sentences down to the necessary information.

In *Flashfire*, the Richard Stark novel just recently published, he writes, "Parker looked at the money, and it wasn't enough." In one of his own novels a few years ago, Donald Westlake wrote, "John Dortmunder and a failed enterprise always recognized one another." Dortmunder, Westlake's recurring character, proposes a Christmas toast this way, "God help us, every one." Parker answers the phone, "Yes."

For years, it was enjoyable and productive to go back and forth between the two voices. Letting the one guy sleep while the other guy stretched helped me avoid staleness, sameness, the rut of the familiar, kept me from being both bored and, I hope, boring.

I missed Stark during his truancy. But finally after fifteen years I did come to the reluctant conclusion that he was as gone as last year's snow. Then an odd thing happened.

I had taken the job of writing the film adaptation of Jim Thompson's *Grifters*, and the director, Stephen Frears, insisted he wanted Richard Stark to write—and sign—the screen-play. He didn't want Westlake, with his grins and winks, his peering around corners. He wanted Stark, blunt-fingered and dogged and with no taste for romantic claptrap.

I demurred, saying I was perfectly capable of writing the screenplay myself, and in any case Stark didn't seem to exist any more. But it remained a bone of contention between us until I finally pointed out that Richard Stark wasn't a member of the Writer's Guild, and I wasn't about to let him scab. In that case, although Stephen might grumble, he was prepared to accept the second best, so I went ahead and wrote the script.

Or did I? Thompson was very much more like Stark than like Westlake, and so was the script. And it was immediately after *The Grifters* that I began to think about and noodle with a new story about Parker. I didn't believe in it, but I went to it anyway, went away from it, went back to it, and all at once there it was. Richard Stark was back.

I sensibly enough called that book *Comeback,* and it was followed by *Backflash* and now *Flashfire.* (The Stark book he and I just completed, to be published next year, is called *Firebreak.* A subtle pattern begins to emerge.)

So was Stephen Frears right after all? Did that screen-writing job wake Stark from his slumbers? Did he actually write that script, with me merely as the union-card-carrying front? I don't really know how I could answer that, one way or the other, for absolutely sure.

Such confusion is rare, however. For instance, this piece is clearly, uh, written by, uh . . .

Before a Rendezvous with the Muse, First Select the Music

Edmund White

I've never willingly written a word without listening to music of some sort. Right now I'm listening to Debussy's "Sonata for Cello and Piano." When pushed by deadlines I've sometimes been obliged to work in silence, on a train or plane or in a cafe. (A Walkman I don't like, since its penetrating sound, piped directly into the cranial bones, is too aggressive and inescapable: booming aural earmuffs.)

Virgil Thomson recognized my condition right away. There are two kinds of writers, he said. Those who demand absolute silence and those, like you, who need to hear music, the better to concentrate.

Perhaps he put his finger on the underlying psychological process, but I have never felt I was blocking out music the better to focus my thoughts. Admittedly I sometimes recognize that at a certain moment during the last ten minutes I must have stopped paying attention to the music filling the room, but more often than not I experience music as a landscape unscrolling just outside the window whenever I look up, or as a human drama unfolding across the courtyard when I peek out, or as a separate but beloved presence, an intimate friend sitting in a matching chair, thinking and feeling. Music for me is a companion during the lonely (and why not admit it? the boring) hours of writing.

Music is also in stark contrast to writing. Music is already perfect, sure-footed, whereas I'm struggling to remember a word, frame a description, invent an action. If for me music is the secret sharer, it is a friend who has no needs and encourages me to trust that beauty can be achieved in this life, at least theoretically.

Music is always living out its own vivid, highly marked adventure, which is continuous and uninterrupted. It exists as a superior way of transcribing emotions, or rather of notating shifting balances, repeating motifs, accumulating tensions, deferred resolutions and elaborated variations. As the composer Roger Sessions once put it, music communicates in a marvelously vivid and exact way the dynamics and the abstract qualities of emotion, but any specific emotional content must be supplied from without, by the listening writer in this case.

Like fiction, music is an art that exists in time. Like fiction, music is always promising an imminent conclusion and then introducing complications. Like fiction, music can be plain to the point of plainsong or as intricate as counterpoint, and both extremes can be satisfying. Just as the novelist must keep all his strategies aloft and not allow the reader to forget a character or lose sight of the house, the ha-ha or the wilderness beyond, or skip over a crucial turn in the plot, in the same way the composer must teach the listener to recognize the key themes, the shifts in harmonic progression and the division of the composition into parts. Of course there are also signal differences between fiction and music. In music the blocks of sound are so insubstantial to the listener (I dare say even to the composer) that repetition of some sort, even a full, literal recapitulation, is always welcome, whereas the reader of fiction can tolerate variations on themes but never straight-out repetition. Fiction includes a large admixture of journalism: anecdotes, scandals, novelties, those gruesome daily horrors the French call *faits divers*. Music, on the other hand, imitates no external reality and is closer to mathematics than is any other art.

Unlike fiction, music is not about mothers-in-law or failed marriages. Of course opera and ballet and program music can be narrative but only because they are adulterated by literature, the libretto or the scenario.

In the nineteenth century music had so obviously leapt ahead of all the other arts that poetry, especially, aspired to the condition of music, i.e., toward abstraction, though a verbal art made up entirely of signifiers can never be abstract by definition, even if the French poet Mallarmé made memorable attempts to violate the fundamental nature of language.

Perhaps the German philosopher Schopenhauer explained the difference best. He said that music was entirely independent of the phenomenal world, ignored it altogether, could to a certain extent exist if there were no world at all, which cannot be said of the other arts. For Schopenhauer the other arts, including literature, imitate reality, whereas music has a status as valid and independent as reality itself. Music and reality are parallel lines that never converge.

In the morning I might listen to Ian Bostridge singing Bach's "Christ unser Herr zum Jordan kam" in order to dig spurs of rectitude into my sloth or to lighten my gloom. In the afternoon if I put on *Parsifal*, it means I'm in for the long haul. I want to stay at my desk and be accompanied and challenged by a masterpiece that is as elevating and demanding as it is long. Sometimes I program my moods: a bit of "Wiener Blut" to bring a smile to the lips, Stravinsky's *Agon* to introduce rigor into the composing process, Chopin's *Nocturnes* to make me more introspective after a jarring conversation.

Sometimes the music even has a direct effect. In my novels and stories I love brisk, dry conclusions, the feeling that once the last peg has fallen into place, there's no reason to linger, a taste I learned from the logical, dedramatizing late Stravinsky. Editors invariably ask me to rewrite and pad out my brisk codas, as if they had been conditioned by late Romantic bombast. The Russian scholar Simon Karlinsky, who has the distinction of being both a composer and a literary critic, once paid me the compliment of spotting the exact piece of music on which I'd based a literary strategy (a Brahms intermezzo).

I seldom listen to pop music because it's too monotonous rhythmically and too coarse harmonically to interest me for long; it depresses me and fails to connect me to a better, nobler society. When I write, I want to feel I could belong, at least in my dreams, to a world in which art must be puzzled out, a realm that believes that beauty is difficult. Of course this limitation on my part is doubtless a function of the generation I belong to.

I was born in 1940 and grew up in a house flooded after dark with music. My father was a misanthrope who worked all night at his desk and slept by day in order to avoid contact with people other than family members.

When I wasn't in school or working a summer job, I'd sit in his office at home and listen to the 78 rpm records he liked to play on his old blond mahogany Meisener: Beethoven chamber music, *La Mer* of Debussy, the Brahms Double Concerto, Kathleen Ferrier singing Bach, the violinist Fritz Kreisler playing his own *Liebeslied.* Dad disliked opera and rejected most twentieth-century music, but he did respect the Stravinsky of *The Firebird,* and he loved Mahler. I can well remember the stack of twelve heavy records that represented the Mahler *Resurrection* Symphony.

During those long, idle nights I first started writing as my father swiveled from his desk to his calculating machine to his file cards. He was making money, and I was writing stories, but we were both living—richly, constantly, invisibly—a second life, the life of unremitting and transporting music.

God Says You Are

Understanding Your Identity in Christ

Jeremy Bouma

BroadStreet
PUBLISHING

BroadStreet Publishing Group
Racine, Wisconsin, USA
www.broadstreetpublishing.com

GOD SAYS YOU ARE

Understanding Your Identity in Christ

© 2015 Jeremy Bouma

ISBN-13: 978-1-4245-5078-4 (hard cover)
ISBN-13: 978-1-4245-5079-1 (e-book)

Scripture quotations marked TPT are taken from *The Psalms: Poetry on Fire, Proverbs: Wisdom from Above, Matthew: Our Loving King, Luke and Acts: To the Lovers of God, John: Eternal Love, Romans: Grace and Glory, Letters from Heaven by the Apostle Paul,* and *Hebrews and James: Faith Works*, The Passion Translation®, copyright © 2014. Used by permission of BroadStreet Publishing Group, LLC, Racine, Wisconsin, USA. All rights reserved. Scripture taken from the Holy Bible, NEW INTERNATIONAL VERSION®, NIV® Copyright © 1973, 1978, 1984, 2011 by Biblica, Inc.® Used by permission. All rights reserved worldwide. Scripture quotations are from the ESV® Bible (The Holy Bible, English Standard Version®), copyright © 2001 by Crossway, a publishing ministry of Good News Publishers. Used by permission. All rights reserved. Scripture quotations are taken from the Holy Bible, New Living Translation, copyright ©1996, 2004, 2007, 2013 by Tyndale House Foundation. Used by permission of Tyndale House Publishers, Inc., Carol Stream, Illinois 60188. All rights reserved. Scripture taken from the New King James Version®. Copyright © 1982 by Thomas Nelson. Used by permission. All rights reserved. Scripture quotations marked HCSB®, are taken from the Holman Christian Standard Bible®, Copyright © 1999, 2000, 2002, 2003, 2009 by Holman Bible Publishers. Used by permission. HCSB® is a federally registered trademark of Holman Bible Publishers.

Cover design by Chris Garborg at www.garborgdesign.com
Typesetting by Katherine Lloyd at www.TheDESKonline.com

Stock or custom editions of BroadStreet Publishing titles may be purchased in bulk for educational, business, ministry, fundraising, or sales promotional use. For information, please e-mail info@broadstreetpublishing.com.

Printed in China
15 16 17 18 19 20 5 4 3 2 1

CONTENTS

Introduction. 4

ABLE 6

ABUNDANT 9

ACCEPTED 11

ADOPTED 13

ALIVE 16

BEFRIENDED. 19

BLAMELESS 21

BLESSED 24

CALLED. 27

CHERISHED 29

CHOSEN 31

CREATED 34

DEFENDED 37

DELIVERED. 39

FAMILY 42

FORGIVEN. 44

FOUND 47

FREE 50

FULFILLED 53

GIFTED. 56

GRACED 58

GUIDED. 61

GUILTLESS 64

HEARD 66

HEAVEN-BOUND 69

HOLY. 72

KNOWN 75

LIBERATED. 78

LOVED. 81

POWERFUL 84

PROSPEROUS 87

PURPOSEFUL 90

REBORN 93

RECONCILED 96

REMEMBERED 98

RESCUED 101

RESTORED 104

RIGHTEOUS 107

SAFE 110

SAVED 113

SECURE. 116

SINLESS 118

STABLE 120

STRONG 122

SUPPORTED 125

TRANSFORMED 128

UNITED. 130

UNASHAMED 132

VALUABLE 135

VICTORIOUS. 138

WISE 141

Introduction

When I was a teenager I was bullied. For all of junior and most of high school I wasn't "Jeremy Bouma." Instead, my identity was entirely defined by the names my bullies called me. Twenty years later, I still find myself struggling with knowing who I really am. Maybe you can relate.

Whether you're fifteen or fifty, every day we're fed countless messages from a host of people telling us who we are. Work says we're slow. Society says we don't measure up. That inner voice tells us we're not good enough.

But who does God say you are? The One who made and saved you, the God who knows you better than you know yourself?

It's only been in the past few years that I've been able to fully understand the depths of that question—and its answers. What I've discovered is when you know who you really are, you won't want to be anyone else. And who you really are is who God says you are!

Here is your guide to your true identity in your Creator and Savior. It organizes all of who God says you are from the Bible in relevant topics, making it the perfect reference when you need God's reassurance most. Short devotions at the beginning of each topic will breathe new life into how you see yourself and understand your identity.

So who are you, *really*? Able and accepted, cherished

and chosen, forgiven and free, known and not guilty, secure and strong, whole and wholly his.

This is what I've been discovering is true about myself. The more I dive deeply into God's Word, the more I realize what God says about me is what ultimately matters. Not people, not myself—God.

I hope you discover the same liberating truth.

ABLE

One of the most insidious lies of our Enemy is the two-word phrase: "You can't." You *can't* be the kind of parent your child needs; you *can't* get the job done; you *can't* provide food and clothing and the occasional vacation for your family.

Guess what? God says otherwise!

"I can" is one of the most important lessons we can learn from our identity in our Creator and Savior. In story after story throughout God's Word, we see people who thought they couldn't, yet God proved them wrong. They were able to do what they could do because God was with them and empowered them.

Moses thought he couldn't lead God's people out of Egypt, but God said otherwise. David wondered if he could survive King Saul's manhunt, but God said he could. Jeremiah didn't think he could stand up to God's people, but God said he was able.

In the Bible we learn we are able because God is strong, he helps his faithful ones, and he has empowered us to accomplish what he's called us to do.

Samuel's words remind us we can "scale any wall." David tells us with God's help we can do mighty things and walk through anything that devastates us. God raises us up and helps those who fail. And Paul boldly declares we are able to do all things because of God's mighty strength and power.

Our Enemy is wrong: You can, because God says you are *able*!

❖

In your strength I can crush an army;
with my God I can scale any wall.
2 SAMUEL 22:30 NLT

Cast your cares on the LORD
and he will sustain you;
he will never let
the righteous be shaken.
PSALM 55:22 NIV

God said to me once and for all,
"All the strength and power you need flows from me!"
PSALM 62:11 TPT

With God's help we will do mighty things,
for he will trample down our foes.
PSALM 108:13 NLT

Through your mighty power
I can walk through any devastation,
and you will keep me alive, reviving me.
Your power set me free from the hatred of my enemies.
PSALM 138:7 TPT

The LORD helps all who fall;
He raises up all who are oppressed.

PSALM 145:14 HCSB

I know what it is to be in need, and I know what it is to have plenty. I have learned the secret of being content in any and every situation, whether well fed or hungry, whether living in plenty or in want. I can do all this through him who gives me strength.

PHILIPPIANS 4:12–13 NIV

ABUNDANT

There is this often told story about the way hunters capture monkeys in India. As the story goes, they set baskets filled with peanuts beneath trees to lure the wily, wiggly creatures from hiding.

What's important about these baskets is the opening at the top. It is just large enough for the monkey to reach his arm into the basket to grab a handful of peanuts. When it does, the hunter merely walks over, grabs the monkey, and stuffs it in his sack. The monkey's hand is so full of peanuts that it can't remove its arm. It is so intent on keeping those peanuts, that it would rather get caught than drop them to find freedom—to stay alive!

The first time I heard this story it was in the context of scarcity and abundance. The speaker said that sometimes we are so blinded by a scarcity mentality—the belief we are in a state of lack and have nothing or risk losing something—that we can't see how much we have, how much *abundance* we have.

Dwelling and focusing on our lack ruins our lives—much like the monkey who couldn't let go, and paid the ultimate price.

It's also a lie. Because as the Bible tells us, in Christ we are abundant, enriched in every way; the storehouses of heaven have been poured out on us in plenty, a love gift from our Father. The lovers of God have more than enough!

The next time that inner voice tries to trick you into believing your life lacks, remember instead that you are abundant!

◈

The LORD is my shepherd;
I have all that I need.

PSALM 23:1 NLT

The lovers of God will have more than enough,
but the wicked will always lack what they crave.

PROVERBS 13:25 TPT

For God has proved his love by giving us his greatest treasure, the gift of his Son. And since God freely offered him up as the sacrifice for us all, he certainly won't withhold from us anything else he has to give.

ROMANS 8:32 TPT

I always thank my God for you because of his grace given you in Christ Jesus. For in him you have been enriched in every way—with all kinds of speech and with all knowledge.

1 CORINTHIANS 1:5 NIV

And God will generously provide all you need. Then you will always have everything you need and plenty left over to share with others.

2 CORINTHIANS 9:8 NLT

Everything heaven contains has already been lavished upon us as a love gift from our wonderful heavenly Father, the Father of our Lord Jesus—all because he sees us wrapped into Christ. This is why we celebrate him with all our hearts!

EPHESIANS 1:3 TPT

Accepted

One of my lifelong struggles has been a struggle for acceptance. Perhaps it stems from my teenage years and the rejection I endured from my peers. Well into adulthood, I have longed for community and for people to accept me.

Yet what I'm beginning to realize is that the acceptance I've been longing for most of my life has been mine all along! That's because God himself accepts me—just as I am. Look at how his Word to us describes this acceptance.

King David writes that God treats and accepts us as a "friend." We have received the Spirit of Full Acceptance, so that we will never again be orphaned; we find a faithful, accepting father in our heavenly Father! While others may reject us, God doesn't; we are his, we are his "darlings." Perhaps most important of all, we are God's children. We have received everything from our heavenly Father that a genuine earthly child receives from their earthly one, including acceptance.

It's taken me awhile to realize it, but I am not abandoned or rejected. I am accepted—by my heavenly Father, by my *Creator*. That is who I really am. I am accepted.

I've found that when I fully lean into and trust this part of my identity, it makes all the difference!

The LORD is a friend to those who fear him.
He teaches them his covenant.

PSALM 25:14 NLT

"For a brief moment I abandoned you,
but with great compassion I will take you back."

ISAIAH 54:7 NLT

And you did not receive the "spirit of religious duty," leading
you back into the fear of never being good enough. But you
have received the "Spirit of Full Acceptance," enfolding you
into the family of God. And you will never feel orphaned,
for as he rises up within us, our spirits join him in saying the
words of tender affection, "Beloved Father, Abba!"

ROMANS 8:15 TPT

Remember the prophecy God gave in Hosea:
"To those who were rejected
and not my people, I will say to them:
'You are mine.'
And to those who were unloved I will say:
'You are my darling.'"

ROMANS 9:25 TPT

Now you are no longer a slave but God's own child. And since
you are his child, God has made you his heir.

GALATIANS 4:7 NLT

ADOPTED

It's been said when someone takes leave of God we should ask, "What sort of God did they leave behind?"

For some of us, the God we've always known is a dictator or taskmaster—commanding us to do this or that, and punishing us when we mess up.

But what if there is a different way to view God? The view of a loving Father relating to his adopted children?

It's a remarkable picture, isn't it? Adoption is arguably one of the purest expressions of love, because a person or a couple intentionally brings a child who is not personally theirs into their very personal family life. That's the picture God gives of how he relates to us; he is an adoptive Father to us, his adopted children!

Paul tells us in Ephesians that at one point in history God decided to adopt us into his family—and we are *fully* adopted children. Not a quarter of the way there, not halfway adopted—fully. John says it best: "See how very much our Father loves us, for he calls us his children, and that is what we are!" (1 John 3:1 NLT).

It might be unusual or even difficult to picture your identity in this way, but according to God's Word you really are God's child; God says you are *adopted*!

Which means you have all of the rights and privileges

that come from being a full son or daughter of God: his comfort and care, his provision and protection, his love and acceptance.

❖

For all who are led by the Spirit of God are children of God.

ROMANS 8:14 NLT

The Spirit Himself testifies together with our spirit that we are God's children, and if children, also heirs—heirs of God and co-heirs with Christ—seeing that we suffer with Him so that we may also be glorified with Him.

ROMANS 8:16–17 HCSB

It is not merely the natural offspring of Abraham who are considered the children of God; rather, the children born because of God's promise are counted as descendants.

ROMANS 9:8 TPT

"I will be a Father to you,
And you shall be My sons and daughters,
Says the LORD Almighty."

2 CORINTHIANS 6:18 NKJV

But when that era came to an end and the time of fulfillment had come, God sent his Son, born of a woman, born under the written Law. Yet all of this was so that he would redeem and set free all those held hostage to the written Law so that we would receive our freedom and a full legal adoption as his children.

GALATIANS 4:4–5 TPT

God decided in advance to adopt us into his own family by bringing us to himself through Jesus Christ. This is what he wanted to do, and it gave him great pleasure.

EPHESIANS 1:5 NLT

See how very much our Father loves us, for he calls us his children, and that is what we are!

1 JOHN 3:1 NLT

ALIVE

Many days I don't feel alive. Perhaps you understand what I mean.

Maybe it's because of my temperament, but often I feel beaten down by life—not enlivened by life. From work responsibilities to home improvement projects to bills and loan payments, sometimes I struggle just to survive.

And sometimes I need God to remind me who I am at the beginning, middle, and end of my day—that I'm not beaten down, dying, or even dead! No. My true identity is as a child of God who has been made *alive*! We are alive in Christ now and we will be fully alive in Christ later.

Jesus reminds us that if we believe in him we will live forever. Paul reminds us that the same God who raised Christ from the dead will raise us from the dead, too. Because Jesus is alive, we've been birthed into a "living hope" brimming with a living inheritance.

But this aliveness isn't merely for the *after*life; we're alive right now, *before* life-after-death! Our old selves have been killed off, so that right now we are alive in new ways with the very presence of Christ living in us. Through God's matchless grace and mercy, not only have we been saved from our sins, but also we've been made alive with Christ in *this* life.

Sometimes life can get us down; we can feel dead and hollowed out. But take heart: God's Word to us reminds us that we are in fact alive—now and forever!

❖

"I am the Resurrection, and I am Life Eternal. Anyone who clings to me in faith, even though he dies, will live forever. And the one who lives by believing in me will never die. Do you believe this?"

JOHN 11:25–26 TPT

But you are not in the flesh but in the Spirit, if indeed the Spirit of God dwells in you . . . And if Christ is in you, the body is dead because of sin, but the Spirit is life because of righteousness. But if the Spirit of Him who raised Jesus from the dead dwells in you, He who raised Christ from the dead will also give life to your mortal bodies through His Spirit who dwells in you.

ROMANS 8:9–11 NKJV

My old self has been crucified with Christ. It is no longer I who live, but Christ lives in me. So I live in this earthly body by trusting in the Son of God, who loved me and gave himself for me.

GALATIANS 2:20 NLT

Because of his great love for us, God, who is rich in mercy, made us alive with Christ even when we were dead in transgressions—it is by grace you have been saved.

EPHESIANS 2:4–5 NIV

Praise the God and Father of our Lord Jesus Christ. According to His great mercy, He has given us a new birth into a living hope through the resurrection of Jesus Christ from the dead and into an inheritance that is imperishable, uncorrupted, and unfading, kept in heaven for you.

1 PETER 1:3–4 HCSB

Befriended

Who are your friends, the people you rely on most when times get tough? Are they the same people who've walked with you through most of your life? Or have your friends come and gone over the years?

Did you know that on average most adults have only two close friends? While the advent of new technology services like Facebook and Twitter gives the illusion of community, many adults feel relationally disconnected and lonelier than ever.

Whether you have a solid, reliable crew or struggle to connect and feel alone, there is one Friend you can be sure to rely on who is the same yesterday, today, and forever. Which means part of who you are is *befriended*, because God is your friend.

The Bible reminds us that we are God's people, and he is our God. Jesus calls us his "intimate friends"—not servants, but friends. This is a relationship that was restored through his life, death, and resurrection. This offer of friendship is extended to anyone who opens the door of their heart up to God, inviting him to do life with them.

We are not alone; we have not been abandoned. Those are lies from our Enemy! And when it seems as though the world has left you behind, you can be sure one Friend will stand with you all the way to the end.

You are befriended. That is who you really are. You are a friend of God.

"You will be My people,
and I will be your God."

JEREMIAH 30:22 HCSB

Jesus answered and said to him, "If anyone loves Me, he will keep My word; and My Father will love him, and We will come to him and make Our home with him."

JOHN 14:23 NKJV

"I have never called you 'servants,' because a master doesn't confide in his servants, and servants don't always understand what the master is doing. But I call you my most intimate friends, for I reveal to you everything that I've heard from my Father."

JOHN 15:15 TPT

Since our friendship with God was restored by the death of his Son while we were still his enemies, we will certainly be saved through the life of his Son.

ROMANS 5:10 NLT

"Here I am! I stand at the door and knock. If anyone hears my voice and opens the door, I will come in and eat with that person, and they with me."

REVELATION 3:20 NIV

BLAMELESS

Guilty! That's what any of us would expect to hear from the throne of God for the things we've done against him and others.

Often that's exactly what I hear from the inner voice that accuses and condemns. Whether it's something I say or want to say, something I think or do, the Enemy is quick to point out my sin. He's quick to *define* me by my sin as a guilty sinner!

Amazingly, though, "Guilty!" is the farthest thing from the lips of our heavenly Father. Guilty isn't who God says we are because guilty isn't who we are!

Consider these words from an old, powerful hymn that remind us of our true identity:

"When Satan tempts me to despair and tells me of the guilt within, Upward I look and see Him there who made an end of all my sin. Because the sinless Savior died my sinful soul is counted free. For God the just is satisfied to look on Him and pardon me."[1]

What this means is that not only am I not guilty, it means I am *blameless*! In Christ I am not blamed for my sin. You see, Jesus took the fall for all our rebellious acts when he climbed up on the cross and bore our punishment. He took all the blame for all we've done and will ever do!

---

1 Charitie L. Bancroft, "Before the Throne of God Above," 1863, public domain.

The next time Satan tempts you to despair, accusing you of being guilty sinner, remember who God says you are: no longer condemned, no longer guilty, fully justified, completely blameless!

◈

"I speak to you an eternal truth: if you embrace my message and believe in the One who sent me, you will never face condemnation, for in me, you have already passed from the realm of death into the realm of eternal life!"

JOHN 5:24 TPT

Jesus was left alone with the woman still standing there in front of him. So he stood back up and said to her, "Dear woman, where are your accusers? Is there no one here to condemn you?"
Looking around, she replied, "I see no one, Lord."
Jesus said, "Then I certainly don't condemn you either. Go, and from now on, be free from a life of sin."

JOHN 8:10–11 TPT

So then, as through one trespass there is condemnation for everyone, so also through one righteous act there is life-giving justification, for everyone.

ROMANS 5:18 HCSB

So now there is no condemnation for those who belong to Christ Jesus.

ROMANS 8:1 NLT

Who will bring any charge against those whom God has chosen? It is God who justifies.

ROMANS 8:33 NIV

For it is with your heart that you believe and are justified, and it is with your mouth that you profess your faith and are saved.

ROMANS 10:10 NIV

BLESSED

It seemed like 2014 was the year of curses for my family.

At the start of the year I discovered I had thyroid cancer, and in early February I had surgery to remove my whole thyroid. During her pregnancy, my wife developed gestational diabetes on top of her genetically high blood pressure. Our newborn son had bad reflux on par with colic. The church I'd been pastoring for a few years closed. And to top it off, both of our bikes were stolen out of our garage!

And yet time and time again I felt God breathing into me, deep down, this truth about my identity: "My cup overflows with blessing" (Psalm 23:5 NLT).

This, dear friend, is what is true about who you are in Christ!

I understand sometimes it doesn't feel that way. The car breaks down on the way to work—then you break down thinking about how to pay for it. A job falls through or a relationship falls apart and you wonder if somehow you're cursed.

You're not. For the Word of God declares the Lord blesses his lovers and surrounds them with favor. He says the works of our hands and our journeys through life are blessed. Jesus declares a whole host of people are highly favored by God: the poor in spirit, the mourners, the meek, those who thirst for righteousness, the merciful, the peacemakers, and the persecuted.

Through the deepest, darkest valleys, God was gracious to remind me each and every day who I really am. And who I am, who *you* are, is blessed.

◈

The LORD your God has blessed you in all the work of your hands. He has watched over your journey through this vast wilderness. These forty years the LORD your God has been with you, and you have not lacked anything.

DEUTERONOMY 2:7 NIV

Blessed is the one
who does not walk in step with the wicked
or stand in the way that sinners take
or sit in the company of mockers,
but whose delight is in the law of the LORD,
and who meditates on his law day and night.

PSALM 1:1–2 NIV

For You, LORD, bless the righteous one;
You surround him with favor like a shield.

PSALM 5:12 HCSB

You prepare a feast for me
in the presence of my enemies.
You honor me by anointing my head with oil.
My cup overflows with blessings.

PSALM 23:5 NLT

"Blessed are the poor in spirit,
For theirs is the kingdom of heaven.
Blessed are those who mourn,
For they shall be comforted.
Blessed are the meek,
For they shall inherit the earth.
Blessed are those who hunger and thirst for righteousness,
For they shall be filled.
Blessed are the merciful,
For they shall obtain mercy.
Blessed are the pure in heart,
For they shall see God.
Blessed are the peacemakers,
For they shall be called sons of God.
Blessed are those who are persecuted for righteousness' sake,
For theirs is the kingdom of heaven."

MATTHEW 5:3–10 NKJV

"Write: 'Blessed are those who are called to the marriage supper of the Lamb!'" And he said to me, "These are the true sayings of God."

REVELATION 19:9 NKJV

CALLED

There is an interesting Latin word that sits at the root of our English one: *vocatio*. The word may sound like *vocation*, and that's because it is. We think of vocation in the context of our work or job, an occupation a person is especially drawn to or trained for.

Did you know this word has a far less earthly and humanistic flavor to it, and a much more heavenly and divine meaning? In the Middle Ages, *vocatio* was a summons, an invitation to do God's work. It wasn't necessarily about picking and choosing the next job or work assignment from a list of LinkedIn openings. It was about discovering what God himself had divinely called you to do.

Because, you see, that's who God says we are: called. Every one of us has been divinely summoned and equipped to do the work of God, whatever that may be.

Jesus, the Son of God, called people to his divine mission of people-fishing. He taught that those who believed in him were called and empowered to do the things that he was doing. Paul instructed Christians in Corinth to give their all to their calling—whatever that was—because their labor was not in vain. And Jesus reminds us all that just as he was sent into the world, so are we. We could say God says we're *sent* as much as he says we are *called*.

No matter who you are or what you're doing, know deep down that you haven't just chosen a job; you have been divinely summoned by the King of kings and Lord of lords!

❖

Jesus called out to them, "Come, follow me, and I will show you how to fish for people!"

MARK 1:17 NLT

"From everyone who has been given much, much will be demanded; and from the one who has been entrusted with much, much more will be asked."

LUKE 12:48 NIV

"I bestow on you a kingdom, just as My Father bestowed one on Me, so that you may eat and drink at My table in My kingdom. And you will sit on thrones judging the 12 tribes of Israel."

LUKE 22:29–30 HCSB

"I tell you the truth, anyone who believes in me will do the same works I have done, and even greater works, because I am going to be with the Father."

JOHN 14:12 NLT

Jesus repeated his greeting, "Peace to you!" And he told them, "Just as the Father has sent me, I'm now sending you."

JOHN 20:21 TPT

Always give yourself fully to the work of the Lord, because you know that your labor in the Lord is not in vain.

1 CORINTHIANS 15:58 NIV

CHERISHED

My home study has large bookcases filled with hundreds of old and new hardcovers and paperbacks—all lovingly, meticulously organized and arranged by category, and in alphabetical order by author.

I cherish them for what they represent: knowledge and information. I cherish them for whom they represent: people I aspire to be and who mentor me from afar.

Consider that word, *cherish*. The word means "to protect and care for someone lovingly, to hold something dear." Other words for cherish include: *adore, hold dear, love, dote on, be devoted to, revere, esteem, admire.*

What and whom do you cherish?

Consider the emotion you feel for that special someone or those special things, and realize that when God looks at you he feels the same way—but magnified infinitely more! The Bible says every single moment God is thinking about us, cherishing us constantly in his thoughts. His desire is toward us, and he carries us close to his heart. Paul reminds us that nothing will ever be able to separate us from God's love!

Who you really are, as God's child and God's image-bearer, is someone who he lovingly protects and cares for. He holds you dear, he adores you, and he is eternally devoted to you.

Books and trinkets are nothing, but you are *everything*—because God says you're *cherished.*

Every single moment you are thinking of me!
How precious and wonderful to consider,
that you cherish me constantly in your every thought!
O God, your desires toward me are more
than the grains of sand on every shore!
When I awake each morning,
you're still thinking of me.

PSALM 139:17–18 TPT

The Lord directs the steps of the godly.
He delights in every detail of their lives.
Though they stumble, they will never fall,
for the Lord holds them by the hand.

PSALM 37:23–24 NLT

I am my beloved's,
And his desire is toward me.

SONG OF SOLOMON 7:10 NKJV

He tends his flock like a shepherd:
He gathers the lambs in his arms
and carries them close to his heart;
he gently leads those that have young.

ISAIAH 40:11 NIV

I am sure that neither death nor life, nor angels nor rulers, nor
things present nor things to come, nor powers, nor height nor
depth, nor anything else in all creation, will be able to separate
us from the love of God in Christ Jesus our Lord.

ROMANS 8:38–39 ESV

CHOSEN

Do you remember the "schoolyard pick" in elementary school, or even later in high school? I sure do.

During recess my classmates and I would organize various games—ones like red rover and baseball, and others we made up. Before we could play, though, we had to divide up into teams, usually using this dreaded method.

Two captains were chosen who then chose people for their teams. One by one kids would be picked for one team and then the other—all the way until the last person standing was "picked" by default.

Often I was that last-picked kid.

It's no fun not being picked, not being *chosen*. Unfortunately, that feeling lives on through a number of experiences well into adulthood: Someone else is picked over you for a dream job or promotion. The one you hoped would choose you to date chooses someone else. As with childhood, often these kinds of experiences take a toll on our self-esteem and identity. Yet when we look at Scripture, we should look at ourselves entirely differently than we often do.

The Bible tells us that we have been chosen by God to be his treasured possessions. Before the very foundations of the world were laid, he chose us in Christ to be like his Son. We truly are a chosen people, God's special possession.

While life can provide one rejection after another, this

isn't who you really are; you aren't rejected, you are chosen. That's who God says you are!

For you are a people holy to the LORD your God. The LORD your God has chosen you to be a people for his treasured possession, out of all the peoples who are on the face of the earth.

DEUTERONOMY 7:6 ESV

And the LORD has declared today that you are a people for his treasured possession, as he has promised you, and that you are to keep all his commandments, and that he will set you in praise and in fame and in honor high above all nations that he has made, and that you shall be a people holy to the LORD your God, as he promised.

DEUTERONOMY 26:18–19 ESV

For God knew his people in advance, and he chose them to become like his Son, so that his Son would be the firstborn among many brothers and sisters.

ROMANS 8:29 NLT

Even before he made the world, God loved us and chose us in Christ to be holy and without fault in his eyes.

EPHESIANS 1:4 NLT

For we know, brothers and sisters loved by God, that he has chosen you, because our gospel came to you not simply with words but also with power, with the Holy Spirit and deep conviction.

1 THESSALONIANS 1:4–5 NIV

But you are a chosen people, a royal priesthood, a holy nation, God's special possession, that you may declare the praises of him who called you out of darkness into his wonderful light.

1 PETER 2:9 NIV

So, dear brothers and sisters, work hard to prove that you really are among those God has called and chosen. Do these things, and you will never fall away. Then God will give you a grand entrance into the eternal Kingdom of our Lord and Savior Jesus Christ.

2 PETER 1:10–11 NLT

CREATED

It may seem odd we need to be reminded that we are *created*. Yet in a world that tells us we're the product of random chance and chaos, it can be easy to miss the deep, biblical reality that every single person on the planet has been crafted in the image and likeness of their Creator.

Including you.

We're not merely the most highly advanced species in a long line of organisms. We are statues of the Creator who were placed here on this earth to rule on God's behalf.

In Genesis 1, we are told: "God created mankind in his own image." This language reflects the ancient culture of the time. When Genesis was written, it was common for kings to create statues of their "image" and place them around their kingdom—especially newly conquered lands. Such a practice reminded people who their rulers were and to whom the people were responsible.

That's the background to the language God uses to talk about our human identity—we're carefully crafted statues of God, placed on this earth in our unique way to fulfill our unique role as his image bearers! Repeatedly the Word of God reminds us who we really are—that God formed us, that we've been marvelously made.

While the secular world might try and convince you

otherwise, you are not the product of random chance and chaotic evolution. You are a Statue of the Divine, for you are created.

That is who you are—who *God* says you are!

❦

Then God said, "Let us make mankind in our image, in our likeness, so that they may rule over the fish in the sea and the birds in the sky, over the livestock and all the wild animals, and over all the creatures that move along the ground."
So God created mankind in his own image,
in the image of God he created them;
male and female he created them.

GENESIS 1:26–28 NIV

The Spirit of God has made me;
the breath of the Almighty gives me life.

JOB 33:4 NIV

You have made [mankind] a little lower than the angels
and crowned them with glory and honor.
You made them rulers over the works of your hands;
you put everything under their feet:
all flocks and herds,
and the animals of the wild,
the birds in the sky,
and the fish in the sea,
all that swim the paths of the seas.

PSALM 8:5–8 NIV

Know that the LORD is God.
It is he who made us, and we are his;
we are his people, the sheep of his pasture.

PSALM 100:3 NIV

Your hands made me and formed me;
give me understanding
so that I can learn Your commands.

PSALM 119:73 HCSB

For you created my inmost being;
you knit me together in my mother's womb.

PSALM 139:13 NIV

I thank you, God, for making me so mysteriously complex!
Everything you do is marvelously breathtaking.
It simply amazes me to think about it!
How thoroughly you know me, Lord!
You even formed every bone in my body
when you created me in the secret place—
carefully, skillfully shaping me
from nothing to something.

PSALM 139:14–15 TPT

DEFENDED

Sometimes life can feel like a helpless sapling doing everything it can to stay put in the middle of a hurricane. The wind blows violently, the waters are rising, and the tree is left wondering if it has the devices to find safety, security, and help.

Where do you turn for help when you need it most—whether emotionally, relationally, financially, or spiritually?

Do you look to a trusted friend? Perhaps you turn to your parents. Or maybe you don't have anyone to turn to.

When we turn the ear of our heart toward God's Word, we're reminded we aren't helpless, we aren't *defenseless*. God says we're the opposite; we're *defended*.

At every turn of the page to God's glorious story about himself and his people, we witness the God who defends and a people who are defended through every force of wind and rising tide. So are we.

We're protected with salvation-armor, Samuel declares. David reminds us the Lord's massive arms are wrapped around us—covering us, protecting us, *defending* us. The prophet Jeremiah reminds us our persecutors have no leg to stand on when they come against us; they will be humiliated and shamed in the face of our sure, divine defense.

Sometimes life can leave us feeling naked and exposed. Yet God reminds us that's not who we are. In reality we are defended—by the Lord of Angel Armies himself!

You protect me with salvation-armor;
you touch me and I feel ten feet tall.

2 Samuel 22:36 msg

But You, O Lord, are a shield for me,
My glory and the One who lifts up my head.
I cried to the Lord with my voice,
And He heard me from His holy hill.

Psalm 3:3-4 nkjv

His massive arms are wrapped around you, protecting you.
You can run under his covering of majesty and hide.
His arms of faithfulness are a shield keeping you from harm.

Psalm 91:4 tpt

God sends angels with special orders
To protect you wherever you go,
Defending you from all harm.

Psalm 91:11 esv

But the Lord is with me like a violent warrior.
Therefore, my persecutors will stumble and not prevail.
Since they have not succeeded, they will be utterly shamed,
an everlasting humiliation that will never be forgotten.

Jeremiah 20:11 hcsb

DELIVERED

When I was a young adult living and working in Washington DC, I had the bad habit of getting tickets for parking too long in zoned parking. Because I wasn't the most responsible young man back then, one day I got a nice, fat orange "boot" slapped on my car—a steel vehicle immobilization device that prevented me from driving home for the weekend after work.

At the time I didn't have enough money on hand to pay the few hundred dollars I'd amassed in tickets and late fees. So I figured I would pay my bill to the DC government at the end of the week when I got paid. Yet when I returned to see if my car was okay Monday morning, it was gone! It'd been towed for failure to pay within twenty-four hours.

I was in big trouble. So I did what any young adult would do: I phoned home! Thankfully, my dad wired me the money to deliver me from financial crisis. He lent me what I needed to pay my fines and retrieve my car.

Like my earthly one, we have a heavenly Father who delivers us from our many troubles and who has brought us ultimate deliverance through his Son Jesus. Samuel describes our Deliverer as a rock and fortress. The prophet Joel describes our future as one of ultimate deliverance. And Paul speaks of this same future, where God will not only continue to deliver us from evil, but will ultimately deliver us from death.

As a young adult I was pretty irresponsible, resulting in lots of trouble. We've all experienced trouble at one point or another—maybe you're there now. Yet we can be sure that in Christ, who we are is delivered.

⬦

The LORD is my rock, my fortress and my deliverer.

2 SAMUEL 22:2 NIV

The righteous person may have many troubles,
but the LORD delivers him from them all.

PSALM 34:19 NIV

The LORD helps [the righteous] and delivers them;
he delivers them from the wicked and saves them,
because they take refuge in him.

PSALM 37:40 NIV

He is my faithful love and my fortress,
my stronghold and my deliverer.

PSALM 144:2 HCSB

And everyone who calls
on the name of the LORD will be saved;
for on Mount Zion and in Jerusalem
there will be deliverance,
as the LORD has said,
even among the survivors
whom the LORD calls.

JOEL 2:32 NIV

He has delivered us from such a terrible death, and He will deliver us. We have put our hope in Him that He will deliver us again.

2 Corinthians 1:10 hcsb

And my Lord will continue to deliver me from every form of evil and give me life in his heavenly kingdom. May all the glory go to him alone for all the ages of eternity!

2 Timothy 4:18 tpt

FAMILY

Several years ago I led a missions trip to a Christian orphanage in Romania. This is a country known for its massive orphan problem. It isn't that thousands of parents have died. Instead parents frequently abandon their children at birth, filling up hospitals and state orphanages.

For some reason two particular children gravitated to me during our week of ministry: a four-year-old girl, Pamilla, and a two-year-old boy, Emil. I was especially fond of Emil and spent much of my time getting into trouble with him: we wrestled, romped in puddles, and pulled the legs off of bugs—you know, the stuff boys do!

One day this sweet little boy kissed me on the cheek and called me "Papa." I melted! Here was a kid who wanted nothing more than to be wanted, to have a daddy all his own, to be *family* to someone.

Isn't that what most of us want? To be known, to be loved, to be family to a people?

Remarkably, that's who we are with God! The Bible tells us that in Christ we are God's children through our faith in him. Though we might be forsaken by our own family, we are received by God into *his*; we really are sons and daughters of God!

When it was time for me and my team to leave the Romanian orphanage, one of the workers explained to Emil what was happening—and he lost it. He clung to my neck and sobbed, not wanting me to go. Because he wanted a papa—me to be his papa; Emil wanted family.

❦

Family. That's who God says you are!
Though my father and mother forsake me,
the LORD will receive me.

PSALM 27:10 NIV

So in Christ Jesus you are all children of God through faith.

GALATIANS 3:26 NIV

So now you Gentiles are no longer strangers and foreigners. You are citizens along with all of God's holy people. You are members of God's family.

EPHESIANS 2:19 NLT

Jesus, the Holy One, makes us holy. And as sons and daughters, we now belong to his same Father, so he is not ashamed or embarrassed to introduce us as his brothers and sisters!

HEBREWS 2:11 TPT

Once you were not a people, but now you are the people of God; once you had not received mercy, but now you have received mercy.

1 PETER 2:10 NIV

FORGIVEN

On October 2, 2006, a shooting occurred at the West Nickel Mines School, an Amish schoolhouse in Nickel Mines, Pennsylvania. The shooter took ten girls hostage, killing five of them before killing himself.

While this incident made national news, the news of a school shooting wasn't what was remarkable about this story; the aftermath made this story newsworthy.

CNN quoted Jack Meyer, who explained the response of the community: "I don't think there's anybody here that wants to do anything but forgive and not only reach out to those who have suffered a loss in that way but to reach out to the family of the man who committed these acts."[1]

Remarkable—otherworldly, really! That's because it is: These Amish Christians forgave a killer because they themselves have been forgiven.

We do, too, because that's who we really are! Because of Christ we are not guilty, and we are not condemned. Our sin and past failures aren't held over our heads. We're forgiven.

David reminds us that, in spite of all we've done, God's forgiveness has "kissed our hearts" (Psalm 103:3 TPT).

Isaiah announces that God forgives people freely when they turn from their ways. To make the point that Jesus was given authority to both heal and forgive people of their sins, he heals a lame man—as if to put an exclamation point on the end of his forgiveness. And Paul announces from the rooftops in his letters that our sins have been cancelled, and what remains is forgiveness all the way down!

The Amish in Lancaster, Pennsylvania, could only forgive the heinous acts in 2006 because they knew who they really were: forgiven.

May we know, deep down, that's who we really are, too.

❖

You kissed my heart with forgiveness, in spite of all I've done.

PSALM 103:3 TPT

As far as the east is from the west,
So far has He removed our transgressions from us.

PSALM 103:12 NKJV

The Lord our God is merciful and forgiving, even though we have rebelled against him.

DANIEL 9:9 NIV

The LORD has taken away your punishment,
he has turned back your enemy.
The LORD, the King of Israel, is with you;
never again will you fear any harm.

ZEPHANIAH 3:15 NIV

Since we are now joined to Christ, we have been given the treasures of salvation by his blood—the total cancellation of our sins—all because of the cascading riches of his grace.

Ephesians 1:7 tpt

You were dead because of your sins and because your sinful nature was not yet cut away. Then God made you alive with Christ, for he forgave all our sins. He canceled the record of the charges against us and took it away by nailing it to the cross.

Colossians 2:13–14 nlt

I am writing to you, dear children,
because your sins have been forgiven on account of his name.

1 John 2:12 niv

FOUND

If you've ever lost something, you know how absolutely frustrating it can be.

I once lost my wedding ring. Correction, I *misplaced* my wedding ring. It was right where I left it. I just forgot where I left it.

As you can imagine I turned the house upside down looking for that thing: turned over every couch cushion, turned all my pants pockets inside out—even drove forty miles to a location I thought my not-lost-only-misplaced ring might have been.

Perhaps you can relate to doing everything possible to find what's been lost. Do you know this is what God is like? Did you know this is what God did for each of us?

Jesus says that God is like a shepherd, a woman, and a father. They lost a sheep, a coin, and a son, respectively. Consider this imagery: A shepherd does everything to find and rescue that one lost sheep; a woman turns over every table to find and recover that one missing coin; and a father goes to great lengths to welcome his one lost son back into the family.

Sometimes we may feel lost—relationally, professionally, spiritually. In reality, we have everything we need to find ourselves again and find where we need to go. David reminds us God is a revealing God who helps us find our way by flooding our path with guidance to lead us to truth and life. Jesus' parables about the shepherd, woman, and father remind us what God did to find us, too.

God is a God who guides; he is a God who rescues us from our lostness. Which means who we really are is found!

◈

You reveal the path of life to me;
in Your presence is abundant joy;
in Your right hand are eternal pleasures.

PSALM 16:11 HCSB

God, all at once, you turned on a floodlight for me!
You are the revelation light in my darkness,
and in your brightness I can see the path ahead.

PSALM 18:28 TPT

"Suppose one of you has a hundred sheep and loses one of them. Doesn't he leave the ninety-nine in the open country and go after the lost sheep until he finds it? And when he finds it, he joyfully puts it on his shoulders and goes home ... I tell you that in the same way there will be more rejoicing in heaven over one sinner who repents than over ninety-nine righteous persons who do not need to repent."

LUKE 15: 4–7 NIV

"Suppose a woman has ten silver coins and loses one. Doesn't she light a lamp, sweep the house and search carefully until she finds it? And when she finds it, she calls her friends and neighbors together and says, 'Rejoice with me; I have found my lost coin.' In the same way, I tell you, there is rejoicing in the presence of the angels of God over one sinner who repents."

LUKE 15:8–10 NIV

 "'My son,' the father said, 'you are always with me, and everything I have is yours. But we had to celebrate and be glad, because this brother of yours was dead and is alive again; he was lost and is found.'"

LUKE 15:32 NIV

FREE

A pastor friend of mine has a favorite quote on his Facebook page: "When Jesus came, he blew everything to pieces, and when I saw where the pieces fell, I knew I was free."

I'm not sure if it's originally his or from someone else, but I love it! It's built on the basic belief that Jesus came to set us free. From sin, yes, but it's more than just about *sinning*.

Scripture declares that Jesus has freed us from sin's *power* and sin's *guilt*. Sin used to be our master; we had no choice but to submit to its demands. Before we met Jesus we were also in bondage to the shame and guilt that come with the memory of our past mistakes—the way we've treated God and our neighbor, privately and publicly.

But when Jesus showed up—not merely back then in first-century Israel, but in each and every one of our own individual stories—this all changed!

Jesus blew to smithereens every aspect of our life that was out of sync with God's intent for us. In the process he crushed the shackles that used to hold us down—the shame and guilt from our past, the sins that trip us up, the lies we believe about ourselves, the very power that draws and compels us to rebel against God in the first place. And in place of both the power and guilt of sin, when the dust settled, there was nothing left but the liberating love of our heavenly Father.

If you're a child of God, you are not a slave. Because Jesus blew apart your chains, you are not living a life of bondage either to sin's power or sin's guilt. In Christ, you are *free*!

◆

But the Lord has paid for the freedom of his servants,
and he will freely pardon those who love him.
He will declare them free and innocent
when they turn to hide themselves in him.

PSALM 34:22 TPT

Jesus replied, "I tell you the truth, everyone who sins is a slave of sin. A slave is not a permanent member of the family, but a son is part of the family forever. So if the Son sets you free, you are truly free."

JOHN 8:34–36 NLT

"Everyone who believes in him is set free from sin and guilt—something the law of Moses had no power to do."

ACTS 13:39 TPT

Death once held us in its grip, and by the blunder of one man, death reigned over humanity. But now we are held in the grip of grace and reign as kings in life, enjoying our regal freedom through the gift of perfect righteousness in the one and only Jesus, the Messiah!

ROMANS 5:17 TPT

God has united you with Christ Jesus. For our benefit God made him to be wisdom itself. Christ made us right with God; he made us pure and holy, and he freed us from sin.

1 CORINTHIANS 1:30 NLT

Now the Lord is the Spirit, and where the Spirit of the Lord is, there is freedom.

2 CORINTHIANS 3:17 HCSB

You have died with Christ, and he has set you free from the spiritual powers of this world.

COLOSSIANS 2:20 NLT

FULFILLED

Where do you go to find fulfillment? To whom or what do you turn to satisfy yourself?

Some of us turn to food or drink when we're in need of satisfaction. Others of us look to work, entertainment, and other activities to fulfill us. Then there are relationships— with friends, family, or even anonymous people.

Blaise Pascal, a French philosopher from the seventeenth century, is often quoted as saying, "There is a God-shaped vacuum in the heart of every man which cannot be filled by any created thing, but only by God the Creator, made known through Jesus Christ."[1]

Did you know you have everything you need to be satisfied and fulfilled? As Pascal reveals, that fulfillment lies entirely with our heavenly Father.

One of the great lies our Enemy tells us is that the things of this world will bring fulfillment—whether who we're dating, what we're doing with our time, or where we're working. The Word of God tells us, however, that who we are is already fulfilled—we don't need to look anywhere else for what we already have in Christ!

Proverbs reminds us that through our awe-filled worship we are ushered into a world of satisfaction. The prophet Joel

---

1 In Chris Lutes's "The Secret That Will Change Your Life," *Christianity Today*, http://www.christianitytoday.com/iyf/hottopics/faithvalues/8c6030.html.

makes known that God's people have more than enough and are more than satisfied in and through him. And Jesus beckons everyone to his side to experience soul-quenching rivers of his unending life—a life that you and I have right this very minute!

The things of this world will never be enough. In reality, we have everything we already need to be satisfied—because God says we're fulfilled.

❖

Blessed are those who find wisdom,
those who gain understanding,
for she is more profitable than silver
and yields better returns than gold.
She is more precious than rubies;
nothing you desire can compare with her.
Long life is in her right hand;
in her left hand are riches and honor.
Her ways are pleasant ways,
and all her paths are peace.

PROVERBS 3:13–17 NIV

The fear of the LORD leads to life,
And he who has it will abide in satisfaction;
He will not be visited with evil.

PROVERBS 19:23 NKJV

"You shall eat in plenty and be satisfied,
And praise the name of the LORD your God,

Who has dealt wondrously with you;
And My people shall never be put to shame."

JOEL 2:26 NKJV

"God blesses those who hunger and thirst for justice,
for they will be satisfied."

MATTHEW 5:6 NLT

Jesus said to them, "I am the Bread of Life. Come every day to
me and you will never be hungry. Believe in me and you will
never be thirsty."

JOHN 6:35 TPT

Jesus stood and shouted out to the crowds—"All you thirsty
ones, come to me! Come to me and drink! Believe in me,
so that rivers of living water will burst out from within you;
flowing from your innermost being, just like the Scripture
says!"

JOHN 7:37–38 TPT

Oh, the depth of the riches
both of the wisdom and the knowledge of God!
How unsearchable His judgments
and untraceable His ways!

ROMANS 11:33 HCSB

GiFTED

Growing up in the Midwest, we boys were expected to play some sort of sport. Football was number one on the list, followed closely by basketball and baseball. Since I was from Michigan, which might as well be Canada, hockey was also a big one. Soccer hadn't yet hit mass adoption, so it was near the end of the list.

Except here's the thing: I hated sports.

I have a vivid memory of sobbing in the boys' bathroom as a fifth grader because my elementary teacher tried to force me to play football. During sign-ups I hid in the bathroom, but she found me and stood outside trying to coax me out and force me to play—hence the breakdown!

I hated sports mostly because I wasn't athletically gifted. I was more interested in creating things and using my mind. It wasn't until years after my fifth grade breakdown that I realized I was gifted in ways God designed.

Some of us need this reminder: that who God says we are is *gifted*.

The Bible makes it clear that God has imparted to each us some sort of gift—both personal abilities and spiritual gifts. Paul says these gifts are given to each of us so we can help other people. These gifts are not one-size-fits-all gifts, but specially crafted to fit our own unique shape.

What are your gifts? The ones that make you uniquely

you? The ones God himself has given you to use for his glory and kingdom?

❥

God's marvelous grace imparts to each one of us varying gifts and ministries that are uniquely ours.

ROMANS 12:6 TPT

Now you have every spiritual gift you need as you eagerly wait for the return of our Lord Jesus Christ.

1 CORINTHIANS 1:7 NLT

A spiritual gift is given to each of us so we can help each other.

1 CORINTHIANS 12:7 NLT

To one there is given through the Spirit a message of wisdom, to another a message of knowledge by means of the same Spirit, to another faith by the same Spirit, to another gifts of healing by that one Spirit, to another miraculous powers, to another prophecy, to another distinguishing between spirits, to another speaking in different kinds of tongues, and to still another the interpretation of tongues. All these are the work of one and the same Spirit, and he distributes them to each one, just as he determines.

1 CORINTHIANS 12:8–10 NIV

And he has appointed some with grace to be apostles, and some with grace to be prophets, and some with grace to be evangelists, and some with grace to be pastors, and some with grace to be teachers. And their calling is to nurture and prepare all the holy believers to do their own works of ministry, and as they do this they will enlarge and build up the body of Christ.

EPHESIANS 4:11–12 TPT

GRACED

Do you know the difference between justice, mercy, and grace?

Justice is getting what we deserve. If I'm clocked going sixty in a residential area, I deserve to have my license clipped on the spot—and spend some time in the clink!

Mercy is not getting what we deserve. A merciful judge would give me back my license and send me home instead of jail. Grace, though—grace is a whole other deal! Grace is getting what we *don't* deserve. Imagine after I was given back my license and sent back home the judge gives me a police escort, and waiting for me in my driveway is a nice shiny new Rolls-Royce and a lifetime of free gas.

Absolutely absurd, I know. But that's what grace is— absurd, loving favor. And that's who we are: graced, by the absurd, loving favor of God.

How else could you describe what we've received through Jesus' life, death, and resurrection? Not only have we been forgiven of all of our rebellious acts against God, but also we've been brought into his family and made heirs of the promises of Christ!

David reminds us how absurd this loving favor is when he says that God hasn't dealt with us or repaid us as our sins deserved. Paul tells of the freedom we live under because of this grace. He calls this grace "superabundant" and "generous." It's a loving favor that has made us righteous, released within us all kinds of understanding, and is all-sufficient for our needs.

While our Enemy would try and convince us otherwise, saying we're condemned and guilty, God says we are graced—the absurd, loving favor of God's love has been poured out on us!

◈

He has not dealt with us as our sins deserve
or repaid us according to our offenses.

PSALM 103:10 HCSB

Sin is no longer your master, for you no longer live under the requirements of the law. Instead, you live under the freedom of God's grace.

ROMANS 6:14 NLT

"My grace is sufficient for you, for power is perfected in weakness."

2 CORINTHIANS 12:9 HCSB

This superabundant grace is already powerfully working in us and flooding into every part of our being, releasing within us all forms of wisdom and practical understanding.

EPHESIANS 1:8 TPT

Together with Christ Jesus He also raised us up and seated us in the heavens, so that in the coming ages He might display the immeasurable riches of His grace through His kindness to us in Christ Jesus.

EPHESIANS 2:6–7 HCSB

He generously poured out the Spirit upon us through Jesus Christ our Savior. Because of his grace he declared us righteous and gave us confidence that we will inherit eternal life.

TITUS 3:6–7 NLT

GUIDED

There is this ancient spiritual practice called the labyrinth. Maybe you've used this practice yourself in your own spiritual life. It's a practice stretching back to the early Church. The earliest known labyrinth is in a church in Algeria from AD 350.

At first glance, the path of a labyrinth looks like a maze, but there are no dead ends—it only looks that way. Created out of hedges or simple stone tiles, the path of a labyrinth has multiple twists and turns as it winds its way into the center, taking the Christian to an area for resting, prayer, and meditation.

The labyrinth is meant as a metaphor for our lives: While the path twists and turns, it marches forward with purpose to carry us toward the center destination, and back out again. As you engage this practice you realize that who you are as a child of God is a *guided* child. You're not left alone, wandering in the dark. The twists and turns of the labyrinth path create a confusing, uncertain experience, yet they always end in a clear destination. The same is true for life.

The prophet Samuel declares the Lord is our lamp who lightens our darkened journey. David felt the guiding presence throughout his life, saying God is a God who guides us with his counsel until we die. The writer of Proverbs says

God guides us on straight paths, similar to our spiritual practice. And Jesus says he is our life-giving light, so that none of us walk in darkness.

Though life may seem twisty and foggy, it isn't—because our true identity is a child guided by a loving Father.

For you are my lamp, O Lord,
and my God lightens my darkness.

2 Samuel 22:29 esv

For that is what God is like.
He is our God forever and ever,
and he will guide us until we die.

Psalm 48:14 nlt

You guide me with your counsel,
and afterward you will take me into glory.

Psalm 73:24 niv

I am teaching you the way of wisdom;
I am guiding you on straight paths.
When you walk, your steps will not be hindered;
when you run, you will not stumble.

Proverbs 4:11–12 hcsb

"I am the Lord your God,
who teaches you for your benefit,
who leads you in the way you should go."

Isaiah 48:17 hcsb

Then Jesus said, "I am light to the world and those who embrace me will experience life-giving light, and they will never walk in darkness."

JOHN 8:12 TPT

He is the perfect Father who leads us all, works through us all, and lives in us all!

EPHESIANS 4:6 TPT

GUILTLESS

Growing up I had an imaginary friend. His name was conscience.

Don't laugh; it's true! I'm not sure why I called him that. That was just his name.

I would talk with my trusted friend about a variety of things. Mostly he—meaning me—talked to me about the bad things I did. He was like my own Jiminy Cricket sitting on my shoulder, an inner voice shaking his finger at the eight-year-old things that got me in trouble.

Unfortunately, many adults have their own version of my trusted friend who condemns and shames them at every turn. If they don't read their Bible or pray one day, if they run a red light or let a curse word slip, their own Jiminy shakes his pointy finger, sneering, "Guilty!"

But here's the thing: In Christ, we're not!

John makes it clear that those who believe in Jesus don't live under any condemnation. Paul's teachings snuff out that inner voice with the verdict: "Not guilty!" In fact, he says Jesus is praying for us at God's side, not condemning us. And John reminds us again that even though our imaginary friend might condemn us, we're not condemned.

Even if we feel guilty, God is greater than our feelings. Our own Jiminy Cricket is silenced. Who we really are is who God says we are—and he says we're guiltless.

"So now there is no longer any condemnation for those who believe in him, but the unbeliever already lives under condemnation because they do not believe in the name of God's beloved Son."

JOHN 3:18 TPT

[Righteousness] will be credited to us who believe in Him who raised Jesus our Lord from the dead. He was delivered up for our trespasses and raised for our justification.

ROMANS 4:24–25 HCSB

And this free-flowing gift imparts to us much more than what was given to us through the one who sinned. For because of one transgression, we are all facing a death sentence with a verdict of "Guilty!" But this gracious gift leaves us free from our many failures and brings us into the perfect righteousness of God—acquitted with the words "Not guilty!"

ROMANS 5:16 TPT

Who then is left to condemn us? Certainly not Jesus, the Anointed One! For he gave his life for us, and even more than that, he has conquered death and is now risen, exalted, and enthroned by God at his right hand. So how could he possibly condemn us since he is continually praying for our triumph?

ROMANS 8:34 TPT

Our actions will show that we belong to the truth, so we will be confident when we stand before God. Even if we feel guilty, God is greater than our feelings, and he knows everything.

1 JOHN 3:19–20 NLT

HEARD

One of the clearest illustrations of who we are comes from the movie *Anna and the King*, staring Jodi Foster and Chow Yun-Fat.

Foster plays Anna, a British schoolteacher who attends to the children of the king of Siam, played by Chow. In one scene Anna's son gets into a fight with the king's son in the middle of class. King Mongkut's young daughter runs to fetch her papa to intervene, which gives us a fascinating illustration of prayer.

The camera pans to King Mongkut's throne room, where a number of diplomats, government officials, and other businesspeople are gathered. They are silent and prostrate before the king seated high on his throne. All of a sudden the doors to the chamber fly open, the little girl runs down the red carpet and past the people paying homage to her father, she ascends the stairs, and she whispers something into the king's ear.

At the beckoning of his sweet daughter, the king immediately stands up, runs past the attendants and dignitaries, and rushes through the doors and out to the schoolhouse.

The most powerful man in the land dropped everything to listen to the heart's desires and cares of his little girl. His daughter was heard because she was his priority.

Friends, *that's* who we are, too. God says we're *heard*

because we're *his* priority. He listens to our every word!

David says that at the start of the day God listens when he voices his requests. He goes on to say the Lord hears his pleas, his distress over his problems, and his calls for help. Jesus is emphatic that whenever and whatever we ask our heavenly father, we will be heard.

Our God is a listening God. Know that you are heard.

❖

In the morning, LORD, you hear my voice;
in the morning I lay my requests before you
and wait expectantly.

PSALM 5:3 NIV

The LORD has heard my plea;
the LORD will answer my prayer.

PSALM 6:9 NLT

Evening, morning and noon
I cry out in distress,
and he hears my voice.

PSALM 55:17 NIV

"Then you will call on me and come and pray to me, and I will
    listen to you.
You will seek me and find me when you seek me with all your
heart."

JEREMIAH 29:12–13 NIV

"So it is with your prayers. Ask and you'll receive. Seek and you'll discover. Knock on heaven's door, and it will one day open for you. Every persistent person will get what he asks for. Every persistent seeker will discover what he needs. And everyone who knocks persistently will one day find an open door."

LUKE 11:9–10 TPT

"I assure you: Anything you ask the Father in My name, He will give you. Until now you have asked for nothing in My name. Ask and you will receive, so that your joy may be complete."

JOHN 16:23–24 HCSB

Now this is the confidence we have before Him: Whenever we ask anything according to His will, He hears us.

1 JOHN 5:14 HCSB

HEAVEN-BOUND

The first funeral I officiated was for a thirty-three-year-old man who died of cancer fourteen months after his diagnosis. He left behind a young wife and two twin boys who were three years old at the time. This young man died far too young.

My message centered on the hope this young man had, the hope of the gospel. This gospel-hope reminds us that the troubles of this world and the death that awaits us all won't have the final word in our story, because it didn't have the final word in *Jesus'* story.

Because of Jesus' death, resurrection, and exaltation, we're all awaiting our final place of rest at our Savior's side in heaven before he returns to restore this broken, busted world and resurrect us on a brand-new earth.

This is true of my congregant's story as much as our own story. Who he was in Christ is who we are in Christ: heaven-bound!

Jesus promised he was going to go prepare a place for his children. Paul spoke of this place, an eternal home from God not built by human hands. He reminded us that our ultimate citizenship is heaven. It's a place God has prepared for all those heroes of the faith Hebrews speaks of—the same place God has prepared for us and for the young man I buried.

In his first letter to the Thessalonian church, Paul reminded those Christians that they don't grieve over the death of their loved ones like the world, because of their identity in Christ. We share that same identity. God says we're heaven-bound, all because Jesus lives.

❖

"So, now, go and sell what you have and give to those in need, making deposits in your account in heaven, an account that will never be taken from you. Your gifts will become a secure and unfailing treasure, deposited in heaven forever. Where you deposit your treasure, that is where your thoughts will turn to—and your heart will long to be there also."

LUKE 12:33–34 TPT

"Don't let your hearts be troubled. Trust in God, and trust also in me. There is more than enough room in my Father's home. If this were not so, would I have told you that I am going to prepare a place for you?"

JOHN 14:1–2 NLT

For we know that if the earthly tent we live in is destroyed, we have a building from God, an eternal house in heaven, not built by human hands.

2 CORINTHIANS 5:1 NIV

For our citizenship is in heaven, from which we also eagerly wait for the Savior, the Lord Jesus Christ, who will transform our lowly body that it may be conformed to His glorious body, according to the working by which He is able even to subdue all things to Himself.

PHILIPPIANS 3:20–21 NKJV

When the Messiah, who is your life, is revealed, then you also will be revealed with Him in glory.

COLOSSIANS 3:4 HCSB

But now they desire a better, that is, a heavenly country. Therefore God is not ashamed to be called their God, for He has prepared a city for them.

HEBREWS 11:16 NKJV

HOLY

One day the prophet Isaiah was fulfilling his duties in the Lord's temple when all of sudden the curtain dividing his reality from God's was pulled back. Isaiah saw God lifted high and exalted on his throne. All around him heavenly beings were flying and calling to one another: "Holy, holy, holy is the Lord Almighty; the whole earth is full of his glory" (Isaiah 6:3 NIV).

When they spoke the doorposts and thresholds of the temple shook and smoke filled the room. Isaiah was both dazzled and frightened! "Woe to me!" he cried. "I am ruined! For I am a man of unclean lips, and I live among a people of unclean lips, and my eyes have seen the King, the Lord Almighty."

Remarkably, one of those heavenly beings took a live coal from the temple altar, flew down to Isaiah, touched the coal to Isaiah's mouth, and said, "your guilt is taken away and your sin atoned for" (Isaiah 6:7 NIV).

Isaiah was frightened because of the holiness of God. But because of God's atonement, Isaiah was made holy to stand in his presence.

The same is true for us.

Paul declares that in our union with Christ we've been made pure and holy. Through Jesus' death, not only has our relationship with God been restored, but also Christ presents us as holy and blameless before God's throne. The writer of Hebrews goes further, saying it was God's will all along that we would be made holy through Christ's sacrifice. Peter joins these voices by declaring the same: "You are a chosen race, a royal priesthood, a holy nation" (1 Peter 2:9 HCSB).

Maybe you feel dirty, polluted, and *un*holy. Yet like Isaiah, you've been cleansed. God says you, like Isaiah, are *holy*!

◈

"Woe to me!" I cried. "I am ruined! For I am a man of unclean lips, and I live among a people of unclean lips, and my eyes have seen the King, the Lord Almighty."

Then one of the seraphim flew to me with a live coal in his hand, which he had taken with tongs from the altar. With it he touched my mouth and said, "See, this has touched your lips; your guilt is taken away and your sin atoned for."

ISAIAH 6:5–7 NIV

God has united you with Christ Jesus. For our benefit God made him to be wisdom itself. Christ made us right with God; he made us pure and holy, and he freed us from sin.

1 CORINTHIANS 1:30 NLT

But now He has reconciled you by His physical body through His death, to present you holy, faultless, and blameless before Him.

COLOSSIANS 1:22 HCSB

For God's will was for us to be made holy by the sacrifice of the body of Jesus Christ, once for all time.

Hebrews 10:10 nlt

But you are a chosen race, a royal priesthood,
a holy nation, a people for His possession,
so that you may proclaim the praises
of the One who called you out of darkness
into His marvelous light.

1 Peter 2:9 hcsb

KNOWN

For most of junior high and high school I felt invisible. I wasn't a jock or part of the "in" crowd; I wasn't popular or wealthy. I was an average, pimply-faced, overweight teenager who just didn't stand out. Then after college I moved to a large city, where I knew no one and no one knew me.

As of 2013, there are more than seven billion people in the world. In America alone there are more than 310 million. You and I are just drops in an ocean of people. While social media connects us in ways we never thought possible, we're still just numbers in a constant stream of updates populating our status feeds.

No wonder many of us feel so alone—so *unknown*.

Yet the truth about who we are is the opposite: God says we're *known* because God himself knows us—by name!

The writer Job tells us that God pays attention to us— every morning he *inspects* us. David reminds us that the Creator of the universe knows everything there is to know about us. From our innermost being to our outer actions, God is intimately aware of us. God told the prophet Jeremiah that before he was even formed in his mother's womb, God knew him and set him apart to accomplish his work. And Jesus himself teaches that the very hairs on our head are all accounted for because of God's intimate awareness of us.

During the times I've felt most alone and unknown, God's Word has been the balm I've needed. For in it God has reminded me who I really am: I am known. And by my Creator!

◆

What is man, that You think so highly of him
and pay so much attention to him?
You inspect him every morning,
and put him to the test every moment.

JOB 7:17–18 HCSB

Lord, you know everything there is to know about me.
You've examined my innermost being with your loving gaze.
You perceive every movement of my heart and soul,
and understand my every thought before it even enters my
    mind.
You are so intimately aware of me, Lord.
You read my heart like an open book
and you know all the words I'm about to speak
before I even start a sentence!
You know every step I will take.

PSALM 139:1–4 TPT

You saw me before I was born.
Every day of my life was recorded in your book.
Every moment was laid out before a single day had passed.

PSALM 139:16 NLT

"Before I formed you in the womb I knew you,
before you were born I set you apart;
I appointed you as a prophet to the nations."

JEREMIAH 1:5 MSG

"Aren't two sparrows sold for a penny? Yet not one of them falls to the ground without your Father's consent. But even the hairs of your head have all been counted. So don't be afraid therefore; you are worth more than many sparrows."

MATTHEW 10:29–31 HCSB

LIBERATED

I have this reoccurring nightmare that I am sent away to prison for a crime I didn't commit. Sometimes this fear is exacerbated when I watch a TV show or movie that features someone in prison.

Can you imagine being locked away in a six-by-eight-foot cell for years—for a lifetime? I shudder just writing about it! The thought of losing my freedom, losing access to the outdoors, and losing my relationships sends jolts of fear down my spine.

Every day we hear stories of people who were finally released after years—decades!—for crimes they didn't commit. There was the Dallas man who served thirty-one years in prison for a rape he didn't do. A Mississippi woman spent years on death row for killing her nine-year-old son—except she was later exonerated.

One day they were guilty and imprisoned. The next, not guilty and liberated.

Unlike these people, we were all guilty for our crimes—the crime of rebelling against God. But like them, we've been acquitted and set free!

Through Isaiah, God tells us to "Come out in freedom" because of what he's done for us. Jesus tells us when we believe in him, freedom is released into our lives. A major theme of Paul's letters is this same message of freedom;

when he says we've been acquitted and liberated, we are freed people.

Reading God's Word reminds me that I am not imprisoned, I am not guilty, I will not be punished for my sins. I should be. Yet by God's grace I've been set free and will escape punishment.

This is what's true about me, what's true about you. God says you're liberated!

◈

"I will say to the prisoners, 'Come out in freedom,'
and to those in darkness, 'Come into the light.'
They will be my sheep, grazing in green pastures
and on hills that were previously bare."

ISAIAH 49:9 NLT

Jesus said to those who believed in him, "When you continue to embrace all that I teach, you prove that you are my true followers. For if you embrace the truth, it will release more freedom into your lives."

JOHN 8:31–32 TPT

Through his powerful declaration of acquittal, God freely gives away his righteousness. His gift of love and favor now cascades over us, all because Jesus, the Anointed One, has liberated us from the guilt, punishment, and power of sin!

ROMANS 3:28 TPT

And God is pleased with you, for in the past you were servants of sin, but now your obedience is heart deep, and your life is being molded by truth through the teaching you are devoted to. And now you celebrate your freedom from your former master—sin. You've left its bondage, and now God's perfect righteousness holds power over you as his loving servants.

ROMANS 6:17–18 TPT

For the "law" of the life-giving Spirit flowing through the anointing of Jesus has liberated us from the "law" of sin and death.

ROMANS 8:2 TPT

The one who was a slave when called to faith in the Lord is the Lord's freed person; similarly, the one who was free when called is Christ's slave.

1 CORINTHIANS 7:22 NIV

It is for freedom that Christ has set us free. Stand firm, then, and do not let yourselves be burdened again by a yoke of slavery.

GALATIANS 5:1 NIV

LOVED

"God loves you."

Read those three words again. Sit with them. Meditate on them.

The entire story of God's Word boils down to those three words.

Even though I grew up in the church and went to a Christian college, I didn't always believe them. I mean, I knew God loved me, but I didn't *know* it; God's love was head deep, not heart deep.

You see for a long time I believed I had to be a spiritual rock star in order for God to love me. Yes, deep down I knew I wasn't saved by the things I did, but by God's grace. I had this nagging sense, though, that God wouldn't truly love me unless I did the right spiritual things.

It wasn't until February 10, 1999, that I finally understood the depths of these three words. I'd been reading the book of Romans my freshman year in college, and all of a sudden one night this wave of love washed over me. I felt that I—even *I*—was loved by God. Not because of what I did or didn't do. But just because.

"For God so loved the world" begins one of the most well-known verses. Paul writes that Jesus proved God's passionate love for us when he died for us—while we were still sinners. He declares that nothing in the entire world could ever separate us from this love, a love that surpasses knowledge. John teaches this kind of love—that God sacrificed his Son for our sins—actually *defines* love.

God is love and he says the same about you: God says you're loved. It took me awhile to realize this about myself, and it took me longer to *fully* realize it. But when I did . . . it changed everything!

Many are the woes of the wicked,
but the LORD's unfailing love
surrounds the one who trusts in him.

PSALM 32:10 NIV

My beloved speaks and says to me: "Arise, my love, my beautiful one, and come away, for behold, the winter is past; the rain is over and gone. The flowers appear on the earth, the time of singing has come."

SONG OF SOLOMON 2:10–12 ESV

For God so loved the world that he gave his one and only Son, that whoever believes in him shall not perish but have eternal life.

JOHN 3:16 NIV

Now, who of us would dare to die for the sake of a wicked person? We can all understand if someone was willing to die for a truly noble person, yet who has ever heard of someone dying for an evil enemy? But Christ proved God's passionate love for us by dying in our place while we were still lost and ungodly!

ROMANS 5:7–8 TPT

I pray that you, being rooted and firmly established in love, may be able to comprehend with all the saints what is the length and width, height and depth of God's love, and to know the Messiah's love that surpasses knowledge, so you may be filled with all the fullness of God.

EPHESIANS 3:17–19 HCSB

We know what real love is because Jesus gave up his life for us.

1 JOHN 3:16 NLT

God showed how much he loved us by sending his one and only Son into the world so that we might have eternal life through him. This is real love—not that we loved God, but that he loved us and sent his Son as a sacrifice to take away our sins.

1 JOHN 4:9–10 NLT

POWERFUL

I love a good underdog story.

Two little hobbits give it all they've got until they nearly die climbing Mount Doom to save Middle-earth—and they do. How about the story of the young shepherd who fights a massive giant-of-a-man with nothing but a sling and some rocks—and wins, rescuing Israel from the Philistines?

In many ways our stories are also underdog stories. And like these other underdogs, we have all the power we need to live the life we've been called to—because our power is from God himself.

Jesus taught his disciples that he was their life, the power that causes them to be fruitful—like branches in a vine. He also taught that power is given to his disciples when the Holy Spirit comes on them. Paul reminds us that we have great power straight from God—a power that demolishes strongholds, wins arguments, and takes every thought captive for obedience. He says we have no reason to doubt this power is ours and at work in and through us.

Sometimes it feels as though we are the most powerless beings on the planet—like Frodo struggling against the might and power of Sauron, or David against Goliath. Don't be afraid and don't lose heart! Because as Paul says, "God will never give you the spirit of cowardly fear, but the Holy Spirit who gives you mighty power."

You are not powerless; that isn't who you are. Who you really are is *powerful*; that's who *God* says you are!

❖

"I am the sprouting vine and you're my branches. As you live in union with me as your source, fruitfulness will stream from within you—but when you live separated from me you are powerless."

JOHN 15:5 TPT

He said to them: "It is not for you to know the times or dates the Father has set by his own authority. But you will receive power when the Holy Spirit comes on you; and you will be my witnesses in Jerusalem, and in all Judea and Samaria, and to the ends of the earth."

ACTS 1:7–8 NIV

We now have this light shining in our hearts, but we ourselves are like fragile clay jars containing this great treasure. This makes it clear that our great power is from God, not from ourselves.

2 CORINTHIANS 4:7 NLT

For though we live in the body, we do not wage war in an unspiritual way, since the weapons of our warfare are not worldly, but are powerful through God for the demolition of strongholds. We demolish arguments and every high-minded thing that is raised up against the knowledge of God, taking every thought captive to obey Christ.

2 CORINTHIANS 10:3–5 HCSB

[Christ] was crucified in weakness, but He lives by God's power. For we also are weak in Him, yet toward you we will live with Him by God's power.

2 Corinthians 13:4 hcsb

Never doubt God's mighty power to work in you and accomplish all this. He will achieve infinitely more than your greatest request, your most unbelievable dream, and exceed your wildest imagination! He will outdo them all, for his miraculous power constantly energizes you.

Ephesians 3:20 tpt

For God will never give you the spirit of cowardly fear, but the Holy Spirit who gives you mighty power, love, and sound judgment!

2 Timothy 1:7 tpt

PROSPEROUS

While much of my childhood was a comfortable middle-class one, there were times of financial struggle.

One winter when I was eight or nine my family was struggling for money. And one evening we took a family trip to McDonald's to dine on Happy Meals and Big Macs and play on the jungle gym.

That winter McDonald's was running one of their big prize contests—the ones with the little peel-y things on the sides of drink cups and fry containers. While my sister and I were enjoying our Happy Meals, my mother peeled off the tab on the side of her drink. Her eyes widened when she looked at it.

"Is this right?" she asked Dad. "Is this what I think it is?"

She didn't want to get her hopes up so, she went to the front counter for confirmation. She was right: A $100 prize was stuck to the side of my mom's McDonald's cup!

What makes this story so great is that my sister and I needed new winter coats, and my parents had no idea how they were going to buy them. Yet through God we lacked no good thing!

When we think of prosperity we often think of the super wealthy. But in the Bible, prosperity is linked more with success, flourishing, and lacking no good thing. This is what God promises his people.

In Deuteronomy God promises us we will find abundance in every aspect of life. David says that in everything the righteous will flourish and never lack any good thing— God will provide it all. And Paul reminds us that every one of our needs will be supplied out of the storehouses of God's riches.

You may not be rich, but you are prosperous. That's who God says you are!

◈

The LORD your God will make you prosper abundantly in all the work of your hands with children, the offspring of your livestock, and your land's produce. Indeed, the LORD will again delight in your prosperity, as He delighted in that of your fathers, when you obey the LORD your God by keeping His commands and statutes that are written in this book of the law and return to Him with all your heart and all your soul.

DEUTERONOMY 30:9–10 HCSB

The God of heaven will make us prosper, and we his servants will arise and build.

NEHEMIAH 2:20 ESV

[The righteous] is like a tree
planted by streams of water
that yields its fruit in its season,
and its leaf does not wither.
In all that he does, he prospers.

PSALM 1:3 ESV

The righteous will flourish like a palm tree,
they will grow like a cedar of Lebanon;
planted in the house of the LORD,
they will flourish in the courts of our God.

PSALM 92:12–13 NIV

Those who walk along his paths with integrity
will never lack one thing they need, for he provides it all!
O Lord of Heaven's Armies,
what euphoria fills those who forever trust in you!

PSALM 84:12 TPT

And my God will supply every need of yours according to his riches in glory in Christ Jesus.

PHILIPPIANS 4:19 ESV

PURPOSEFUL

On days when I question my life purpose, I often consider the story of Esther, one of the more encouraging stories of Scripture.

Esther is the only book of the Bible where God isn't explicitly mentioned. But it's clear from the story that he's guiding the events that unfold according to his divine purpose—which includes the heroine of the story, Queen Esther.

As the story goes, King Xerxes of the Persian empire chose a successor to his wife, Queen Vashti, after she refused to obey his command to appear at his party and display her beauty. Jewish exile Esther was the one he chose as her replacement.

During the course of her tenure, Esther's cousin Mordecai uncovers a plot to exterminate the Jews living within the Persian empire by the king's advisor, Haman. Mordecai gets word to Esther and encourages her to make an urgent plea to Xerxes on behalf of her people, even though it could result in her death.

Understandably she hesitates. Her cousin, though, suggests it was "for such a time as this" that God had purposefully placed Esther in her royal position.

Mordecai reminded Esther who God said she was when she needed it most: She was *purposeful*.

Isaiah declares as much when he says we're all the work of God's hands. Paul says God molds and shapes every aspect of our life to fulfill his designed purpose. He goes on to say that he has placed each of us right where he wants us—we are an integral part of his plans and purposes!

God has created each of us, like Esther, on purpose and with purpose. And God will complete this good work in your life—just as he did in Esther's.

❖

Mordecai told the messenger to reply to Esther, "Don't think that you will escape the fate of all the Jews because you are in the king's palace. If you keep silent at this time, liberation and deliverance will come to the Jewish people from another place, but you and your father's house will be destroyed. Who knows, perhaps you have come to your royal position for such a time as this."

ESTHER 4:13–14 HCSB

Yet LORD, You are our Father;
we are the clay, and You are our potter;
we all are the work of Your hands.

ISAIAH 64:8 HCSB

So we are convinced that every detail of our lives is continually woven together to fit into God's perfect plan of bringing what is good into our lives, for we are his lovers who have been invited to fulfill his designed purpose.

ROMANS 8:28 TPT

Yes, the body has many different parts, not just one part. If the foot says, "I am not a part of the body because I am not a hand," that does not make it any less a part of the body. And if the ear says, "I am not part of the body because I am not an eye," would that make it any less a part of the body?

1 Corinthians 12:14–16 nlt

But in fact God has placed the parts in the body, every one of them, just as he wanted them to be. If they were all one part, where would the body be?

1 Corinthians 12:18–19 niv

And I am sure of this, that he who began a good work in you will bring it to completion at the day of Jesus Christ.

Philippians 1:6 esv

REBORN

In the movie *The Matrix*, one of my favorite scenes is the "red pill, blue pill" scene when Morpheus offers Neo the chance to remain in the Matrix or be unplugged from it.

Given the choice, Neo takes the red pill and awakens in the real world, where he is forcibly ejected from the liquid-filled chamber in which he has been lying unconscious for years as a slave to sentient machines. In many ways, the red pill is Neo's rebirth—the point when he passes over from a virtual death to life again.

Such is the case for anyone who chooses to follow Jesus, too. They are reborn and experience newness of life. As Jesus says, they become "children born not of natural descent, nor of human decision or a husband's will, but born of God." It was God's choice to give us this new birth through the gospel. The apostle John says we know we've experienced this new birth when we do what is right by loving God and neighbor. Everyone who believes Jesus is the One God sent to rescue us receives this rebirth.

When Neo is reborn he becomes a new person who experiences a new way of living. The same is true of us! "Flesh gives birth to flesh," Jesus says, "but the Spirit gives birth to spirit" (John 1:6 NIV).

While it may sound remarkable—the Pharisee Nicodemus sure thought it was!—that's who God says we are: We are *reborn*!

❖

"Yet to all who did receive him, to those who believed in his name, he gave the right to become children of God—children born not of natural descent, nor of human decision or a husband's will, but born of God."

JOHN 1:12–13 NIV

Do you not know that all of us who have been baptized into Christ Jesus were baptized into his death? We were buried therefore with him by baptism into death, in order that, just as Christ was raised from the dead by the glory of the Father, we too might walk in newness of life.

ROMANS 6:3–4 ESV

By His own choice, He gave us a new birth by the message of truth so that we would be the firstfruits of His creatures.

JAMES 1:18 HCSB

If you know that he is righteous, you know that everyone who does what is right has been born of him.

1 JOHN 2:29 NIV

No one who is born of God will continue to sin, because God's seed remains in them; they cannot go on sinning, because they have been born of God.

1 JOHN 3:9 NIV

Dear friends, let us love one another, because love is from God, and everyone who loves has been born of God and knows God.

1 JOHN 4:7 NIV

Everyone who believes that Jesus is the Christ is born of God, and everyone who loves the father loves his child as well.

1 JOHN 5:1 NIV

RECONCILED

If you've been at odds with someone, you know how hard it is when that relationship is broken and strained.

Another holiday looms and your gut twists thinking about how you'll get through it, because you haven't talked with your sibling for months. Or you fight with your spouse just before leaving for work. As you drive you already anticipate how unproductive the day will be as you continuing stewing, how lonely the evening will be when you return home.

Such pain of estrangement is only outmatched by the sweetness of reconciliation. When you apologize for your part in an argument, when your grievances are expressed and you feel heard, and when the two of you are reunited, the feeling takes you to heights of relief and satisfaction.

Consider the moment when you were reconciled with God. That moment when you crossed over from being his enemy to being his friend.

Do you realize that is who you are? A friend of God? Look at how the Bible describes this repaired relationship.

Paul says that we have been made right with God and have peace with God because of Jesus. He says it's more than that, though, because we've been *reconciled*—which goes deeper than merely ending conflict. In fact, he says this relational repair extends to the entire world. He reminds us that at one point we were God's enemy, but now because of Jesus we're not. And now we have the joy and job of acting as agents of reconciliation in the world, drawing others back to God, too.

With our human relationships, we tend to fall in and out of a good relational standing because of conflict. With God it's different, because who God says you are is reconciled—both now and forevermore!

Therefore, since we have been made right in God's sight by faith, we have peace with God because of what Jesus Christ our Lord has done for us.

ROMANS 5:1 NLT

We also rejoice in God through our Lord Jesus Christ, through whom we have now received reconciliation.

ROMANS 5:11 ESV

Everything is from God, who reconciled us to Himself through Christ and gave us the ministry of reconciliation.

2 CORINTHIANS 5:18 HCSB

In Christ, God was reconciling the world to Himself, not counting their trespasses against them, and He has committed the message of reconciliation to us.

2 CORINTHIANS 5:19 HCSB

Once you were alienated from God and were enemies in your minds because of your evil behavior. But now he has reconciled you by Christ's physical body through death to present you holy in his sight, without blemish and free from accusation.

COLOSSIANS 1:21–22 NIV

Remembered

One year I forgot my dad's birthday. Totally just dropped off my brain. It wasn't until my mom said something a few days later about them going out to dinner that I remembered. I felt horrible.

Luckily I haven't forgotten my anniversary yet—it's only been five years, so give me time! I have forgotten to take out the trash; to get that one thing I was sent to the grocery store to get, after picking up a basketful of other items; and to pay a bill—or two.

We are a forgetful people, aren't we? Aren't you glad there's Someone who never forgets, who always remembers and is faithful to the memory of his promises?

Sometimes we may believe that God has forgotten about us, but he says otherwise! We are not forgotten because God says we're remembered.

One of the surest, most enduring signs of his promise of remembrance is that multicolored bow in the sky, which God placed there as a sign that we are remembered. In fact, the Hebrew Scriptures say that God remembers the covenants he's made with us forever, from generation to generation. David reiterates this everlasting remembrance in several of his poems—a remembered covenant that extends to provision so that those who are hungry are fed. Jesus himself proved God remembers when one of the men hanging next to him asked to be remembered eternally; Jesus assured him he was remembered, which gives us a lasting hope.

Though people are forgetful and faithless, failing to remember important dates and action items, promises and people, God is totally different. And because God remembers, our identity is as remembered people!

❖

And God said, "This is the sign of the covenant I am making between Me and you and every living creature with you, a covenant for all future generations: I have placed My bow in the clouds, and it will be a sign of the covenant between Me and the earth. Whenever I form clouds over the earth and the bow appears in the clouds, I will remember My covenant between Me and you and all the living creatures: water will never again become a flood to destroy every creature."

GENESIS 9:12–15 HCSB

He remembers his covenant forever,
the promise he made, for a thousand generations,
the covenant he made with Abraham,
the oath he swore to Isaac.

1 CHRONICLES 16:15–16 NIV

Now this is what the Sovereign LORD says: "I will give you what you deserve, for you have taken your solemn vows lightly by breaking your covenant. Yet I will remember the covenant I made with you when you were young, and I will establish an everlasting covenant with you."

EZEKIEL 16:59–60 NLT

He remembers his covenant forever,
the word that he commanded, for a thousand generations,
the covenant that he made with Abraham,
his sworn promise to Isaac,
which he confirmed to Jacob as a statute,
to Israel as an everlasting covenant.

PSALM 105:8–10 ESV

He provides food for those who fear him;
he remembers his covenant forever.

PSALM 111:5 NIV

The LORD remembers us and will bless us.
He will bless the house of Israel;
He will bless the house of Aaron.

PSALM 115:12 HCSB

Then he said, "Jesus, remember me when You come into Your kingdom!"

And He said to him, "I assure you: Today you will be with Me in paradise."

LUKE 23:42–43 HCSB

RESCUED

When I was about six years old, I nearly drowned.

One summer, my family visited my grandparents who were camping along the lakeshore in northern Michigan. After feasting on buckets of KFC chicken and mashed potatoes, we went for a stroll on the beach. We took off our shoes to dip in along the periphery of the lake, and apparently I got a little too close.

I vaguely remember one minute splashing in a puddle of water after a wave receded. The next moment I was splashing, gasping for breath, and choking on a mouthful of lake water a few feet out.

My dad took quick action before the situation got any worse. He dragged me to the shore and helped me catch my breath. He rescued me from drowning, from dying.

Maybe you haven't had as obvious of a rescue experience, but if you are in Christ you *are* a rescued person. God has done so once and for all, and he continues to do so at life's every turn.

King David says that God is a mighty God who rescues us over and over again. Matthew says God is like a shepherd who gives all it takes to rescue the one lost sheep. Zechariah declares that through his Son, God has rescued us from powerful enemies. John writes this Son was sent not to shake his finger at the world, but to extend the helping hand of rescue. And Paul tells us God has rescued us from one dark and evil realm, and brought us into an entirely different realm—the kingdom of the Son he loves.

God saved us through the cross, and continues to save his children when the undercurrents of life try to drag us down.

In Christ, you are *rescued*!

◈

Our God is a mighty God who saves us over and over!
For the Lord, Yahweh, rescues us
from the ways of death many times.

PSALM 68:20 TPT

"Look at it this way. If someone has a hundred sheep and one of them wanders off, doesn't he leave the ninety-nine and go after the one? And if he finds it, doesn't he make far more over it than over the ninety-nine who stay put? Your Father in heaven feels the same way. He doesn't want to lose even one of these simple believers."

MATTHEW 18:12–14 MSG

"He has rescued us from the power of our enemies!
This fulfills the sacred oath he made with our father Abraham.
Now we can boldly worship God with holy lives,
living in purity as priests in his presence every day!"

LUKE 1:73–75 TPT

"God did not send his Son into the world to judge and condemn the world, but to be its Savior and rescue it!"

JOHN 3:17 TPT

May God our Father and the Lord Jesus Christ give you grace and peace. Jesus gave his life for our sins, just as God our Father planned, in order to rescue us from this evil world in which we live.

GALATIANS 1:3–4 NLT

He has rescued us from the domain of darkness and transferred us into the kingdom of the Son He loves.

COLOSSIANS 1:13 HCSB

RESTORED

My parents love antique furniture; they have a house full of it. All of our bedroom furniture growing up—from bed to dresser to desk—were certifiable antiques. They even have a nearly century-year-old upright radio the size of a small refrigerator.

One summer my mother spotted a small drop leaf table at the end of our neighbor's driveway sitting next to several trash bags. Other than severe paint stains, it was in fine condition. So she asked our neighbor if she could have it. One person's trash is another person's treasure, as they say.

When my dad came home from work he discovered he had been commissioned to restore a small drop leaf table! So Saturday he stripped off the paint and old stain. Then he gently sanded the old wood before applying a nice honey oak stain and a thin coat of varnish. The end product was a beautifully restored table.

It took the loving attention and care of my mom and dad to restore what years of neglect had ruined and what the original craftsman intended for this table.

The same is true of us.

Isaiah writes that God restores peoples' crushed spirits and removes their disgrace. He cleanses and restores us from our impurities. Ezekiel says the Lord gives us new breath and makes us live again. Joel tells us that God restores those aspects of our lives that "the swarming locust" has eaten. And John gives us a beautiful picture of the end of the age, when Jesus comes to ultimately put us and this world back together again.

No matter how we may feel or what lies our Enemy might breathe into our ears, in Christ we have been lovingly restored to the way our heavenly Father intended when he created us!

❦

The Lord GOD will wipe away the tears
from every face
and remove His people's disgrace
from the whole earth,
for the LORD has spoken.

ISAIAH 25:8 HCSB

The high and lofty one who lives in eternity,
the Holy One, says this:
"I live in the high and holy place
with those whose spirits are contrite and humble.
I restore the crushed spirit of the humble
and revive the courage of those with repentant hearts."

ISAIAH 57:15 NLT

"But the time is coming," says the LORD, "when people who are taking an oath will no longer say, 'As surely as the LORD lives, who rescued the people of Israel from the land of Egypt.' Instead, they will say, 'As surely as the LORD lives, who brought the people of Israel back to their own land from the land of the north and from all the countries to which he had exiled them.' For I will bring them back to this land that I gave their ancestors."

JEREMIAH 16:14–15 NLT

"I will also sprinkle clean water on you, and you will be clean. I will cleanse you from all your impurities and all your idols."

EZEKIEL 36:25 HCSB

This is what the Sovereign LORD says: "Look! I am going to put breath into you and make you live again! I will put flesh and muscles on you and cover you with skin. I will put breath into you, and you will come to life. Then you will know that I am the LORD."

EZEKIEL 37:5–6 NLT

"So I will restore to you the years
    that the swarming locust has eaten,
The crawling locust,
The consuming locust,
And the chewing locust,
My great army which I sent among you."

JOEL 2:25 NKJV

I saw the Holy City, the new Jerusalem, coming down out of heaven from God, prepared as a bride beautifully dressed for her husband. And I heard a loud voice from the throne saying, "Look! God's dwelling place is now among the people, and he will dwell with them. They will be his people, and God himself will be with them and be their God. He will wipe every tear from their eyes. There will be no more death or mourning or crying or pain, for the old order of things has passed away."

REVELATION 21:2–4 NIV

RIGHTEOUS

Martin Luther, a sixteenth century monk, spent as many as six hours every single day confessing his sins. Every time he confessed a sin he would be crushed again because he remembered yet *another* sin. So he'd start the confession all over again. Confession, guilt, repeat.

What was his deal? The problem wasn't that he was a spiritual slacker. And the kinds of sins this guy committed weren't the kind that would get you on *The Jerry Springer Show*. The problem was he saw how far even his best deeds fell short of God's perfect standard.

One day Luther was reading a passage from Paul's letter to the Church of Rome, and he had this major "Aha!" moment. He saw something about God's love he hadn't seen before. Here is what he read: "For in the gospel the righteousness of God is revealed—a righteousness that is by faith from first to last, just as it is written: 'The righteous will live by faith'" (Romans 1:17 NIV).

Luther had read this passage before, but on this day he realized who he really was because of what God had done in his life: He was righteous.

Paul reminds us that independent of religious works, the righteousness of God is tangible and brought to light through Jesus and given to everyone as a gift. We can't rely on ourselves for this righteousness. We are made righteous and made right with God all because of Jesus.

Luther wrote that this passage of Paul became a gate of heaven for him. He felt himself to be reborn and to have gone through open doors into paradise.

May we hear this day the powerful declaration Luther himself heard: "You are now righteous in my sight" (Romans 5:9 TPT).

❧

For in the gospel the righteousness of God is revealed—a righteousness that is by faith from first to last, just as it is written: "The righteous will live by faith."

ROMANS 1:17 NIV

But now, independently of the law, the righteousness of God is tangible and brought to light through Jesus, the Anointed One. This is the righteousness that the Scriptures prophesied would come. It is God's righteousness made visible through the faithfulness of Jesus Christ. And now all who believe in him receive that gift. For there is really no difference between us.

ROMANS 3:21–22 TPT

And there is still much more to say of his unfailing love for us! For through the blood of Jesus we have heard the powerful declaration, "You are now righteous in my sight."

ROMANS 5:9 TPT

For just as through one man's disobedience the many were made sinners, so also through the one man's obedience the many will be made righteous.

ROMANS 5:19 HCSB

Having determined our destiny ahead of time, he called us to himself and transferred his perfect righteousness to everyone he called. And those who carry his perfect righteousness he co-glorified with his Son!

ROMANS 8:30 TPT

For Christ has already accomplished the purpose for which the law was given. As a result, all who believe in him are made right with God.

ROMANS 10:4 NLT

I no longer count on my own righteousness through obeying the law; rather, I become righteous through faith in Christ. For God's way of making us right with himself depends on faith.

PHILIPPIANS 3:9 NLT

SAFE

I live on the edges of what's called Tornado Alley. We don't get nearly as many tornados as states like Kansas or Missouri, but I've had my fair share of freaky weather experiences.

One year at college in Ohio we heard the sirens not once, not twice, but three times. Each time the wind would pick up, rain and hail would pummel our dormitory, and then it would all suddenly stop and get quite calm. Within seconds the sirens would blare and we'd scurry to our tornado shelter—the interior bathroom on the first floor.

The next day we learned the storm had produced an F4 tornado only a few miles away! It killed one person, injured one hundred more, and left a trail of devastation. We were fortunate to have escaped without injury or damage.

For states prone to tornadoes, the basement or some interior closet is our refuge, our place of safety. God is sort of like that basement. The Bible says he is our bedrock and castle, our mountain of hiding and pathway of escape. He is a tower of rescue, our strength and shield. God is a safe place to hide. Everyone who is of God dwells in safety by him; he shelters them all day long. David tells us God holds our lives safely in his hands; in him we are safe.

Sometimes life can feel like an F4 tornado—or a category 5 hurricane or a 9.0 earthquake. Yet we have nothing to fear! Because part of who we are is a sheltered, protected child of God. In Christ, we are *safe.*

❖

The beloved of the LORD shall dwell in safety by Him,
Who shelters him all the day long;
And he shall dwell between His shoulders.

DEUTERONOMY 33:12 NKJV

You're as real to me as Bedrock beneath my feet,
Like a Castle on a cliff, my forever firm Fortress,
My Mountain of hiding, my Pathway of escape,
my Tower of rescue where none can reach me,
my secret Strength and Shield around me,
you are Salvation's Ray of Brightness shining on the
    hillside,
always the Champion of my cause.

PSALM 18:2 TPT

God, you're such a safe and powerful place to hide!
You're a proven help in time of trouble,
more than enough and always available whenever I need you.

PSALM 46:1 TPT

There's no doubt about it;
God holds our lives safely in his hands.
He's the One who keeps us faithfully following him.

PSALM 66:9 TPT

You're the only place of protection for me.
I keep coming back to hide myself in you,
for you are like a mountain-cliff-fortress where I'm
    kept safe.

PSALM 71:3 TPT

You'll even walk unharmed among the fiercest powers
    of darkness,
trampling every one of them beneath your feet!

PSALM 91:13 TPT

SAVED

Several years ago I heard about a friend of a friend who was going through a tough time with drugs and alcohol. This person's brother was so concerned about him that he moved his family from one part of the city to the house next door so he could walk with him through his struggles. He stepped into his brother's life in order to save him from a life of addiction and eventual death, and to save him for the life he was meant to live.

That's what God did for us: He stepped into our lives— literally, by becoming one of us in order to save us from sin and death, and save us for the lives he meant for us when he created us.

"You are saved by grace through faith," Paul says. Perhaps you memorized this key verse at an early age like I did. In many ways it is the foundation of our very faith. It is also the foundation of our identity in Christ.

David reminds us the Lord is a saving God. Jesus tells us while a situation of salvation may seem humanly impossible, it is more than possible with God. Paul declares that if anyone declares "Jesus is Lord" and believes God raised him from the dead, they will be saved.

Of course, God saved us from our sins, death, and eternal separation. But it's not enough to know what we're saved *from*; we need to know what we're saved *for*. Hebrews tells us Jesus is able to fully save us from circumstances in life now, as well as throughout all eternity.

Jesus saves us from death and for the life he always meant for us—eternal life. That's who God says you are. You are saved!

But I call to God,
and the LORD will save me.

PSALM 55:16 ESV

Jesus saw his disappointment, and looking right at him he said, "It is next to impossible for those who have everything to enter into the kingdom realm of God. Nothing could be harder! It could be compared to trying to stuff a rope through the eye of a needle."

Those who heard this said, "Then who can be saved?"

Jesus responded, "What appears humanly impossible is more than possible with God. For God can do what man cannot."

LUKE 18:24–27 TPT

If you declare with your mouth, "Jesus is Lord," and believe in your heart that God raised him from the dead, you will be saved.

ROMANS 10:9 NIV

When you heard the message of truth, the gospel of your salvation, and when you believed in Him, you were also sealed with the promised Holy Spirit.

EPHESIANS 1:13 HCSB

For you are saved by grace through faith, and this is not from yourselves; it is God's gift—not from works, so that no one can boast.

EPHESIANS 2:8–9 HCSB

But Jesus permanently holds his priestly office, since he lives forever and will never have a successor! So he is able to save fully from now throughout eternity, everyone who comes to God through him, because he lives to pray continually for them.

HEBREWS 7:24–25 TPT

SECURE

When I was a kid growing up, there was a time when I prayed the sinner's prayer almost every Sunday. I would talk back to my parents or do something mean to my sister during the week, and the next Sunday I was remorseful and scared I'd be sent to hell.

It wasn't because of anything my pastor or parents said or did that caused me to doubt my salvation. I just wasn't all that sure about the *security* of my salvation. Of course the more I grew in faith the more I realized what the Bible says about my life in Christ: I am secure, both for my eternal life and for my earthly life.

"He sets me securely on the heights," David says. By God's power I will always be safe and secure. Which means I don't need to fear a thing—whether by night or by day, whether in this life or the next. Proverbs declares the Lord keeps me so secure I won't be caught in traps laid for me. And here's a promise for my childhood self, as much as my adult self: The Holy Spirit has sealed us in the family of God, as a deposit guaranteeing our inheritance and redemption!

If I've learned anything between those years as a child and now, it's that I am not vulnerable to attack, I am not in danger, I am not at risk of hell. God is a God who really can be trusted to keep me safe and secure. And who you are is who God says I am: God says you are *secure*!

He makes my feet like the feet of a deer
and sets me securely on the heights.

PSALM 18:33 HCSB

Though many wish to fight and the tide of battle turns against me,
by your power I will be safe and secure;
peace will be my portion.

PSALM 55:18 TPT

Don't fear a thing! Whether by night or by day,
demonic danger will not trouble you,
nor the powers of evil launched against you.
For God will keep you safe and secure;
they won't lay a hand on you!

PSALM 91:6 TPT

The LORD is your security.
He will keep your foot from being caught in a trap.

PROVERBS 3:26 NLT

We know that God's children do not make a practice of
sinning, for God's Son holds them securely, and the evil one
cannot touch them.

1 JOHN 5:18 NLT

When you heard the message of truth, the gospel of your
salvation, and when you believed in Him, you were also sealed
with the promised Holy Spirit. He is the down payment of our
inheritance, for the redemption of the possession, to the praise
of His glory.

EPHESIANS 1:13–14 HCSB

SINLESS

"I'm just a sinner saved by grace."

This popular Christian saying has a nice ring of piety to it, doesn't it? I know I've said it before. Wasn't it Jonathan Edwards who suggested we were like spiders dangling over the licking flames of hell, one divine flick away from eternal oblivion? This "sinners in the hands of an angry God" sentiment probably has a lot to do with this view.

For much of my life this was how I viewed myself: just a rotten sinner, who happened to be saved by grace through faith. Probably because that's what I heard from many of the Christians around me.

But what if it isn't true? What if who we really are isn't *just a sinner* saved by grace?

Yes, we're born sinners. And we're 100 percent saved by God's absurd, loving favor and 0 percent saved through our own merit. But on the other side of this crazy grace, are we *just sinners* who happen to be saved by grace?

When I read God's Word, that doesn't seem right.

The apostle Paul, who called himself the chief of sinners, teaches that we've passed away from sin; we're dead to it. He goes so far as to say our sins have been completely washed away. So does the apostle John, who reminds us that God's Son has purged all of our sins from us, so that they are taken away.

Again, we're saved and rescued from sin and death not because of anything we've done, but purely because of God's grace. But that doesn't mean we're still rebellious sinners. In Christ, we're far more glorious than "just a sinner saved by grace."

Instead, we are sinless. That's who God says we are!

❧

We have passed away from sin once and for all, as a dead man passes away from this life. So how could we live under sin's rule a moment longer?

ROMANS 6:2 TPT

Count yourselves dead to sin but alive to God in Christ Jesus.

ROMANS 6:11 NIV

When God our Savior revealed his kindness and love, he saved us, not because of the righteous things we had done, but because of his mercy. He washed away our sins, giving us a new birth and new life through the Holy Spirit.

TITUS 3:4–5 NLT

But if we walk in the light as He Himself is in the light, we have fellowship with one another, and the blood of Jesus His Son cleanses us from all sin.

1 JOHN 1:7 HCSB

But you know that he appeared so that he might take away our sins. And in him is no sin.

1 JOHN 3:5 NIV

STABLE

In 2012 Hurricane Sandy ripped along the shores of New Jersey, causing $30 billion in damage and damaging or destroying 346,000 homes. Some of the most dramatic images came from Seaside Heights, where Casino Pier crumbled, roller coasters floated away, and houses slid into the sea.

Sometimes life can feel that way—as though you're crumbling, sliding, and floating away into oblivion because of your circumstances.

A surgery goes differently than you were told, bringing physical limitations you didn't expect. Job loss threatens your financial stability. The threat of divorce unhinges your family life. When life takes a turn we need to be reminded who God says we are in his Word.

The prophet Samuel says that God makes our feet like the feet of deer, setting us securely up on high. He plants his children in secure places so they won't be disturbed. We won't ever be shaken because God remembers us, acting as a secure fortress and fortified city of refuge. Paul reminds us when we wear God's armor nothing will be able to shake us, and we will be able to stand our ground.

After Jesus' famous Sermon on the Mount he declares that anyone who listens to him and obeys him "is like a wise man who built his house on the rock" (Matthew 7:24

NIV). The lesson: Disciples of Jesus are standing on solid ground!

While you may feel the total opposite because of life circumstances, who God says you are in Christ is *stable*.

❖

He makes my feet like the feet of a deer
and sets me securely on the heights.

2 SAMUEL 22:34 HCSB

And I will provide a homeland for my people Israel, planting them in a secure place where they will never be disturbed.

1 CHRONICLES 17:9 NLT

Surely the righteous will never be shaken;
they will be remembered forever.

PSALM 112:6 NIV

Whoever fears the LORD has a secure fortress,
and for their children it will be a refuge.

PROVERBS 14:26 NIV

"Today I have made you a fortified city, an iron pillar and a bronze wall to stand against the whole land—against the kings of Judah, its officials, its priests and the people of the land."

JEREMIAH 1:18 NIV

Therefore put on the full armor of God, so that when the day of evil comes, you may be able to stand your ground, and after you have done everything, to stand.

EPHESIANS 6:13 NIV

STRONG

Sometimes I wish I were Popeye. You know, the spinach-eating Sailor Man with superhuman strength from the mid-twentieth-century cartoon and comic strip. He made strong look easy. I mean, what could be easier than powering up with a can of spinach—as horrid as that sounds?

I wish being strong was that simple—not only because I can barely curl twenty-five-pound dumbbells, but also because I often can be so emotionally and spiritually weak.

Take fear. I know God really can be trusted. He's proven himself over and over and over again. But when a client hasn't checked in with work projects or my health feels a little off, the tentacles of fear wrap around my heart. It's in moments like these and countless others that I need God to remind me who he says I am. In Christ I am not weak; God says I'm strong!

Deuteronomy tells us not to fear because God goes with us everywhere we go—which should give us strength and courage in life. He is the strength of our heart, David says. Isaiah says young people may get tired and fall, but God promises to strengthen the weary and powerless. And of course Paul gave the final word on the subject: "When I am weak, then I am strong."

Sometimes I feel so weak, and am so prone to think

of myself that way. But when I come to God's Word I'm reminded who I really am.

◈

Be strong and courageous. Do not fear or be in dread of them, for it is the LORD your God who goes with you.

DEUTERONOMY 31:6 ESV

My flesh and my heart fail;
But God is the strength of my heart and my portion forever.

PSALM 73:26 NKJV

He gives strength to the weary
and strengthens the powerless.
Youths may faint and grow weary,
and young men stumble and fall,
but those who trust in the LORD
will renew their strength.

ISAIAH 40:29–31 HCSB

The LORD God is my strength;
He will make my feet like deer's feet,
And He will make me walk on my high hills.

HABAKKUK 3:19 NKJV

I take pleasure in weaknesses, insults, catastrophes, persecutions, and in pressures, because of Christ. For when I am weak, then I am strong.

2 CORINTHIANS 12:10 HCSB

I have written to you who are God's children
because you know the Father.
I have written to you who are mature in the faith
because you know Christ, who existed from the beginning.
I have written to you who are young in the faith
because you are strong.
God's word lives in your hearts,
and you have won your battle with the evil one.

1 JOHN 2:14 NLT

SUPPORTED

Steve Jobs and Steve Wozniak. Michael Jordan and Scottie Pippen. Frodo Baggins and Samwise Gamgee.

You could argue Steve Jobs, Michael Jordan, and Frodo Baggins were successful only because of the support from their partners.

Frodo and Sam make up one of my favorite partnerships. Despite the trials and terror of their journey, Sam stood by his friend—even when Frodo turned on him. A case could be made that Sam was the real hero of the story, because without him Frodo never would have been able to complete his mission.

You are also supported. That's who God says you are.

The Bible tells us that we have nothing to fear or dread, because the Lord our God is with us. David reminds God's people that God supports them; when they stumble God is right there to lift them up. Because God will always sustain us and never let us be shaken, we are invited to bring all of our cares to him to find the support we need. God lived our life, understands our life, and is waiting to support our life at every turn.

One of the best moments in the Lord of the Rings trilogy is when Sam and Frodo are on the side of Mount Doom. Frodo is struggling to ascend the mountain to do what he came to do: destroy the ring of power. He's exhausted, spent. He can't go another step. But his trusted, faithful friend can: "Come, Mr. Frodo!" Sam cries. "I can't carry it for you, but I can carry you."

What a perfect picture of support, the kind of support we have from our trusted, faithful heavenly Friend.

◆

Be strong and courageous. Do not fear or be in dread of them, for it is the LORD your God who goes with you.

DEUTERONOMY 31:6 ESV

The little that the righteous man has is better
than the abundance of many wicked people.
For the arms of the wicked will be broken,
but the LORD supports the righteous.

PSALM 37:16–17 HCSB

The steps of the God-pursuing ones
follow firmly in the footsteps of the Lord.
And God delights in every step they take to follow him.
If they stumble badly they will still survive,
for the Lord lifts them up with his hands.

PSALM 37:23–24 TPT

Cast your cares on the LORD
and he will sustain you;
he will never let
the righteous be shaken.

PSALM 55:22 NIV

So then, we must cling in faith to all we know to be true.
For we have a magnificent King-Priest, Jesus Christ, the Son
of God, who rose into the heavenly realm for us, and now
sympathizes with us in our frailty. He understands humanity,
for as a Man, our magnificent King-Priest was tempted in
every way just as we are, and conquered sin. So now we come
freely and boldly to where love is enthroned, to receive mercy's
kiss and discover the grace we urgently need to strengthen us
in our time of weakness.

HEBREWS 4:14–16 TPT

·

TRANSFORMED

When I was a pastor there was this running joke about my road rage with my congregation. Well, *rage* might be too strong a word; I'd say it was more road *angst*. Either way, I'd often weave my struggle with controlling my irritation with fellow drivers into sermons. It was sort of this funny way to show I had a long way to go to get to where I knew God wanted me!

Do you ever feel like me? Like you're walking one step forward and forty-seven steps backward in your Christian life?

One year I decided I was sort of tired of the joke, because I was tired of the person who was telling it; I was done being *that guy* on the road. What helped me change this aspect of my character was coming to grips with who God says I really am in Christ.

In Christ we have everything we need to live the new life we all long to live, because in Christ we're *already* transformed as much as we're *being* transformed.

In the Hebrew Scriptures, Ezekiel prophesied that God would remove our stone-cold heart and give us a new fresh one. Paul tells us that in Christ we are being transformed into the image of Christ. This is possible because in him we are literally new creatures; the old person has gone and the new person has come! He reminds us that at one time we were full of darkness, but now we are people full of light.

The Christian life is often forward movement followed by stumbles backward. But I'm learning that's okay. I don't need to give in to self-loathing, because who God says I am is transformed—both right now and inch-by-inch.

I will give you a new heart and put a new spirit within you; I will remove your heart of stone and give you a heart of flesh.

EZEKIEL 36:26 HCSB

For when we were in the flesh, the sinful passions operated through the law in every part of us and bore fruit for death. But now we have been released from the law, since we have died to what held us, so that we may serve in the new way of the Spirit and not in the old letter of the law.

ROMANS 7:5–6 HCSB

We all, with unveiled faces, are looking as in a mirror at the glory of the Lord and are being transformed into the same image from glory to glory; this is from the Lord who is the Spirit.

2 CORINTHIANS 3:18 HCSB

Therefore, if anyone is in Christ, he is a new creation; old things have passed away, and look, new things have come.

2 CORINTHIANS 5:17 HCSB

For as many of you as have been baptized into Christ have put on Christ like a garment.

GALATIANS 3:27 HCSB

For once you were full of darkness, but now you have light from the Lord. So live as people of light!

EPHESIANS 5:8 NLT

UNiTED

There's nothing like a good sporting event to divide even the most loving of families. In my home state, the Michigan vs. Michigan State game is usually the culprit. But the list of things that bring division could circle the Earth: Democrats vs. Republicans; Mac vs. PC; iPhone vs. Android; Ford vs. Chevy; Starbucks vs. Everyone Else.

Do you know what the main dividing line in Jesus' day was? Jews vs. non-Jews, or as Israel called them, Gentiles. Israel separated people based on their ethnic and religious heritage. Anyone who was not Jewish was shunned and labeled "unclean."

All of us have been on one dividing line or another. We've all experienced the feeling that comes from being in the "out" group. In Christ, however, we are not divided and or separated. Instead, God says we're *united*.

Jesus himself says that his sheep from all over the earth are joined together into one flock, with him as the one shepherd. Paul reminds us that though the church has many different members, in Christ we are all united together in one body. He goes on to say that all distinctions between people in the church—whether ethnic, social, or gender—are abolished in and through Jesus. Finally, Peter reminds us that we all participate together in the divine nature of the Trinity, the great unifier.

Though our world likes to try to separate us and fosters

division at every turn, division and separation don't define us. Instead, who God says we really are is *united*.

❖

"And I have other sheep that I will gather which are not of this Jewish flock. And I, their shepherd, must lead them too, and they will follow me and listen to my voice. And I will join them all into one flock with one shepherd."

JOHN 10:16 TPT

For as in one body we have many members, and the members do not all have the same function, so we, though many, are one body in Christ, and individually members one of another.

ROMANS 12:4–5 ESV

There is neither Jew nor Greek, there is neither slave nor free, there is neither male nor female; for you are all one in Christ Jesus.

GALATIANS 3:28 NKJV

Although you were once distant and far away from God, now you have been brought delightfully close to him through the sacred blood of Jesus—you have actually been united to Christ!

EPHESIANS 2:13 TPT

Through these he has given us his very great and precious promises, so that through them you may participate in the divine nature, having escaped the corruption in the world caused by evil desires.

2 PETER 1:4 NIV

Unashamed

One Christmas I wanted a radio controlled car. My friends had them and I'd seen commercials for them, so I dropped hints to Mom and Dad that this was what I wanted above *anything* else.

In the weeks leading up to Christmas I wondered if my parents had gotten the hints. I couldn't contain my curiosity, so one morning I snuck into my parents' bedroom, opened their closet, and peeked under the white sheet covering our gifts.

There it was: a shiny red radio-controlled car!

Delight quickly turned into despair, however, when I remembered Mom told me not to look in her closet, and if I did she'd return my presents to the store. I ran out of their room and downstairs, trying to play it cool. Mom saw this from the kitchen, and she knew what happened; moms know these things.

When she asked if I'd looked in her closet I denied it, but eventually confessed. I was so ashamed. She returned my radio-controlled car.

Shame is a feeling that has haunted me throughout my life. I still struggle with it when I think about the things I've done in rebellion against God, the things I've done that have hurt my neighbor. Perhaps you understand that feeling. Yet the Bible breathes so much hope into our shame-filled hearts.

David tells us that whoever looks to the Lord is never covered with shame. God's children have no reason to be afraid of him because we won't ever be put to shame. By God's grace, instead of shame, we receive an abundance of blessing. John tells us when we confess our sins we are cleansed and forgiven.

Shame isn't from God; it's from our Enemy. The next time you feel ashamed, remember: God says you are *unashamed*!

❖

Those who look to him are radiant;
their faces are never covered with shame.

PSALM 34:5 NIV

Do not be afraid, for you will not be put to shame;
don't be humiliated, for you will not be disgraced.
For you will forget the shame of your youth,
and you will no longer remember
the disgrace of your widowhood.

ISAIAH 54:4 HCSB

"Instead of your shame you will receive a double portion,
and instead of disgrace you will rejoice in your inheritance.
And so you will inherit a double portion in your land,
and everlasting joy will be yours."

ISAIAH 61:7 NLT

On that day you will no longer need to be ashamed,
for you will no longer be rebels against me.

I will remove all proud and arrogant people from among you. There will be no more haughtiness on my holy mountain.

ZEPHANIAH 3:11 NLT

If we confess our sins, He is faithful and righteous to forgive us our sins and to cleanse us from all unrighteousness.

1 JOHN 1:9 HCSB

VALUABLE

Think about something that is of great worth to you. Could be an expensive watch or piece of jewelry. Maybe it's a collection of rare items, like paintings or coins. Perhaps it's not even a thing, but a memory—from childhood or a vacation.

My dad would probably say his record collection is valuable to him. He's got hundreds of primo vinyl, ranging from Bach to the Beatles, Miles Davis to the Mamas and the Papas. If a fire tore through his house, I think he'd cry most for his lost record collection and hi-fi equipment!

As much value as you might place on something—as much as my dad might value his vintage vinyl—did you know you are infinitely more valuable and of far greater worth?

That's right, because who God says you are is *valuable*.

Throughout the Bible God says his children are incredibly valuable to him. We are God's beloved, and his desire is directed toward us. He has paid an infinitely precious price for our ransom, because that's who we are to God—precious. I especially love how Jesus compares us to birds: He says if God provides for them beyond what they need, how much more will he do for us because we are far more valuable than birds! Finally, God calls us his masterpiece, because that is what each of us is; we are God's handiwork.

Sometimes it's hard to remember our worth. People call us names, society tells us we're not good enough, or an inner voice criticizes every movement. Just remember who God says you really are—and what he says is what ultimately matters!

❖

He will take pity on the weak and the needy
and save the needy from death.
He will rescue them from oppression and violence,
for precious is their blood in his sight.

PSALM 72:13–14 NIV

I am my beloved's,
And his desire is toward me.

SONG OF SOLOMON 7:10 NKJV

"Do not be afraid, for I have ransomed you.
I have called you by name; you are mine.
When you go through deep waters, I will be with you.
When you go through rivers of difficulty, you will not drown.
For I am the LORD, your God,
the Holy One of Israel, your Savior.
I gave Egypt as a ransom for your freedom;
I gave Ethiopia and Seba in your place.
Others were given in exchange for you.
I traded their lives for yours
because you are precious to me.
You are honored, and I love you."

ISAIAH 43:1–4 NLT

"Consider the ravens: They do not sow or reap, they have no storeroom or barn; yet God feeds them. And how much more valuable you are than birds!"

LUKE 12:24 NIV

For we are God's masterpiece. He has created us anew in Christ Jesus, so we can do the good things he planned for us long ago.

EPHESIANS 2:10 NLT

Victorious

At chapel in Bible college we would often recite this triumphal declaration together: "I've got the victory, halle-lujah!"

Do you believe that? That you stand in victory, that you are victorious in Christ?

Life can sometimes feel everything but victorious. We fail an important test or lose a prestigious promotion. We blow up at our kids or give in to temptation. We lose a close friend to cancer or nearly lose our own life in a car accident.

Yet when we turn to God's Word, we are reminded who we really are. We are not defeated, because God says we are *victorious*! The Bible says we have the victory over three areas: circumstances, sin, and death.

David declares that victory comes from the Lord for all his anointed ones. He answers them from his throne with victorious power. He crowns his people with victory. John tells us that through faith in Jesus every child of God defeats this world. Paul reminds us that through Jesus we have victory over both sin and death, reciting that ancient battle cry:

"Where, O death, is your victory?
Where, O death, is your sting?" (1 Corinthians 15:55 NIV).

The next time you're in the shower or driving in the car

and you're despairing over your circumstance, your sin, or even your mortality, join with me in shouting my college declaration: I've got the victory, hallelujah!

Amen? Amen!

◈

Now this I know:
The LORD gives victory to his anointed.
He answers him from his heavenly sanctuary
with the victorious power of his right hand.

PSALM 20:6 NIV

I wait quietly before God,
for my victory comes from him.

PSALM 62:1 NLT

See, God has come to save me.
I will trust in him and not be afraid.
The LORD GOD is my strength and my song;
he has given me victory.

ISAIAH 12:2 NLT

When the perishable has been clothed with the imperishable, and the mortal with immortality, then the saying that is written will come true: "Death has been swallowed up in victory."

"Where, O death, is your victory?
Where, O death, is your sting?"

1 CORINTHIANS 15:54–55 NIV

But thank God! He gives us victory over sin and death through our Lord Jesus Christ.

1 CORINTHIANS 15:57 NLT

For every child of God defeats this evil world, and we achieve this victory through our faith. And who can win this battle against the world? Only those who believe that Jesus is the Son of God.

1 JOHN 5:4–5 NLT

Wise

Sometimes life can be confusing: Do I take this job or that job? Should I say "yes" to that first date—or second? Does it matter what major I choose?

Sometimes life's questions are as deep as they are confusing: Where did I come from and why am I here? What is the meaning of life? Why are things so messed up—and what's the fix?

Sometimes life's questions are as spiritual as they are deep and confusing: Who is God and what is he like? If God is so good why is life so bad? How can I understand this God and get to know him, like I would a new friend?

Thankfully, we are not left on our own to navigate life's important questions. God has given us his Word and his Spirit to make us wise.

As the Bible says, we find light and understanding in God's words, when we unwrap them like we would a present. God promises that we will gain knowledge and understanding of him when we listen to his wisdom and cry out for insight. Paul tells us that if we've decided to follow Jesus, we have received God's very Spirit so that we may understand who God is and what he desires from us. And James declares that we have direct access to wisdom at anytime; all we have to do is ask God, who gives generously!

God has given us his Word and his Spirit. So the next

time you're facing a confusing situation or are unsure about the answers to life's big questions, remember who you really are.

In Christ, you are wise because you have everything you need to *be* wise.

❦

The unfolding of your words gives light;
it gives understanding to the simple.

PSALM 119:130 NIV

Tune your ears to wisdom,
and concentrate on understanding.
Cry out for insight,
and ask for understanding.
Search for them as you would for silver;
seek them like hidden treasures.
Then you will understand what it means to fear the LORD,
and you will gain knowledge of God.

PROVERBS 2:2–5 NLT

Do not let wisdom and understanding out of your sight,
preserve sound judgment and discretion;
they will be life for you.

PROVERBS 3:21–22 NIV

What we have received is not the spirit of the world, but the Spirit who is from God, so that we may understand what God has freely given us.

1 CORINTHIANS 2:12 NIV

We are asking that you may be filled with the knowledge of His will in all wisdom and spiritual understanding, so that you may walk worthy of the Lord, fully pleasing to Him, bearing fruit in every good work and growing in the knowledge of God.

COLOSSIANS 1:9–10 HCSB

If any of you lacks wisdom, let him ask God, who gives generously to all without reproach, and it will be given him.

JAMES 1:5 ESV